Maggie Günsberg explores the intersection of gender portrayal and other social categories of class, age and the family in the Italian theatre from the Renaissance to the present day. She examines the developing relationship between patriarchal strategies and the formal properties of the dramatic genre such as plot, comedy and realism, and also conventions specific to drama in performance, including images of both femininity and masculinity. An interdisciplinary approach, drawing on semiotics, psychoanalysis, philosophy, theories of spectatorship and dramatic theory from a feminist perspective, informs Günsberg's critique of landmarks in Italian theatrical history, including work by Machiavelli, Ariosto, Goldoni, D'Annunzio and Pirandello. The book concludes with a chapter on the plays of Franca Rame, assessing the impact of this important figure on contemporary Italian theatre.

GENDER AND THE ITALIAN STAGE

GENDER AND THE ITALIAN STAGE

From the Renaissance to the present day

MAGGIE GÜNSBERG

University of Sussex

CAMBRIDGE
UNIVERSITY PRESS

PUBLISHED BY THE PRESS SYNDICATE OF THE UNIVERSITY OF CAMBRIDGE
The Pitt Building, Trumpington Street, Cambridge CB2 1RP, United Kingdom

CAMBRIDGE UNIVERSITY PRESS
The Edinburgh Building, Cambridge CB2 2RU, United Kingdom
40 West 20th Street, New York, NY 10011–4211, USA
10 Stamford Road, Oakleigh, Melbourne 3166, Australia

First published 1997

Printed in the United Kingdom at the University Press, Cambridge

Typeset in Baskerville no. 2 11/12½ pt [CP]

A catalogue record for this book is available from the British Library

Library of Congress cataloguing in publication data
Günsberg, Maggie.
Gender and the Italian stage: from the Renaissance to the present day / Maggie Günsberg.
p. cm.
Includes bibliographical references and index.
ISBN 0 521 59028 0 (hardback)
1. Italian drama – History and criticism. 2. Sex role in literature.
3. Sex in literature. I. Title.
PQ4136.G86 1997
852 .008'3538 – DC21   97–5750   CIP

ISBN 0 521 59028 0 hardback

For Ruth Fornelli, my mother, no stranger to the
stage herself as a dancer in opera houses in 1930s
Austria and Poland

Contents

Illustrations

Acknowledgments

I am grateful to the following for reading various sections of this book as it took shape, and for combining encouragement with constructive critique in the process: Richard Andrews, Zygmunt Barański, Peter Brand, Joseph Farrell, Anna Laura Lepschy and Giulio Lepschy. Seminar discussions involving students at Sussex have filtered into the final chapter on Franca Rame (in particular, Katrina Tilmann, Dagmar Vinz, and students on my 1995–6 course on Italian theatre and cinema). A number of people have ensured in various ways that sanity prevailed during the gestation of this book, especially George and Betty James, and Elaine Smith. Others have reminded me that insanity also has its rewards, particularly when translated into jigs and reels, and for this I have to thank Phil and Mandy Berthoud, John Brewins, Dave Flewitt, Neil Hamer, Roger Leach, Nick Pynn and Vincent Purcell. All translations are my own, unless otherwise stated. In the interests of clarity, elegance of expression in translation has on occasion given way to a strictly literal approach.

Bertie provided me with much love and affection, but sadly died as the book was in its final stages.

Introduction

The purpose of this book is to offer a new, up-to-date perspective on Italian theatre by examining the representation of gender in a range of plays from the comedies of the Renaissance to the one-woman satires of Franca Rame in the 1970s, 80s and 90s. An interdisciplinary approach informs textual analyses to produce a set of feminist readings in which gender is seen to interact with other social categories, particularly those of class, age and the family. This approach is in line with feminist research which crosses the boundaries separating disciplines and social categories in order to elucidate their actual interaction in the overriding context of a dominant patriarchal ideology. One of the earliest such cross-overs was that of materialist feminism, which recognized the importance of the economic sphere in determining not only the position of women in society according to their class, age, race, colour, working and familial status, but also the reinforcement of this position by cultural texts. More recently, feminist discussion of western civil society has drawn attention to the effects on women of social relations as governed by market relations in a capitalist economy subtended by the ideology of patriarchy.[1]

The interdisciplinary approach followed in this book draws on areas as varied as semiotics, psychoanalysis, philosophy and dramatic theory. One main line which runs through all these areas to provide continuity and coherence is that of materialism. This will be noted in the constant consideration of the socioeconomic context in its effects on the dramatic representation of gender as perceived through an interdisciplinary range of areas. Within this socioeconomic context, attention is focussed on the interface between ideology and culture; in other words, between patriarchal strategies and the formal properties of the dramatic genre as exemplified by structures of plot, comedy, realism and conventions specific to drama as performance. Particularly evident in all the plays is patriarchy's adherence to gender difference as

I

informed by traditional western epistemology, most notably in the
form of the binary structure, with its oppositional, rather than relational, implications.[2]

Given the broad historical span covered by the book, the socioeconomic context for the production of Italian theatre ranges from the
early development of a capitalist market economy during the
Renaissance, through to the post-boom years of industrial capitalism
within which Franca Rame's plays are situated. One important issue
which arises throughout is the effect of a changing socioeconomic climate on dramatic gender representation. At the same time, patriarchal
ideology can be observed to remain relatively constant, changing its
face only superficially to accommodate varying socioeconomic patterns. What changes and what similarities can be detected across the
centuries? The first two chapters show how the Renaissance comedies,
written during a period of expanding market capitalism but strongly
influenced by the pre-capitalist plays of Plautus and Terence, retain the
fundamental patriarchal definitions of femininity, while constructing
different variants of them in accordance with the development of early
capitalism. Other questions to be addressed are how, if at all, does subversion find its way on to the stage at different periods, given the changing perceptions of sexuality over time? What are the possibilities of
counter-reading or deconstructing dramatic texts, given that the text is
now no longer viewed as monolithic and univocal, but, rather, as a site
of conflicting ideologies and contestation of meanings? And in the light
of the recent shift of emphasis back on to the addressee of the text not as
passive recipient, but as active participant in meaning-construction,
how can we be sure to historicize correctly our reconstruction of spectator readings of the performance text?[3]

The questions raised by the diachronic nature of this book are made
more complex by elements of regionalism, a factor peculiar to the history of a country which did not unify until 1870, and which, even after
unification, has resolutely favoured regional rather than centralized,
national identity. As a result, a certain degree of regional variation
occurs in both socioeconomic and cultural spheres, adding a further
dimension to the historical variation taking place over the five centuries
spanned by this study. For example, gender portrayal in the comedies of
Goldoni (1707–1793), the subject of chapter three, is informed by overly
materialist and moralist concerns in a specifically eighteenth-century
Venetian context. This chapter examines Goldoni's inflection of
the generic notions of morality – good and bad, virtue and vice:

terms which acquire a special patriarchal resonance in the context of eighteenth-century Europe in general, and Venice in particular. The specifically Venetian issues of permissiveness and gambling can be seen to particularly affect gender portrayal in these realist urban comedies. By contrast, the decadent plays of D'Annunzio (1863–1938) dramatize both pre-capitalist and capitalist, urban and non-urban preconditions for their particularly extreme problematization of femininity. The focus in this chapter is on difference as dominance, given the overt workings of power in D'Annunzio's plays. A hierarchical dynamic informs gender relations in a way which is much more covert in other eras, and in other dramatists not so influenced by Nietzsche's philosophy of will to power. Of central significance is the crucial role of a decadent variant of patriarchal femininity in helping to define the D'Annunzian superman as it interacts with masculine fears and superstitions. A comparison with the realist plays of Verga (1849–1922) helps to highlight the particular features of gender portrayal to be found in decadent theatre.

Both rural and urban Sicily of the late nineteenth and early twentieth centuries supply the context within which Pirandello (1867–1936) wrote the plays examined in chapter five. The workings of patriarchy are again in evidence despite, or perhaps as a reaction to, the growing women's movement in Italy. This writer was well aware of feminism's demands for wider working horizons for women, and registered his disapproval in an article entitled 'Feminismo' in 1909 (Pirandello 1965). The movement did little, however, to modify the continued socio-economic and cultural hegemony of market relations and their patriarchal underpinning in a slowly industrializing Italy, while Sicily itself remained locked in the primary sector of agricultural and mining production. While the tertiary, public sector developed significantly in Italy in the 1920s and 30s, and many more women joined the labour force as office workers, Pirandello's plays resolutely exclude this particular contemporary reality. His work illustrates how patriarchy continues to police its own male hierarchy, in both material and sexual arenas, in such a way as to marginalize femininity, and specifically maternity. This chapter concentrates on the age hierarchy in Pirandello's plays, both as it is represented by interactions between male characters, and in its very different implications for femininity. Age as a social category is frequently mentioned as an important factor in gender criticism. However, all too often there is no further development of this issue, a situation which this chapter attempts to remedy.

The socioeconomic line followed throughout this study ends with fully industrialized, post-boom Italy of the 1970s, 80s and 90s, with its well-entrenched market capitalism subtended as ever by patriarchal ideology. It is within her satires of these aspects of modern Italy that Franca Rame (b. 1929), both in collaboration with and independently of Dario Fo, situates her critique of patriarchy. A central aspect of gender portrayal in Rame's work is its highly politicized context, from which it is inseparable on many levels, including those of production, performance, funding and use of profits. Gender portrayal is integrated with representations of contemporary issues; profits from these performances, which have often taken place not in conventional theatres, but in factories and public spaces, have been donated to political causes, as well as being used to finance future productions. Rame herself, moreover, is involved in all these stages, rather than solely those of writing and acting (in itself already quite a unique combination of roles). In all senses, hers is a living, working theatre, which aims not to reaffirm dominant values in elitist settings, but to question the system on all its levels (gender, politics, economics, religion) and in the forum of popular culture. Her particular performance politics ensure that female parts dominate the stage, unlike their sixteenth-century predecessors waiting in the wings during the early period of developing market capitalism.

The selection of Rame, a female playwright/actress/producer, for the final chapter concluding a study of otherwise male dramatists, raises the issue of the choice of plays and playwrights for this volume. This was determined by one major consideration, namely that those chosen are revealing in matters of gender in an interesting variety of ways. Rame was chosen as a deliberate contrast, not simply on account of her gender and the popular theatrical tradition which she continues, but in order to explore how dramatic representation of femininity might function differently in theatre that is contemporary, and that actually aims to unmask and subvert traditional values. The fusion in her work of past dramatic method with present-day concerns makes her an ideal culminating point for this study. Rame is, moreover, a key figure not only in contemporary Italian theatre, but on the world stage. It was felt important to concentrate as much as possible on what may be regarded as landmarks in Italian theatre and, in some cases, theatre history generally. While the main object of study is the representation of gender, this is necessarily also informed by developments in theatre history, particularly in view of the timespan covered.

Any study of theatre must also be prefaced by clarification regarding the type of text on which it is to focus. I am referring to the distinction between the dramatic text (the play in its written form) and the performance text (the play in performance).[4] The dramatic text exists in a single form as matrix for innumerable performance texts, each distinguishable from the other in the light of a complex set of performance factors: producer and stage manager, actresses and actors, vocal and gestural inflections, audience reception, venue etc. The study of the text in performance, and so in its ultimate, authentically theatrical format, although desirable, is, in effect, largely impracticable. While this work therefore deals with the play in its written form, attention is nonetheless paid to the actualities of stage presentation, especially in terms of audience dynamics.

This is particularly the case as far as the early chapters on the Renaissance are concerned. Here recourse is taken to recent theories of spectatorship, as well as accounts of stage and auditorium practices of the time, in order to piece together the overall performance context for which the plays would have been intended. The gender of the performer was a vital aspect of the performance and is crucial to an understanding of gender dynamics on stage and in the auditorium. Chapter two explores the implications, for both female and male spectators in the sixteenth century, of young male actors playing female roles, a scenario which becomes even more complex when female characters, in reality already male, cross-dress as male characters. The performance context itself can of course be seen to change with time. With the passing of the centuries, the play no longer forms merely one part of an entertainment that went on for eleven or twelve hours, as it did during the Renaissance. As a consequence, the immediate context within which gender relations are enacted becomes progressively more variable, making issues of spectatorship even more difficult to unravel.

The overriding aim of this study is to develop a methodological framework for the analysis of gender portrayal on the Italian stage, a methodology informed by the historically-specific patriarchal and socioeconomic context within which Italian theatre has evolved. In so doing, it is intended not only to bring discussion of Italian theatre into the contemporary debate on gender, but also to facilitate the analysis of gender in dramatic works in any language.

CHAPTER ONE

Waiting in the wings: female characters in Italian Renaissance comedy

This exploration of gender on the Italian stage begins with an assessment of the role of female characters in Italian Renaissance comedy. The focal point both in this chapter and the next is the interface between gender portrayal and stage conventions, particularly in view of differences between the sixteenth-century stage and that of today. The relationship between gender portrayal and stage conventions is by no means immediately apparent; nevertheless, social conventions both feed into and are reinforced by traditions of staging. Of particular interest in sixteenth-century erudite comedy is the basic fact that it retained a significant proportion of the stage, and consequently also the social, conventions of the Roman comic theatre out of which it developed. An appraisal of the social mores inscribed in what may appear at first sight to be ideologically innocuous devices of staging, plot and language, throws into sharp relief the position of female in relation to male characters, as well as illuminating the situation of each within their own respective gender hierarchies.

In terms of both genre and corpus of plays chosen, Italian Renaissance theatre is essentially a comic theatre which flowered in the early decades of the sixteenth century, and which proved more popular than other dramatic genres (Scrivano 1986, p. 9; Pietropaolo 1986, p. 35).[1] The plays examined date from 1508 to 1531, and are known variously as classical comedy, erudite comedy (*commedia erudita*), serious comedy (*commedia grave*), sustained comedy (*commedia sostenuta*) and *commedia osservata* (because it observed the rules of classical drama).[2] With its complete written text and, initially at least, performed by amateurs, it is to be distinguished from the *commedia dell'arte* (comedy of the guild or trade), the improvised branch of comedy which was developed towards the middle of the sixteenth century by new professional acting companies. In the history of Italian theatre, the classical Renaissance comedies were preceded by the predominantly religious mediaeval

Plate 1. Female characters at windows or near open doorways in an illustration for
Bibbiena's *La Calandria*, 1526.

sacre rappresentazioni, which continued to be performed during the sixteenth century, but from which the comedies constituted a separate
development in their humanist allegiance to a return to the classical
authors of the pre-Christian era.[3] Numerous performances of the
comedies of Plautus and Terence in the latter part of the fifteenth
century went hand in hand with the writing of Latin and, increasingly,
vernacular plays in the Roman style.[4] Many of the plays in the corpus
under scrutiny are regarded as representing the apotheosis of the
vernacular development of the classical Roman tradition primarily
because of what is perceived as their contemporary social focus, a perception which is particularly relevant to the purpose of this study.

The assessment of the situation of female characters in the social
scene staged by these plays requires the use of certain criteria. Visibility
is one criterion for the evaluation of characters in drama of any period,
and it can be argued that this is especially the case as far as the
Renaissance is concerned. During this era the printed word was still
generally less important as a means of communication than visual
and oral channels. As a result the theatre, in its reliance on both
these means, occupied a special position in Renaissance Europe
(Koenigsberger and Mosse 1968, p. 314). In this context, the visual element in theatre may be said to be of particular significance for the audience of the Renaissance. Study of the art of memory during this period
emphasized the greater impact on an audience of visual rather than
spoken material, so that the audience's perception of a play was determined more by what they saw than by what they heard (Pietropaolo
1986, p. 45). Active presence on stage, in both visual and oral terms, is
central to the dramatic importance of a character.

Another major consideration is that of social status. The characters,
both female and male, vary greatly in terms of class and age, as well as
in marital and household ranking. These differences can be seen to
directly inform the type of stage presence and corresponding audience
attention which they are accorded. Basically, the higher the status of
the female character, the less power and stage presence she can be seen
to have in both visual and oral terms. Highest in social status, but not in
dramatic presence, are young, nubile, virginal, beautiful, well-born
(middle-class or higher) freewomen living in the household of their
fathers or guardians, with nubility during this period beginning at the
age of twelve (Chamberlin 1982, p. 190). Seventeen-year-old Clizia,
living in the home of her guardian in Machiavelli's play *Clizia*, is such a
character. As a ward, her situation was by no means uncommon in the

Renaissance, due to the frequency of plague and warfare. In the fifteenth century a communal office, the *Ufficio de' Pupilli*, was even set up to take charge of wards and the reimbursement of their guardians (Klapisch-Zuber 1985, p. 75). Clizia's father, separated from his daughter twelve years previously during the invasion of Naples by Charles V, appears at the end of the play to relieve Nicomaco of his guardianship. The high-status Clizia, like Licinia in Ariosto's *La Lena*, never appears on stage; she is neither seen nor heard by the audience.

Meanwhile, at the opposite end of the female hierarchy are to be found servantwomen, slavewomen, procuresses and prostitutes. In the middle are wives (whose status is measured in terms of youth and beauty), and, with curious infrequency, mothers. The remarkable paucity of mothers in these plays, as opposed to the ubiquity of fathers or male guardians, is a significant feature. As regards the procuresses and prostitutes at the lower end of the female hierarchy, it is no accident that Lena, in Ariosto's *La Lena*, perhaps the liveliest and most prominent of all the female characters, is an adulteress turned temporary procuress and no longer in her teens. Relevant to this is Herrick's comment on female presence in Roman comedy: 'since representations of respectable young women were virtually barred from the Roman comic stage, the courtesans provided all the feminine charm of the New Comedy' (Herrick 1950, p. 162).

The influence of Roman comedy on the portrayal of female characters in Italian Renaissance comedy is an important consideration. Although intertextuality is now an accepted fact, in that all cultural production is in some way derivative, in this era as in no other the roots of the past are clearly discernible. Whether or not 'respectable' female characters gained prominence on the Italian Renaissance stage in relation to their Roman sisters, who in turn largely mirrored their Greek antecedents, is a debatable point.[5] It would certainly seem to be the case that the four categories of female characters in Roman comedy are replicated in Renaissance comedy: the maid (*ancilla, nutrix*), the courtesan (*meretrix*), the wife (*matrona*) and the young girl (*virgo, puella*). Duckworth's statement that in Roman comedy 'the young girl seldom comes on the stage; those who do appear are usually girls of unknown parentage who are in the power of a slave-dealer' also appears analogous to the Renaissance situation (Duckworth 1971, p. 253). While the situation of these dramatically underprivileged female characters in Roman comedy does not appear to have improved to any significant degree in the erudite comedy of the Italian Renaissance, their portrayal does show evidence of the different socioeconomic context within which they were conceived. Certain developments in staging during this era also helped to introduce at least the beginnings of some possibilities in terms of stage appearance for hitherto invisible heroines.

This analysis of the plays takes into account the notion of audience positions in relation to the hierarchies of gender, class, age and social status displayed by the characters. These positions are determined by the way in which the comedies treat the basic dramatic components encapsulated in the three unities of time, place and action. The dramatists would have worked within these traditional conventions, which they observed at work in Roman comedy (Andrews 1993, p. 26). These conventions have notable implications for certain female characters, whose freedom of movement some of them inherently limit. Of special interest are the social/patriarchal strictures which the dramatic conventions reproduce and reinforce. In addition to the three unities, there is one obvious stage convention which is of special relevance to audience perceptions of gender during the Renaissance, namely the playing of female parts by young male actors. The complex dynamics resulting from this convention will be examined in the next chapter. Suffice it to say at this point that erudite comedy, as a rule, was performed only by male actors in the first half of the sixteenth century. However, the particular context of each individual performance (private or public, papal or court) and the occasion it helped to celebrate (weddings, carnival), were also influential in determining the presence or absence of women in the cast.

SETTING THE SCENE

The adherence by Renaissance dramatists to the unities of time and place, and the concomitant observance of the social conventions implicit in them, held important implications for certain female characters. The attention to norms which characterized an era increasingly burgeoning with treatises thus extended to the social sphere, by which it was itself of course also conditioned.[6] Aristotle called only for unity of plot in *Poetics* x. Yet, despite the fact that he made no reference to unity of place, and observed rather than proscribed that 'as regards length, tragedy tends to fall within a single revolution of the sun', sixteenth-century comic dramatists and theorists considered all three areas (time, space and action) in terms of unities for the purposes of dramatic composition.

The time

The restriction of the fictional timespan of the comedies to twelve or twenty-four hours, in conjunction with plot complexity, inevitably meant that some action had to take place not only in the day, but also during the early morning, late evening, or night time. This affects female characters in a variety of ways, particularly when time of day is considered in relation to place. The stage on which the comedies were performed represented space that was public in more ways than one, and consequently off-limits for certain female characters. In the first place, the performances in themselves were, by definition, public. Secondly, unity of space resulted in the use of only one stage set, and this depicted the public, outside world of the town square. The appearance out of doors in this public space at any time of day by high-status women (young, nubile, virginal, beautiful and well-born) was as little countenanced in the Renaissance comedies as in those of Plautus and Terence. Particularly opprobrious in terms of social convention was such an appearance not only at night, as one might expect, but even at the other extremity of the day. In *Gli ingannati*, for instance, Lelia, dressed as a boy for greater freedom of movement, declares that she is committing a daring act by 'leaving the house alone so early' and describes her apprehension as follows:

I can't think where I found the nerve to come out alone like this at this time of day, knowing what I do about the bad habits of the wicked young men of Modena! It would serve me right if one of those reckless young idiots grabbed hold of me and dragged me into a house somewhere to find out whether I'm really a boy or girl! That would teach me to go out on my own in the early hours like this. (I, 3)

For a female character of high status to be alone out of doors early in the morning is clearly marked as unusual, and occurs only under exceptional circumstances that have to be explained in order to justify the breaking of social convention. Lelia continues:

But the cause of all this turmoil is my love for that ungrateful brute Flamminio . . . And that's why I've come out so early, to consult my nurse. I was looking out of the window, and saw her coming this way, and I want to ask her to help me choose the best course of action. (II, 3)

There are also implications for female characters involved in action which takes place at night. In addition to the fact that appearance in the street at night is even less of a possibility than during the day, action involving a female character that has taken place offstage has to be narrated onstage, either while it is taking place or afterwards. This type of action (for instance, a bedscene), is frequently the climax of the scheme around which the plot is built. Its narration is invariably carried out either by a male character, who may be of any social status, or by a low-status female character. In other words, any participation in the action by a female character of high status is taken over and recounted on her behalf by another character. This ventriloquism by other characters of what can be described as the ideal female voice within patriarchy, is a prominent feature of the comedies, as will be seen on pp. 46–8 below.[7] This is of course also an issue as far as daytime action is concerned. Because of the single public *piazza* scene which framed all onstage action, the private, domestic scenario, namely the conventional domain of the high-status female character, remained unrepresented except through narration.

The identity of the narrator in these instances is a defining factor in the delineation of this ideal, yet absent, female character. While in *Clizia* it is Doria, a female servant, who gives an update on the various phases of the trick (IV, 8; V, 1), which takes place indoors, at night, and involves Clizia herself, it is Nicomaco who recounts the full version of the culmination of the trick (V, 2). Interestingly, several versions of these offstage events are given. In one account, Nicomaco is told that Clizia has become violent and he is thereby thrown off the scent. In reality she has been moved even further from the stage in that she has been removed from the implicit indoor scene behind the scenes, and taken to a nunnery. On the one hand, then, several female characters (Doria, Sostrata and Clizia) have combined forces to successfully outwit the patriarch himself, who is made a figure of ridicule. However, the participation and indeed the entire role of the idealized young virgin is rendered invisible in terms of audience perception, and it is Nicomaco's final lengthy narration of the trick that predominates.

As far as the representation of time is concerned, then, the indications are that while the appearance by high-status female characters was not countenanced in daytime action, the night time does not even come into consideration, and the early morning is regarded as highly unsuitable. These particular female characters are thus bound by a round-the-clock curfew, while all male characters have permanent freedom of movement.[8] Moreover, the meticulous attention paid in various ways to the representation of time in the plays serves to reinforce these social conventions, continually reminding the audience of the time element. This can be observed to take place in both verbal and visual areas of the performance: the speech of the characters and the mechanical stage effects.

References to time punctuate what the characters say, informing the audience of the time of day at which the play opens, the passing of time as the play progresses, the coming of nightfall and, in *La mandragola*, the passing of night and the dawn of the following day. The first two lines of *Clizia*, for example, establish that the play begins very early in the morning (both characters use the phrase *di buon'ora*):

PALAMEDE: You're leaving the house rather early, aren't you?
CLEANDRO: And where are you coming from so early?

La Lena also opens with references to time, as Corbolo remarks on Flavio's early rising: 'Flavio, if you don't mind my asking, where are you going at this time of day? The bell is only just ringing for matins.' Their subsequent dialogue is dominated by the theme of time, as light and dark are used to lead to a discussion of Licinia, with whom Flavio is in love. In *La cassaria*, Volpino warns that 'we have little of the day left' (II, 1) and two acts later night has fallen, as Crisobolo indicates in his remark 'I've lingered so long in Plutero's house, without realizing, that it is now night' (IV, 2). Ligurio in *La mandragola* recommends speed of action, as time is moving on apace: 'But let's not waste any more time; it's already two o'clock' (IV, 2). Fra Timoteo refers to the passing of night at the end of Act IV. The *canzone* following this act and beginning 'O sweet night', also serves to indicate that the bedscene is taking place at night. This is followed by Timoteo's opening statement in Act V to the effect that he has been unable to sleep that night, while Nicia remarks to Lucrezia: 'You're very lively this morning' (V, 4). Chronological references are thus interwoven with the action in such a way as to keep the audience in a state of constant awareness of time. Meanwhile, on the visual plane, mechanical devices such as a mobile sun, sometimes complemented by the use of the same sky for both stage and auditorium, served to enhance these intradiegetic references.[9] With the spatial element similarly given a high profile, the social conventions inherent in the dramatic conventions of both space and time would have been quite emphatically underlined in the minds of the audience.

The place

The single stage setting for the erudite comedies indicates the extent to which the flexibility of mediaeval stage practice, with its multiple stages and scenes, had been forfeited (Firth 1978, p. 65). That this restriction was certainly not for any lack of mechanical expertise is shown by the elaborate devices engineered for the *intermezzi*. In this context, advice on scene changing for the *intermezzi* could easily have been extended to the plays themselves.[10] In the case of comedy, it was the *scena comica*, the public, outdoor *piazza* scene, which was standard during the years covered by our corpus. In yet another return to the classics, architects such as Serlio and Sangallo canonized existing practice by following Vitruvius and dividing scene types into comic, tragic and pastoral. All these scenes were set outdoors, with both comic and tragic scenes having an urban setting, differentiated in terms of the class of buildings depicted (middle class and noble, respectively), whilst the pastoral scene was rustic in style. The comic scene, then, allowed for no indoor action on stage, unlike some early humanist plays (like Pisani's *Philogenia*, 1435–7), which still retained the mediaeval tradition of various onstage 'houses' depicting a variety of scenes. The mediaeval *sacre rappresentazioni* were similarly not limited to one outdoor scene.

The fixed *piazza* scene inevitably restricted the playwright in the type of material which could be portrayed. As Pietropaolo comments: 'There can be no doubt that the Serlian stage was a determining influence on the conventionalization of Renaissance comedy, since the number of situations representable in a city square was quite limited' (Pietropaolo 1986, p. 38).[11] Given the fact that this dramatic convention was also an expression of the social conventions which kept high-status female characters indoors, this meant that male characters, irrelevant of status, occupied a privileged dramatic position from the start.[12] The influence on the dramatic by the social as regards the stage setting is made clear by Burns. Writing on the eventual normalization of the indoor scene, she sees the 'shift in locale from the public to the private sphere as a direct correspondence with an analogous shift of emphasis in social reality' (Burns 1972, p. 71). In this context, the influential Renaissance innovation in stage scenery, namely the introduction of perspective, signalled no increase in dramatic possibilities for high-status female characters. In addition to the element of perspective, one other aspect of Serlian scenery differentiated this outside scene from its lateral, non-perspectival Roman predecessor. This was the inclusion of a church, which did in fact provide a glimmer of hope for these female characters:

Since in the set for comedy the highest building is a church, the newly created upstage area could be used to resolve an important dramaturgical problem in classical comedy, which consisted in finding a way of preserving the decorum of a lady or of a girl of good family engaged in a dialogue with a male character in a public place . . . encounters of this type could now conveniently and decorously take place near the church, as the ladies in question went to or returned from service, confession or prayer. (Pietropaolo 1986, p. 39)

In *La mandragola*, Lucrezia, the beautiful young wife of Messer Nicia, is seen on stage near the church approaching Frate Timoteo with her mother, Sostrata (III, 10), and conversing with him in the next scene. It is his suggestion that both women come to see him, and it is as a direct consequence of this invitation to the church that Lucrezia appears at all in these two scenes. (No such pretext is needed, on the other hand, for the appearance of Sostrata, her mother; her conversation with two male characters contains no references to the church (III, 1)). Lucrezia's reappearance for the final two scenes is again preceded by information, given by Callimaco in the previous scene, that he has arranged to meet her at the church, where she is to go with her mother and husband. In other words, all Lucrezia's stage appearances are carefully placed in a religious context. That she is allowed to appear at all is due to the fact that she is married, and consequently not as closely guarded as a young, unmarried woman would have been. And she has, of course, committed adultery, which automatically lowers her status. Nevertheless, that her appearance at the play's end is again emphasized as linked to the church would seem to be somewhat gratuitous in terms of the plot itself. There is no marriage to be held at the end of this comedy (unless one reads the final scene as a mock celebration of the affair which has begun between Lucrezia and Callimaco).

Another female character who speaks with the friar near his church is the anonymous 'woman' (III, 3). The sexual innuendo with which she expresses her fears of what the Turks might do to her gives this character a comic dimension. However, there are no indications that she is other than 'respectable', and her appearance on stage/out of doors, is associated with meeting another female character in a religious environment. Her actual function in the play is not at all clear. She is superfluous to the plot, which gains nothing from her dialogue. Apart from the possibility that she is introduced to provide a little light relief from the main interest, and at the same time act as a foil to Timoteo's humour, it may indeed be the case that her primary role lies in her final reference to the nearby church, where she catches sight of the woman she wishes to see. This would remind the audience that Timoteo is actually at his church, so that his suggestion a few scenes later that Lucrezia and her mother should visit him would emphasize, yet again, the religious associations of the young wife's appearance on stage.

Lucrezia has apparently attended church with great frequency in order to pray for pregnancy (a detail which sits somewhat awkwardly with her own rather critical reference to her husband's desire for a child, rather than to any desire of her own: 'I have always suspected that Messer Nicia's desire for children would make us make some mistake or other' (III, 10)). It was common practice for women to turn to the Church for help in order to conceive.[13] It is of course the Church, in the form of Friar Timoteo, which contributes to the scheme that results in Lucrezia's presumed future pregnancies, although not in the conventional manner. Indeed, the perpetuation of the tradition of anticlericalism in this play has the effect of reversing the idealized perception of the church as one of the rare permissible outdoor venues for women (it does not as a rule endanger the stake which patriarchy has in female chastity). It is true that Lucrezia will doubtless sooner or later conceive as a result of the intervention of the Church, thereby contenting Nicia, the wealthy patriarch in need of an heir. However, not only does she commit adultery to do so; her frequent churchgoing has in the past made her a target of a friar's sexual advances. Nevertheless, it is the basic patriarchal ideology of the church as a decorous outdoor locus which remains central, not only visually in terms of the perspective of the comic scene, but also as the fantasized norm from which the Church as represented by Timoteo is seen to deviate.[14]

It seems clear that what Pietropaolo, referring to the need in classical comedy to justify the stage appearance of 'respectable' women, describes as a 'dramaturgical problem', is patently also, if not predominantly, a social one. With patriarchal definitions of femininity continuing to hold sway in Renaissance Italy (a continuance, in effect, of many of the Roman social norms), there would be no real impetus to change dramatic rules in any significant way. Moreover, the retention of the single outdoor scene in Renaissance comedies would not in itself necessarily have precluded the presence on stage, and full participation in the action, of all types of female character but, rather, reinforces perceptions of gender current at the time. The introduction of the church into the comic scene, then, can be seen to have increased female access to the stage only to a limited degree.

The ideology linking gender with place which is inscribed in the comic scene is founded on a series of traditional binary opposites: female–male, body–mind, absent–present, inside–outside, private–public.[15] The first important implication of these binaries is an implicit correspondence between the female body and the home. Entry by a male character into a house in which there is a young female character causes alarm precisely because it is equated with sexual entry. Conversely, the presence of such a female character out of doors invariably connotes sexual availability on her part. In order to defuse this connotation, a female character who is on stage/out of doors, has to elaborate on the unusual circumstances which have led her to lay herself open to sexual advances simply by being on the street (as in the case of Lelia in *Gli ingannati*). Alternatively, it must be made abundantly clear that she is heading for a church.

The association of female sexual availability with mere appearance on the street appears to have been formalized in a ritual which took place after Renaissance weddings. Brucker describes the procedure which followed the solemnization of the marriage by a notary: 'Then the bride and her entourage made a formal and festive journey through the city streets to her husband's house where the physical consummation of the marriage occurred' (Brucker 1986, p. 83). The legitimation of the bride's imminent loss of virginity, that precious commodity in the circulation among men of female reproductive power, occurs when she is passed from her father or guardian, the (non-sexual) custodian of her virginity, to her future sexual protector. This sexual passage from one man to another is made public by the appearance of the bride in the street, often with great pomp: 'The bridal procession was not only a means of display, but it also provided the very important opportunity to tell the world that the girl had passed from her father's to her husband's protection. In Florence, spectacular torchlight processions were particularly popular, bride and groom being preceded by trumpets and drums' (Chamberlin 1982, p. 195). In the light of the body/house equation, the female character's lack of control over her body is also symbolized by the fact that the house in which she lives never belongs to her, but to her father, guardian or husband.

This leads to another major factor, namely that femininity is defined by patriarchy exclusively in terms of sexuality. As a result, the possibilities for a female character to appear on stage/out of doors are entirely dependent on the particular phase she has reached in her sexuality, in itself defined in relation to men.[16] Any actual abilities a female character might have are secondary to the sexual considerations which completely circumscribe her identity; and, even then, they are often only those already associated with ideal femininity. In *La mandragola*, Lucrezia is described by Ligurio as 'wise, dignified, and fit to rule a kingdom' (1, 3) (high praise indeed, but somewhat empty in view of the fact that women were not granted citizenship).[17] The particular talents he refers to are the traditional wifely ones concerned with managing the household. Yet not even these are seen in action: there are no indoor scenes. The domestic sphere, moreover, is regarded as inferior to the public world of male transactions (even when these appear to be focussed on women). Alberti, in his fifteenth-century treatise on the family, gives an indispensable insight into the low value accorded to the indoor domain, while also incidentally revealing that women were not classed as citizens:

GIANNOZZO: Since I find it no easy matter to deal with the needs of the household when I must often be engaged *outside with other men* in arranging *matters of wider consequence*, I have found it wise to set aside a certain amount for outside use, for investments and purchases. The rest, which takes care of all the smaller household affairs, I leave to my wife's care. I have done it this way, for, to tell the truth, it would hardly win us respect if our wife busied herself among men in the marketplace, out in the public eye. It also seems somewhat *demeaning to me to remain shut up in the house among women* when I have manly things to do among men, fellow citizens and worthy and distinguished foreigners. (Alberti 1969, p. 207, italics added)

The biological argument is invoked to justify what amounts to the enclosure indoors of women in Renaissance society:

LIONARDO: The character of men is stronger than that of women and can bear the attacks of enemies better, can stand strain longer, is more constant under stress. Therefore men have the freedom to travel with honor in foreign lands acquiring and gathering the goods of fortune. Women, on the other hand, are almost all timid by nature, soft, slow, and therefore more useful when they *sit still and watch over our things*. It is as though nature thus provided for our well-being, arranging for men to bring things home and for women to guard them. The woman, as she *remains locked up at home, should watch over things by staying at her post*, by diligent care and watchfulness. The man should guard the woman, the house, and his family and country, but not by sitting still. (Alberti 1969, p. 207, italics added)[18]

In relation to the difference in mobility between men and women, Brucker records the following plea by Fiorenza, a witness to the case between Giovanni and Lusanna: 'If you have to lie to help me, it will not be a sin, because it is better to help a woman of my condition instead of a man. Unlike a woman, a man can go anywhere' (Brucker 1986, p. 71). Thus at the beginning of *La mandragola*, Callimaco returns to Florence from Paris, where he has been living, while Lucrezia, according to Nicia, 'would be unwilling to leave Florence'. The gender implications of the inside–outside dichotomy in the Renaissance are clear, together with the negative perception of women who attempted to transgress its divide: 'Giannozzo: I often used to express my disapproval of bold and forward females who try too hard to know about things outside the house and about the concerns of their husband and of men in general' (Alberti 1969, p. 207).

The dividing line between these binary opposites structured around the spatial dimension is of great interest, for it is at the juncture between the two that much of the onstage action takes place. Indeed, it might even be said that the hub of the plot is more often than not concerned with the illicit crossing of that divide, as male characters attempt to penetrate the house/body of forbidden female characters. It is on entrances to houses, and on windows and balconies, that audience attention is often made to focus. These areas represent the boundaries of the female body and in particular, points of access to it. In *Gli ingannati*, the sexual interplay which takes place between Isabella and Lelia (disguised as Fabio) in the entrance to the house of Isabella's father, is dangerously situated not merely on one boundary, namely that between the domestic and the public as signified by the doorway. As well as allowing the possibility of lesbian desire to enter the scene, the interaction between these two characters also challenges that most severely policed of all boundaries, that between virginity and its 'loss' at the moment of penetration. One could argue that in this case the threat is defused, or even non-existent, as Fabio is really a woman. However, the phantom of defloration is nevertheless invoked by the scene, particularly as observed with horror by two male servants. Moreover, Lelia/Fabio will later be replaced by her twin brother in Isabella's arms, this time actually inside the house itself, at which point Isabella's dream, and her father's nightmare, become reality.

Other instances of sexually-connotative action at the boundaries of the inside–outside, domestic–public divide, occur at windows and on balconies, both on stage and as reported action. In *La cortigiana*, for example, Messer Maco sees a beautiful woman at a window and falls in love with her, and Togna is reprimanded by her husband for 'flirting at the windows' (IV, 11). In his writings on stage scenery, Serlio remarks that 'Some artists are in the habit of painting supposedly living characters in these scenes – such as a *woman on a balcony or in a doorway*, even a few animals' (Hewitt, 1958, p. 317, italics added).[19] This would seem to be a recognition and formalization of the dramatic possibilities of that particular location for a female character, while at the same time serving to immobilize women within the indoor domain.

It is frequently out of doors that a female character is first seen by the central male character, thereby setting the plot in motion as schemes are hatched in order for him to gain access to her house/body. For example, Erostrato in *I suppositi* first saw Polinesta in the Via Grande. He thereupon exchanged identity with his manservant in order to enter the service of Polinesta's father, as a result of which he has freedom of movement in her house. Once again, the documentation of a real-life Renaissance love affair by Brucker is of interest, in that it indicates the street as one of the more obvious outside places where men would espy the woman of their dreams: 'Antonio recalled that Giovanni would follow his sister [Lusanna] in the streets and would approach her in markets and churches "as lovers are wont to do"' (Brucker 1986, p. 16). Class is an important issue here. Lusanna's father is a tailor, which places her in the artisanal class, and consequently she would have had the freedom to attend markets and other outdoor venues:

While the moral code defined in sermons and in civic legislation did apply to woman like Lusanna, it may have been attenuated or less rigidly enforced by the particular circumstances of her condition. Women from the artisanal class enjoyed a greater degree of social freedom than did their chaperoned, aristocratic sisters. They could move freely in the streets, gossip with neighbours, shop in the markets, attend services in their local church. (Brucker 1986, pp. 90–1)

The romantically involved female characters in the comedies, however, are never from the artisanal classes. Isabella and Lelia in *Gli ingannati*, for instance, are the daughters of wealthy merchants, while Polinesta's father (*I suppositi*) is sufficiently rich to have a household of servants and to aim at a financially advantageous marriage for his daughter.

The inside–outside dichotomy is invoked for the audience by both visual and verbal means, as in the case of the representation of time. In addition to stage scenery depicting a public, outdoor place, the characters constantly talk about going inside, knock on house doors, or observe others coming out or going in. As a result, what are in effect stage directions become part of the dramatic text, to be retained in the performance itself. It is interesting to see how information about place, with its implications for female characters, is integrated into the fabric of onstage speech as one way of dealing with the strict unity of the single outdoor scene. In several plays the outside part of the inside–outside dichotomy becomes paradoxically associated with privacy and secrecy. When characters wish to talk without being overheard, they come out on to the street/stage, thereby providing a pretext for being out of doors, and on stage, rather than indoors, and off stage. *I suppositi* opens in this way, with the Nurse beckoning to Polinesta to come outside:

NURSE: There's no one around; come out, Polinesta, into the street, where we'll be able to see around us, and we'll at least be certain of not being overheard by anyone. I think in our house even the bedsteads, the chests and the doorways have ears.

In this case, the mere appearance of a high-status female character such as Polinesta, albeit just outside her front door and in the company of her maid, is certainly remarkable; however, she never reappears during the course of the play. *La cassaria* also uses the device of justifying an outdoor conversation/the outdoor setting itself, with the motive of secrecy. Act v, scene 3 leads into the next scene as follows:

FULCIO: Tell Crisobolo that Signor Bassa's messenger has something to tell him.
MARSO: Why don't you go into the house?
FULCIO: Ask him to be so kind as to come outside, for reasons of prudence and because I've come on a matter of great importance to him. *Scene 4*
CRISOBOLO: Who's asking for me at this inopportune hour?
FULCIO: Don't be surprised, and pardon me for having called you out here, but as I've something very secret to tell you, I don't trust not being over-heard inside by people who'll then repeat it. Here I can see all around me, and won't have to worry about being overheard by anyone I can't see. But let's come out further into the street, and ask your people to stay indoors.
CRISOBOLO: Wait for me inside, all of you. Now, tell me what's on your mind.

Place references such as these would have been necessitated, at least in part, by the custom of not providing a separate set of stage directions. Their role would have been primarily to inform the actors, as well as the audience, of the precise location on stage of each of the characters in any given scene. Such information would also serve to suggest the existence of an indoor scenario behind the scenes. This would presumably be a necessary allusion if only in terms of verisimilitude, given that in reality life was not lived exclusively out of doors. Of importance is the effect which such reiteration of indoor–outdoor dynamics would have had on the audience. These intradiegetic place references, in conjunction with the outdoor stage set of the comic scene and the spatial dynamics of the characters' movements, would undoubtedly have reinforced the social significance of the inside–outside dichotomy, along with that of other related opposites (private–public, absent–present). Most significantly, the implications of these spatial conventions for female characters would have received repeated confirmation in the minds of the audience.

PLOTTING THE TRICK

The trickster and the tricked

The role of female characters in the plot is crucial in determining audience perceptions of them. The plot of classical comedies is invariably constructed around a central trick or intrigue in the form of a cunning plan conceived with wit (*ingegno*), in which several characters conspire together at the expense of others. The result was a 'comedy of plot designed to entertain and to create wonder' (Beecher 1984, p. 171). The aim of the sixteenth-century comedy of plot was thus to give the audience intellectual as well as visual pleasure. The high value accorded to wit is particularly underlined by Aretino's reference to 'the love which the courtesy of Princes bears to good wits (*buoni ingegni*)' in a letter to the Cardinal of Trento which precedes *La cortigiana*. In assessing the part the female characters played in the plays, it is important to ascertain whether their mental faculties are engaged in this dramatic area. In other words, the purpose of the trick must be established, as well as the extent to which female characters contribute both to its conception and its enaction. In identifying who conspires with and against whom, a distinct hierarchy of male characters also comes into focus.

In general narrative terms, the trick can be described as the device that works to overcome the obstacle at the heart of the plot by stimulating further action upon which the development and progression of the narrative depend. In the specific context of drama, intrigue clearly gives ample opportunity for dramatic irony, with consequent audience omniscience at the expense of certain of the characters.[20] The trick can be defined as essentially competitive in nature: its purpose is that of gaining an advantage or profit either intellectually or materially, but often both. The development of the trick as a pivotal dramatic element was to reach a high point in erudite Italian Renaissance comedy, with the figure of the trickster providing scope for plot variety in the otherwise restrictive context of the dramatic conventions of time and place (Beecher 1986, pp. 53, 55).

The material gain aimed at by the trick appears not only in terms of money and goods (clothes and food), but also, in true Lévi-Straussian style, in terms of female bodies, as will be seen later. Beginning with the intellectual facet of the trick, the most common motive for intrigue is the inaccessibility to a male character of a desired female character who is socially out of bounds and physically out of reach. The aim of the trick is for this male character to gain access, primarily for sexual reasons which are sometimes, but not always, linked to marriage. This often necessitates further scheming as the male character, frequently the young son of a wealthy father, needs to obtain money to buy help in achieving his objective. Both this sub-trick and the main trick involve a variety of devices: 'disguises, false rhetoric, deceptive jargon, fraudulent representation of merchandise' (Beecher 1986, p. 56).

The conception of the trick is interesting in that it is hardly ever the ardent 'hero' who is seen to employ his wit in its creation. One exception is Erostrato's adoption of disguise in *I suppositi* in order to enter household service and thereby gain access to his master's daughter; however, even this takes place not on stage, but before the play begins. More typical is Flavio, the young would-be lover in *La Lena*, who disappears permanently from the stage once he has revealed his desire and engaged help in fulfilling it. Usually it is the hero's male servant whose *ingegno* is the centrepiece of the play. For him the purpose of the trick is to sell his help for material profit; it is also a means of obtaining intellectual satisfaction as he outwits other characters. The characters whom the trick outwits are, basically, any other competitors for the female character in demand, and her male protector (father, husband, guardian, pimp). The extent to which the female character herself is tricked varies from play to play. What is standard, however, is the role of the young, high-status female character as the prize to be won if the trick succeeds. In order to outmanoeuvre other characters, the designer of the stratagem is also part of a conspiratorial team. As well as liaising with his master, for whom the trick is being carried out in the first place, the trickster intrigues with other characters from the servant class and above. Sometimes he enlists the help of a female character, who is either a prostitute or a procuress, or becomes labelled as such. This is the case of Lena, in Ariosto's play of the same name. She is not a regular procuress, but her role in the trick tars her with that brush, particularly in the eyes of male characters who are also involved, yet not pejoratively viewed.

The prologue to *La mandragola* leaves no doubt as to Lucrezia's position in relation to the trick. She is actually introduced in the description of the characters as 'deceived', despite the fact that she is also described as 'shrewd'. Indeed, the fact that she is also, in Ligurio's words, 'wise, dignified, and fit to rule a kingdom', indicates that she is not short of *ingegno*. On the one hand, it could be argued that these attributes, coupled with her chastity, make her even more of a challenge to outwit. However, the important point is that she is not the architect of the play's trick, but its objective, and the shrewdness mentioned as a feature of her personality is never allowed on stage. Lucrezia's role is clearly envisaged from the start as that of being duped, even though she will join the side of the deceivers at the end of the play and well into the foreseeable future (she and Callimaco embark on an affair which will culminate in their marriage on her old husband's death). There is also a sense in which she is the undignified butt of coarse humour when in one scene a urine sample, which she has apparently provided, is flaunted on stage by a group of male characters. They attempt to ascertain the reason for her supposed infertility by peering at its colour, an indecorous act even by Renaissance standards, when bodily functions were not yet the source of social embarrassment which they were later to become.

Lucrezia is of course not alone in being tricked. She is the prize at which the trick is aimed, but in order for Callimaco to claim her, Messer Nicia, her husband, has to be convinced of the efficacy of the *mandragola* as a fertility potion. He also has to be persuaded of the necessity for her to have sexual intercourse with another man in order to draw off its poisonous effects, for his own safety. At this point issues of hierarchy among the male characters come into play, as Ligurio takes great pleasure in duping Messer Nicia. Despite the fact that Nicia is a doctor of law (the title of *messer* was only held by lawyers and nobles), he is portrayed as offensively stupid in a context where wit is highly valued. *Ingegno* was particularly favoured by Machiavelli. In another of his works, *Il principe*, it appears as a variant of *virtú*, and denotes the use of one's own faculties rather than relying on chance (*Fortuna*). Nicia's stupidity, which Ligurio regards as an important aid to facilitating his trick, inspires in the latter a sense of dislike with clear class connotations: 'I don't think there's a more stupid man in the world than this one; and how fortune has favoured him! He's the one with all the money, he's the one with the beautiful woman' (1, 3). Callimaco, the putative 'hero' for whom Ligurio schemes, does have intelligence; however, his behaviour is to a great extent orchestrated by Ligurio, who is his servant.

While the married young Lucrezia is on stage for three scenes, on each occasion decorously near the church, Clizia, the nubile young ward of Nicomaco in *Clizia*, never makes an appearance. She too is the primary object of intrigue, which takes the form of two parallel schemes conceived for two would-be lovers in the form of father and son (Nicomaco and Cleandro). The plot thickens, with distinctly unpleasant implications for Clizia, as two other male characters, servants of Nicomaco and Cleandro, compete as prospective husbands who would allow their masters access to her in return for a house and a financial settlement. It is Clizia's unknown social status which has made these particular machinations possible, a possibility which disappears once her long-lost father appears at the end of the play and she is revealed to be legitimate, well-born, and suitable for marriage to Cleandro. Before this happens, however, Nicomaco's designs on Clizia are thwarted by a crucial trick designed by his wife, Sofronia. Rather unusually, it is a female character whose wit has been used here to devise a successful trick. And it is a female servant, Doria, who relates it. It is important to bear in mind, however, that Sofronia is not a high-status female character; as Nicomaco's wife and Cleandro's mother, she is neither nubile nor young, factors which enable her not only to appear on stage, but even to be seen to have intelligence. Clizia, on the other hand, is a high-status character, and is markedly absent. Her removal to a convent means that she is also excluded from the merriment that follows the successful outcome of Sofronia's plan, as narrated by Doria:

I've never laughed so much, and I don't think I ever will again; in our house we've done nothing all night except laugh, Sofronia, Sostrata, Cleandro, Eustachio, everyone's laughing. (v, 1)

Except for Clizia, that is; absent even from behind the scenes, where she has been invisible anyway, she has been whisked away to a place of safety, presumably in case the trick misfires and she is raped. Laughter, in this comedy as in many of the others, hides a darker side. Moreover, her response to Cleandro's desire for her is never clarified, nor, indeed, is her reaction to their marriage, an event which is planned the very instant of her long-lost father's reappearance. It is this fortuitous event which saves her from direct sexual exploitation (it is by no means certain that Sofronia could have continued to deviate her husband from his designs).

It would seem, then, that female characters who are not of high status are allowed to participate in onstage action (the servant Doria), and even to plot a trick (Sofronia). Two other female characters are notable in this regard. The first is Lena, in Ariosto's play of that name. Unlike Clizia, who gives her name to the title of her play but never appears in it, Lena's presence does make itself felt (in seven out of thirty-six scenes in the first version, and nine out of thirty-eight in the second). Like the male servant who is paid for conspiring to aid his master in his amorous quest in the tradition of the Plautine pimp (*leno*), Lena, who is not young but still attractive, asserts herself vigorously. She sets a firm price on her help and will not be swayed, even by Flavio, the young master himself. In the first six scenes she is a crucial element in his designs on Licinia, to whom she can provide access. Like Clizia, Licinia is a high-status female character who is the object of the trick and who never appears on stage (at one point, her father does address her in the wings, but there is no reply, as she is not there).

However, this dimension of the plot fades into the background as the scheme in which Lena is an important participant gives way entirely to Flavio's inability to raise the necessary twenty-five florins, at which point the focus shifts to the tricks put into play for him to obtain the money. Lena disappears at the end of Act II, to reappear after a prolonged absence of seventeen scenes at the end of Act IV, and then another ten scenes later at the very end of the play. In other words, it is Corbolo, Flavio's servant and plot mechanic, who dominates the play as its arch-schemer, and who implies as much in the following piece of metadiscourse:

What's needed now is the cunning of a manservant, a character whom I've seen played so often in comedies, who knows how to milk this sum from the purse of the old man with fraud and fallacy. (III, 1)

What seems at first sight to be the central trick aimed at getting Flavio access to Licinia, is in fact a pretext for the amplification of a lengthy plot of wit and intrigue which has as its object financial and intellectual competition between men. Even Lena's impotent husband, Pacifico, has an important part to play in the culminating trick which ties together all the plot lines of the play. All the various tricks are linked by his provision of the barrel, a crucial device which short-circuits Lena's part completely by carrying Flavio into Fazio's house and straight to his daughter Licinia. While Lena acquits herself well when she is on stage, she is in the end not as important a participant in the intrigue as Corbolo, her male equivalent.

Another female character of similar note is Alvigia, the low-status procuress and ex-prostitute in Aretino's *La cortigiana* (the usual translation is *Court affairs*, although the title can also mean 'the courtesan'). Although once again the female character plays second fiddle to male intelligence in the form of Rosso, the servant of Signor Parabolano, her mode of self-assertion is emphasized by Rosso's open admiration of her. She is an interestingly powerful character when she is on stage, notably in the way that she comes and goes when she pleases, and is at no one's beck and call. In her role of procuring the services of Togna to impersonate the woman Parabolano has fallen in love with, she is also clearly of central importance to Rosso's schemes. Nevertheless it is he who is the arch-trickster in the play, admired even by his master, whom he has also deceived, along with another servant, Valerio, a Florentine fish merchant and a Jewish clothes seller. In an ending which reasserts the class order, the noble Signor Parabolano pardons both Rosso and Alvigia (a significant event for her, since procuring actually carried the death penalty at the time) (Chamberlin 1982, p. 216).

Two female characters of even lower status than Alvigia, but this time with insignificant parts, are to be found in *La cassaria*. Although once freewomen, they are now slaves kept by the procurer Lucrano, and are the objective of Erofilo and Caridoro. Eulalia and Corisca play no part at all in the intrigue designed by their young men's male servants to carry them off, and appear fleetingly on stage only to speculate about their destiny. When they are present, they express anxiety about being out of doors: Lucrano is not to be crossed in his efforts to keep his sexual merchandise intact (they are still virgins and therefore command a higher price). The central focus of the plot is not even on them, but on the workings of the trick involving the chest, which will result in their liberation from Lucrano and the prospects of piecework prostitution, and assure them of a future as the kept mistresses of Erofilo and Caridoro.

So far it would appear that lower-status but freeborn female characters are allowed to participate in the plot and display wit and intelligence. The higher-status female characters, in descending order, are absent (Clizia, Licinia), present in a peripheral role (Lucrezia), or are allowed partial participation (Sofronia). There is, however, an interesting exception, or rather variation, to this rule, in that cross-dressing enables Lelia in *Gli ingannati* to take part in onstage action and indulge in intrigue. While the full implications of gender disguise will be dealt with in the next chapter, in relation to female participation in the intellectual trickery foregrounded by the comedies, *Gli ingannati* appears progressive in this aspect of the play. However, it is important not to lose sight of the obvious: it is *as a man* that Lelia is allowed to scheme and plot, and she does so at great risk to her reputation *as a woman*. Moreover, her trick does not succeed without the intervention of Clemenzia, her old nurse. Santilla, a high-status female character in *La Calandria*, has been in male disguise since childhood, but although her male identity gives her a fair amount of stage presence, she spends much of her time avoiding the intrigues of others rather than plotting any of her own. Her main priority is to escape a projected marriage with her guardian's daughter, Verginia, a high-status character who never appears on stage. Santilla is released from this marriage not because of her own efforts, but because of the reappearance of her long-lost twin brother, Lidio, who can take her place.

The high-status female characters are married off at the end of the plays: Santilla and Verginia in *La Calandria*, Lelia and Isabella in *Gli ingannati*, Clizia in *Clizia*, Licinia in *La Lena*, and Polinesta in *I suppositi*. Those without a family, namely Eulalia and Corisca in *La cassaria*, are established as mistresses.[21] In the context of tricks and tricksters, the function of the majority of these female characters is to play a passive role in the schemes engineered by male servants who are concerned with gaining a material and intellectual advantage for themselves, and on behalf of their young masters, over rich male protectors (fathers, husbands, guardians, procurers). The female character in question may or may not be duped herself in the process. However, she is invariably in the position of the possession which is forfeited by the male character who finds himself tricked. The daughters of rich fathers (Lelia, Isabella, Clizia, Licinia, Polinesta, Verginia) are literally assets in the context of Renaissance marriage as a business, their high status deriving not merely from their birth, but also from their virginity, which was at a high premium in the marriage market. At the heart of the role which these female characters play in these materialistic comedies lie the twin processes of commodification of the female body and commodity fetishism.

The market and social relations

A materialist base patently informs these plays in a dynamic that works itself out in a complex fashion across the hierarchies of gender, class, age and social status. A recurring factor in plot machinations is the link between money, sex and power, which combine together in financial transactions involving the female body, thereby leading to its commodification.[22] The foregrounding of socioeconomic concerns by the comedies can be seen to stem in part from the characteristics of comedy as a genre. Unlike the 'unworldly mystery' represented by tragedy, it is a 'worldly quality' which features in the comic genre (Howarth 1978, p. 2). According to Cicero, comedy is 'an imitation of life, *a mirror of custom*, and an image of truth' (Howarth 1978, p. 3, italics added). For Donatus, the subject of comedy is 'civic and private concerns'. Howarth notes that 'its protagonists are – unlike the heroes of tragedy – nearly all of "middling fortune": representative men and women, engaged in ordinary pursuits'. This can be interpreted quite literally in class terms as the middle classes and their concerns, as borne out by the class-belonging of the characters in the plays. Howarth continues: 'Even when comedy does involve characters of exalted status, it should still present their "civic and private concerns": courtship, marriage and adultery, the *acquisition of money and social status*, we take to be the common interests of all men, whereas treason, murder and revenge are part of a ruler's prerogative' (Howarth 1978, p. 3, italics added). *La cortigiana* features one of the rare noblemen in these Renaissance comedies, Signor Parabolano, and, true to the conditions mentioned here, it is his private concerns, in the form of love interest, which are central.

The materialist perspective can also be seen to contrast comedy with the pastoral genre. Clubb notes: 'The experience of love, self-knowledge and the vision of harmony which could be felt straining against the limits of *commedia grave* committed to *urban economic realities* could be approached directly and expressionistically in pastoral drama' (Clubb 1986, p. 23, italics added). It is also clear that the ostensibly nonideological classical notions of verisimilitude and decorum which were to be observed by the comic dramatist, serve in effect to ensure the representation of female characters who are patriarchally correct according to the socioeconomic context of their time. Both verisimilitude (mirroring of reality) and decorum (socially appropriate behaviour) thus place social context at the heart of comedy. Realism itself is a standard artistic device for the (re)production and perpetuation of the dominant order, which it reinstates at the end of a plot positing an initial disorder as the narrative problem to be solved.[23] Nonetheless, the prevalence of materialistic concerns in the comedies would seem to exceed even the classical dictum on subject matter.

Female characters in the comedies, especially the young women who act as object of the trick, undergo a process of commodification as a central feature of the plot. The Renaissance playwrights updated the Roman plays to accord with their perception of contemporary socio-economic conditions.[24] In particular, there is a greater emphasis on merchant activity, an increase in the significance of the role of the daughter, especially in terms of a profitable and respectable marriage, and a higher incidence of marriage itself as the 'happy ending' to the plays. However, while the more advanced socioeconomic patterns of the later period may have allowed comparatively greater development of certain female roles, these roles can ultimately be seen merely to reflect a more complex system in which marriageable young daughters were at a premium.

Behind the comedies of the Italian Renaissance, in contrast with their Roman predecessors, lies a highly developed urban economy, based in particular on trade in manufactured goods (in contrast to the corn, oil and wine on which the classical economy largely depended).[25] The dominant mode of production was that of wage (rather than slave) labour, with production for exchange rather than use. By the sixteenth century this system was already well established in Italy as a result of what Anderson describes as 'the premature development of *mercantile capital* in North Italian cities' (Anderson 1984, p. 143). This took the form of bourgeois mercantilism which, in conjunction with banking innovations, led to an accumulation of wealth from the fourteenth century onwards. By then, a city like Florence was a well-established merchant, manufacturing and banking centre, as the Florentine Boccaccio's *Decameron* (1349–51) already shows.

The merchant class dominates sixteenth-century Italian comedy. It does so not only in terms of characters, but also, more endemically, through the prevalence of issues related to commodities in the context of a capitalist market system of exchange. The merchant, no longer the reviled figure of Roman times, was now clearly differentiated from the artisan, in a period when the management of mercantile and banking capital had become much more sophisticated.[26] The specific nature of this socioeconomic habitat from which dramatic portraits of the nubile, middle-class Renaissance woman were drawn, and in particular the crucial role of a profitable marriage in ensuring the growth of capital, is clearly of great relevance to our argument. In the context of wealth rather than birth as the defining factor in terms of social status, daughters became a capital investment, as the existence of marriage brokers would appear to bear out. In *La mandragola*, Ligurio is in fact described by Callimaco as an erstwhile marriage broker. It seems that 'the marriage market was not unlike a modern stock exchange; indeed, marriageable girls were sometimes characterized as "merchandise" (*mercatanzia*)' (Brucker 1986, p. 107).

Whatever the form of the sexual market place, female characters in the comedies do not own their sexual wares: it is the fathers, guardians and procurers who buy and sell, and generally negotiate. Male characters tend to dominate the transaction, whether it concerns marriage (as in *Clizia*, *I suppositi*, *Gli ingannati*, *La Lena*), or other sexual arenas such as seduction (*La Lena*, *La mandragola*, *Clizia*) or prostitution (*La cassaria*, *La cortigiana*). At the end of Machiavelli's *Clizia*, Ramondo, Clizia's long-lost father, reappears to discuss her marriage with Cleandro, the son of her former guardian, Nicomaco. In the final scene, it is Ramondo and Nicomaco, with the help of another male character, Damone, who between them finalize the negotiations. This brings to an end Nicomaco's attempt to purchase access to Clizia by setting up his bailiff in a marital home with the young girl, an arrangement which would, in effect, have commodified her. In Ariosto's *I suppositi*, both Erostrato and Cleandro offer a counter-dowry to Damone in the hope of winning Polinesta's hand in an institutionalized, and therefore respectable, form of female commodification. The play ends with Damone agreeing to allow Erostrato, Filogono's son, to marry his daughter when he is told that Erostrato's father is 'by blood, not inferior to you, but in wealth . . . rather superior' (v, 9). Present at this scene, in addition to Damone, Erostrato, and Filogono are Pasifilo, the parasite who has been involved in the negotiations, and Cleandro, who has withdrawn his offer of marriage to Polinesta. As for Polinesta herself, she is introduced by Damone to Filogono with the words 'and this is your daughter-in-law'. She, however, is absent from the scene.

Both *I suppositi* and *Clizia* include the marriage transaction as an integral part of the play, indeed as its climax. In this area the plays can be seen to have added to the Roman plays on which they are believed to be based (Andrews 1993, p. 39; Radcliff-Umstead 1969, pp. 75, 134). As far as Terence's *Eunuchus* and Plautus' *Captivi*, the models for *I suppositi*, are concerned, in the former, betrothal does follow the rape of a slave who turns out to be a freeborn Athenian (in contrast to the seduction in the Italian play).[27] However, while Chaerea's rape of Pamphila in *Captivi* is the result of a trick devised by his slave, neither this nor the subsequent betrothal appears to hinge on any sort of financial transaction. Moreover, Chaerea reports his betrothal in the manner of a *fait accompli*, accomplished, that is, behind the scenes. The transaction is not foregrounded as it is in _I suppositi_, where it forms the climax and actual ending of the play. Love interest, let alone marriage, is completely absent from the all-male _Captivi_, as the epilogue proudly proclaims. _Clizia_ foregrounds the marriage transaction which is mentioned only briefly as postfact in the epilogue to Plautus' _Casina_. In _Casina_, the equivalent of Cleandro, namely Euthynicus, never appears on stage, and there is consequently no focus on the dismay of a son at the family patrimony going to a servant, the bailiff, rather than to himself.

The introduction of merchant fathers in the Renaissance comedies is in contrast to the unspecified _senex_ who dominates the Roman plays. Thus while Nicomaco (_un vecchio_) in _Clizia_ follows the pattern of Lysidamus (_senex_) in _Casina_, in representing the landowning class (both fathers own farms managed by a bailiff), _I suppositi_, on the other hand, sees the introduction of Filogono, a merchant father (_mercatante_) who was not present in either _Eunuchus_ or _Captivi_. In Gli Intronati's _Gli ingannati_ (1531) a prominent place is given to the merchant class, in comparison with Plautus' _Menaechmi_ (Radcliff-Umstead 1969, p. 198). In the Roman play a merchant is in fact mentioned (the only instance of a merchant in the eight Roman plays under discussion).[28] However, he figures only in the antefact as the dead father of the twin Menaechmi, while the Renaissance play features two merchant fathers as central negotiating characters. Moreover, in _Gli ingannati_ one of the twins is female and the object of a marriage transaction.

Gli ingannati opens with Virginio negotiating the marriage of his daughter, Lelia, with Gherardo. The discussion between the two male characters revolves around money and patrimony, and is couched in mercantile terms, as Virginio swears to Gherardo: 'Don't think, either, that I'm about to go back on my promise to you, provided that the girl is willing; for you know very well that it's not good for merchants to renege on something once they've promised' (I, I). The regard which Virginio shows here for Lelia's feelings disappears once her twin brother is known to be alive and can take his place as Virginio's rightful heir. Virginio later tells Gherardo 'She's yours; do as you will with her; as for me, I give you permission' (IV, 3). Lelia has now been replaced by her brother in her cardinal role in the destiny of her family's patrimony. When an only daughter stands to inherit (such as Isabella in the same play, Polinesta in _I suppositi_, and Clizia in _Clizia_), her placement in a profitable marriage is vital if the patrimony is to be enlarged, or indeed preserved. When a long-lost brother reappears, this process is automatically displaced onto him. The absence of the son, Lelia's brother, also allows her to enjoy an important role during the first four acts of the play.

Gli ingannati can be seen to differ from *Menaechmi* not only in its introduction of two merchant fathers and a female twin. Importantly, the two Menaechmi are both *young* men, and there is no *senex* father figure in this play. There is, moreover, no seduction, rape or prospective marriage in the Roman play, which concentrates on the twins' rediscovery of each other. Menaechmus I is already married and also has a mistress, while Menaechmus II appears to have no romantic interests. The Renaissance play, by contrast, addresses the issue of marriageable daughters and the preservation of the patrimony by a suitable marriage transaction. In view of the crucial introduction in both *Gli ingannati* and *I suppositi* of female heirs who appear on stage (albeit mostly in crossdress in Lelia's case and, in that of Polinesta, only in the opening scene), the dominance of fathers in negotiating their marriages, and indeed the focus on marriage itself, is all the more pointed.

Fathers control marriage transactions in *Gli ingannati*, *I suppositi* and *Clizia*. *La Calandria*, on the other hand, sees the exceptional case of a mother, Fulvia, instead of her husband, Calandro, arranging the marriage of her son, Flamminio. One reason for this may be that the wealth in this family comes from her side, rather than that of her husband, and she is indeed referred to in the play as rich. Her dominance may also be due to the fact that her character is believed to have been based partly on that of the wealthy and resourceful Mona Sismonda who marries the merchant Arriguccio in Boccaccio's *Decameron* VII, 8.[29] Although it is not clear if Calandro himself is involved in trade, a merchant is present in the play in the form of the Florentine Perillo, who tries to arrange a marriage between his daughter, Verginia, and Lelio (in reality a female character in disguise). In Ariosto's *La Lena*, the marriage which ends the play is negotiated, once again, by two fathers, Ilario and Fazio. While Ilario consults with his son, Flavio, Fazio gives no indication that he intends to ask the opinion of Licinia (who has not once appeared on stage). His concern is to redeem his daughter's lost honour, regardless of her views on the matter. It is he, as the owner of his daugher's sexual wares, who has been slighted by Flavio: 'Ilario, it's simply not possible, for God's sake, for me to tolerate your son having done me such a great wrong, and for me not to revenge myself in any way I can' (v, 10).

As in the case of marriage negotiations, the methods whereby male

characters finally arrive at the seduction (or actual rape) of female
characters (which may or may not lead to marriage), can also be seen to
fit into the transaction model in which material wealth changes hands
between male negotiators. Although in *La Lena* it is initially Lena who
negotiates her services as procuress with Flavio, she is soon replaced by
Corbolo in the lucrative plan to seduce Licinia. Callimaco's successful
seduction of Lucrezia in *La mandragola* similarly depends on money
changing hands: Callimaco rewards Ligurio and Siro, and Nicia, her
husband, unwittingly pays Friar Timoteo to further his own cuckold-
ing. Callimaco's warning to Siro to obey Ligurio and keep the seduction plan a secret also clarifies the role of material wealth in the scheme:
'if you hold dear material goods, honour, my life, and your own well-
being' (IV, 5). Timoteo even refers to his dealings as 'my trading'.
Interestingly, the other party to Lucrezia's seduction, her mother,
Sostrata, is not part of the transaction process, and gains no financial
advantage. In *Clizia* the marriage transaction is preceded by conflict,
with financial implications, between her guardian, Nicomaco, and his
son, Cleandro, as they each plot to seduce/rape the unseen young
ward. As Cleandro reflects on his father's plan to disinherit him in
favour of a servant, he bemoans, in the same breath, the loss of his
beloved and his goods.

Male characters dominate sexual transactions. However, female
desire also finds its way on to the stage. Isabella and Lelia in *Gli
ingannati*, Polinesta in *I suppositi*, and Fulvia in *La Calandria*, are all desiring female characters who circumvent the patriarchal authority of
fathers, and in the case of Fulvia, husband, in their pursuit of sexual
satisfaction and/or marriage. Unlike the desiring male characters,
however, who make active use of power and material wealth, these
female characters appear to deal more directly with the object of their
desire. Although Fulvia uses her maidservant to further her designs on
Lidio, there is no mention of any special remuneration, with the mistress making use of her own wits rather than depending on those of the
maidservant (who is portrayed as witless). Isabella communicates her
desires in no uncertain fashion to Fabio (in reality, Lelia), while Lelia
has taken the bold step of cross-dressing to enter the service of the man
she loves in the hope of bringing her designs on him to a positive conclusion. Polinesta pursues a sexual liaison under her father's nose with
Erostrato, the latter having gained entry into her father's household as
a servant, and Fulvia succeeds in prolonging her passionate, adulterous
affair with Lidio.

These active female characters clearly represent positive developments in female characterization. However, complications often arise which they are unable to resolve alone. Isabella has made a fundamental error in that she unwittingly directs her advances at a woman, and in order to achieve her goal she is in need of nothing short of a miracle (the arrival of Fabrizio, the male version of Lelia). Lelia herself cannot bring her desire to regain Flamminio's affections to fruition without the direct intervention of her nurse, Clemenzia. The continuing satisfaction of Polinesta's desire also requires a *deus ex machina*, namely the revelation of her lover's high social status which enables them to marry.

Female desire is not, however, taken into account at all in the case of Clizia and Licinia, and in this the Roman model (as exemplified by *Eunuchus*) is still discernible. As for Lucrezia in *La mandragola*, not only does Callimaco threaten to resort to 'bestial, crude, evil actions' (I, 3) in order to satisfy his desire, but Lucrezia herself is imagined by Ligurio to base her response to a man on his worldly wealth, rather than on any sexual desire of her own: 'Someone might come along who liked Lucrezia as much as you do, someone richer than you, and with more charm, so that . . . she might turn her attentions to another, and not to you' (I, 3). What is more, although in the event she appears to have enjoyed Callimaco's advances, his unexpected apparition in her bed might just as easily have had an unpleasant outcome. Her collusion with Callimaco may also be based on the fear of losing her good reputation should the night's events become public knowledge. Ligurio's instructions to his master include the use of blackmail if she is uncooperative (Callimaco is told to persuade her that 'she can be your friend without bringing shame on herself, and your enemy at great cost to her honour' (IV, 2)).

In comparison with male-led transactions leading to marriage and the seduction/rape of female characters, the procedures of prostitution provide the most overt form of commodification of female sexuality in the plays. Prostitution was one of the two major industries of the Renaissance underworld (alongside gambling) (Chamberlin 1982, p. 213). In its depiction of the prostitution of slave women, Ariosto's *La cassaria* (1508) closely follows the practice of the Roman comedies. However, it differs in its inclusion of two merchant fathers, Crisobolo and Critone. These two characters do not appear in any of the Roman source plays (Terence's *Andria, Phormio, Heautontimorumenos* and Plautus' *Mostellaria*) (Radcliff-Umstead 1969, pp. 66–8). *La cassaria* centres on the chest of goods which is used to trick the procurer, Lucrano (a name based on the Latin *lucrum* meaning 'gain'), out of the two slave women in his possession. Here the male negotiators are Lucrano and the two prospective owners/lovers, Erofilo and Caridoro, while the two women, Eulalia and Corisca, anxiously await the outcome. They are concerned that if they are not sold 'wholesale' (*in grosso*), Lucrano will sell their services 'piecemeal' (*a minuto*). Erofilo, meanwhile, schemes to exchange his father's goods for female bodies: 'cloths, silks, wools, gold and silver material, wine and grain . . . to satisfy my desire for a while' (I, 5).

Although Eulalia and Corisca were freewomen before they were captured during wartime, little dramatic attention is paid to their need for freedom. They continue to be referred to as 'merchandise' and 'stuff', while at one point the equation of 'woman' with 'thing' is accompanied by the comment that she is worth only fifty florins, rather than the 1,000 offered. Indeed, 'a herd of cattle is to be had more cheaply' (IV, 4), calculates the merchant, Crisobolo. Equating women with 'stuff' in a soliloquy in Aretino's *La cortigiana* (1525), Rosso remarks about his master that 'placing good quality stuff in his hands is all that counts' (II, 19) and gloats over the money he will earn as a result of procuring the sexual services of the baker's wife, Togna, for the unwitting Signor Parabolano.

A telling remark about contemporary attitudes to material wealth is made by Cleandro in *I suppositi*. 'I know well', he says, 'that the person who doesn't own things these days is reputed to be a mere beast' (II, 3). Alberti's treatise on the family would seem to bear this out. One of his characters, Adovardo, speaking about Tuscany, says:

Nor does our country admire literary men too much, rather it seems all bent on profit and avid for wealth. Whether because of the character and customs of its past inhabitants, everyone seems bred to the cultivation of profit. Every discussion seems to concern economic wisdom, every thought turns about acquisition, and every art is expended to obtain great riches. (Alberti 1969, p. 56)

The desire for material goods which is played out in the arena of female sexuality focusses on food and clothes, the preferred commodities of the time.[30] Pasifilo in *I suppositi* sells his services as negotiator in marital transactions to the master who will best feed him. Food, in the form of capons, pheasants, bread, wine and cheese, is also used by the servant Corbolo in *La Lena* in an attempt to persuade Lena to forget the twenty-five florins which Flavio has promised her and is now unable to raise. Flavio then sells his valuable clothes in order to pay her.

Food imagery is often used by male characters when speaking of the female body, in a direct metaphor of consumption. In *La Calandria*

Calandro swears that if he ever gets near to Santilla, he will 'devour' her, to which Fessenio replies: 'woman is to be drunk, not eaten' (1, 6). Gherardo in *Gli ingannati* describes Lelia as: 'my sweet Lelia, of sugar, gold, milk and roses' (1, 4). The commodification of women is a problematic situation on which McLuskie comments as follows: 'when sex becomes a matter of commodity relations, women occupy the ambiguous position of sharers in this consumption and the commodity themselves' (McLuskie 1989, p. 217). The exclusion of the commodity from the transaction process depicted by the comedies is clearly essential if this problem is not to become overt and intrusive, and this undoubtedly helps to account for the dramatic absence or marginalization of female characters.[31]

The comedies appear to illustrate, on a variety of levels, the process which Hartsock describes as 'the conceptualisation of women as a social commodity' (Hartsock 1983, p. 36, n. 34). The capitalist market model of commodity exchange can here be seen to mould social exchange, and it is in this context that the female characters of the comedies must be considered if their dramatic function is to be properly understood. The Renaissance comedies are based on market models of social exchange; in other words, social relations in the plays are determined by the mechanics of commodity exchange. This market model is based on the twin assumptions of relations of domination as the norm, and of the individual as inevitably isolated and interest-driven (Hartsock 1983, p. 10). The exchange transaction is therefore inherently competitive, with the participants in opposition to each other. A further effect of this system is that the individual is perceived only in terms of her/his relation to commodities. This explains a major feature, already noted, in the female characters, namely that they are defined exclusively in terms of the utility of their sexuality, to the exclusion of any other qualities (such as, for instance, wit and intelligence). Ellipsis is of course also a feature of the portrayal of male characters in the comedies. The tricks and intrigues of the plays revolve around the dynamics of exchange and its material concerns, and any life which these characters may have outside this sphere is disregarded. However, as subjects rather than objects of the exchange system, the male characters clearly have greater power than the female characters. While the male characters behave as active participants in the market system, high-status female characters in particular are pressed into social relations based on what amounts to a fetishism of commodities.

Commodity fetishism is particularly prominent in eras of expanding capitalism, such as the fifteenth century in the northern Italian states and the late nineteenth century in northern Europe. This concept, first theorized by Marx, draws on anthropological evidence of tribal practices which attributed special powers to inanimate objects, thereby 'fetishizing' them. Commodity fetishism characterizes social relationships that operate between things rather than between people. Importantly, Marx's critique of commodity fetishism refers, as Geras argues, not only to 'substantive domination' but also to the 'ideological mystification' to be found in the comedies (Geras 1979). The concept also carries with it the association of obsession, of an abnormal and excessive attachment to an object which is accorded extraordinary qualities. In this sense, commodity fetishism is related to fetishism as a psychic mechanism, classified by Freud as a perversion (Freud 1962, pp. 147–57).[32] Of particular relevance is the implication of commodity fetishism for the female characters. With virginity as the most prized possession in the marriage market, the exchange value of nubile, middle-class females was of primary importance given the appropriation of female sexuality and reproductive powers into the service of patriarchy. This particular articulation of commodity fetishism notably results in the marginalization of any other qualities which these characters might possess.

Social relations in the comedies, modelled as they are on the market, are thus highly simplistic. As Hartsock argues:

In a society modeled both in fact and in theory on the exchange of commodities, the attainment of a complex and deep-going series of relations with others is indeed difficult. Community itself is only a by-product of activities directed at other ends, and thus the social synthesis that results from exchange is one in which persons are in opposition to each other and associate with each other only indirectly, by means of the exchange of things passed back and forth on the basis of self-interest. (Hartsock 1983, p. 103)

This is the context within which Cleandro withdraws his claim to marry Polinesta on the rediscovery of his long-lost son in *I suppositi*, as he had only courted her 'for the desire of leaving an heir' (v, 9). It also explains why Gherardo, in *Gli ingannati*, is hardly sanguine in his rejoicing at the return of his friend's long-lost son and heir, Fabrizio: 'If this is the case, it doesn't do me any good. Me, I've lost a thousand florins' (IV, 2). His first thought is of the money he will now lose in dowry from his prospective bride, Lelia, as the reappearance of her brother automatically results in the diminution of her share of the patrimony. Even

Virginio's thoughts turn irresistibly to money when he is told that his son is alive: 'God bless you, my son! Just think, I've got to recompense all those who've looked after him' (IV, 3). In these market-modelled relations between the characters of the comedies, whose (self) interest in each other is partial and simplistic, the male characters negotiating in the exchange system occupy a dominant position in relation to the female characters who form the object of the transactions. It is characters such as Polinesta and Lelia, in their exclusively sexual function, who are circulated in the form of commodities among male transacting subjects.

The role of the male trickster, the central schemer to be found in all the comedies, can also be read in market terms. The fact that he sells his wit and intelligence, along with his other services, means that he is commodified in that aspect of his being. However, he is never commodified *in his sexuality*, as are the female characters (whether for the purpose of marriage, seduction or prostitution). In the Roman comedies the buying and selling (or manumission) of slaves, or of captives who are enslaved, is also a transaction which commodifies males as well as females. (In *Captivi*, for example, Hegio's son of four years is reported to have been stolen and sold.) While not as widespread as in the Roman plays, enslavement and manumission are mentioned in the Renaissance comedies. It has been argued that this would not have been implausible in real life, given the Turkish practice of enslaving prisoners (Radcliff-Umstead 1969, p. 82). Dulippo in *I suppositi* was captured as a child by the Turks, whose ship was then taken by Sicilian galleys. He was then bought by Filogono for twenty-four ducats. However, the fact that he was *bought* from the Sicilians would suggest that slavery existed in the Italian states irrespective of Turkish influence.

Market forces also enter the commodification procedures identified in the plays. In this context, Lévi-Strauss' observation that attractive women are always in short supply is highly relevant to the commodification process at work in comedies showing one female character as the focus of attention of more than one male character, but never the converse (Lévi-Strauss 1969, p. 76, n. 36). This is the case whenever a triangle exists, such as that involving Lucrezia, Nicia and Callimaco in *La mandragola*, and Fulvia, Calandro and Lidio in *La Calandria*. In *Clizia* four male characters compete for one female (father, son, and both of their two manservants). In *La cassaria*, the two young men who bid with the procurer Lucrano for the two slavewomen do so in implicit competition with other men, in that Lucrano is determined to get the highest price he can for his merchandise. Lelia in *Gli ingannati* can finally choose between two prospective husbands, Flamminio and Gherardo, while Isabella has spurned Flamminio's attentions in favour of Fabio, and later Fabrizio. The financial aspects of competition for scarce female bodies are particularly highlighted in *I suppositi*, which sees Cleandro and Erostrato competing for Polinesta's hand. In order to further his case, the former offers a sum of 2,000 ducats to Polinesta's father. This *sovradote* amounts to a counter-dowry which, as Herlihy explains, comes into being in periods in history when there is a lack of eligible women and a surplus of men. Unlike the *dos*, or dowry, which passed from the bride's father to the groom, the *donatio*, or counter-dowry, thus took the reverse route in accordance with the demands of the marriage market.[33] It would therefore not be unreasonable to surmise that during the first half of the sixteenth century, when the comedies were composed, there existed either an actual shortage of eligible young women, or an anxiety about the possibility of a shortage of this kind.

The purpose of the exchange of women and the consequent commodification of the female body is, as observed in the case of single daughters, that of increasing or at least preserving the patrimony. On a more fundamental level, it also functions 'to create a community providing greater security for the individual in a hostile world' (Hartsock 1983, p. 276). In addition to the disorder caused by intermittent warfare, everyday life in Renaissance Italy was quite dangerous in terms of criminality.[34] The creation of kin, or *affines*, was thus a prime concern during this time, with the exchange of women functioning 'as a means for transforming strangers into affines or relatives by marriage' (Hartsock 1983, p. 274).[35] Ties of kinship and alliance are seen to be important in the comedies, and find particular expression in the verbal exchanges of fathers in the course of marriage transactions concerning their offspring. These elder male characters with financial responsibilities join forces and become kin to their mutual benefit at the end of many of the plays. One might even begin to wonder whether this is indeed the real goal towards which the plays, by means of an often rather circuitous route, wend their way. At the end of *Clizia*, for example, Ramondo, Clizia's father, says to Nicomaco, father of his prospective son-in-law: 'As for family, nothing would please me more than that the friendship which has arisen as a result of your merits, be maintained through family ties' (v, 7). *I suppositi* also ends on a note of rejoicing in newly-established kinship ties, as Damone tells Filogono: 'I desire family and kinship with you, Filogono, no less than you with me . . . I accept your son as son-in-law, and you as most honoured relation' (v, 9). The usefulness of ties of this kind is made obvious in *La cassaria*, when Fulcio refers to a network of family and friends in the context of personal law enforcement. He relates how Caridoro has threatened Lucrano with a visit by his relations and friends, and how, as a direct result of this, Lucrano has released Eulalia and Corisca, the two slavewomen.

The dominant role of male characters as exchanging subjects is linked to the paucity of mothers as compared to fathers in this corpus of comedies.[36] The only mothers are Sostrata, mother of the married Lucrezia in *La mandragola*, Fulvia, mother of Flamminio in *La Calandria*, and Sofronia, mother of Cleandro in *Clizia*.[37] Clizia herself is motherless, as are Erofilo and Caridoro in *La cassaria*, Polinesta, Erostrato and Dulippo in *I suppositi*, and Isabella, Lelia and Fabrizio in *Gli ingannati*. Sometimes there is a nurse who fills this maternal function (Clemenzia for Lelia, a *nutrice* for Polinesta). All high-status female characters, however, have powerful fathers. Apart from Polinesta's father, Damone, who laments the death of his wife, and Cleandro, who reveals his wife's name *was* Sofronia, in *I suppositi*, mothers are simply not written into these plays. The fundamental reason for this omission may well be that mothers are not readily conceived of as participants in the exchange of daughters and sons, and are thus superfluous to the main concern of the plot.

ADDRESSING THE AUDIENCE

Intertwined with issues of time, place and action, diction is another element of dramatic composition that contributes to gender portrayal in the plays. Looking beyond the classical rule that comic diction should be of the colloquial style, verbal expression of the action also plays its part in shaping audience perception of the hierarchies of gender, class, age and social status. This final section examines audience positioning in relation to female characters as a result of the various types of dramatic speech vehicle used. These speech vehicles (prologue, soliloquy, monologue, aside, dialogue and polylogue) perform different dramatic functions and vary in the degree of intensity or exclusivity of actor–audience communication they generate, with the dialogue and polylogue as the least exclusive forms. In assessing the female characters, it is important to establish whether they have access to the more privileged forms (prologue, soliloquy, monologue and aside). At the other end of the speaking hierarchy are those female characters who never appear, and those who have only minimal speaking parts. Of special interest is the way in which male characters frequently speak for female characters who are absent, and who are consequently often placed grammatically in the direct object position, or referred to using the passive voice.

The issue of audience address is of crucial importance as an integral part of theatre. Without an audience, the theatrical event cannot take place. In the words of Piscator, 'Theatre can be played anywhere, in a market place, in a subway station, as long as there is an audience' (Marker 1977, p. 18). In comedy, the relationship between the audience and the stage is arguably closer than in tragedy:

Tragic actors expect to be applauded as well as comic ones, but nevertheless the word 'plaudite' at the end of a Roman comedy, the invitation to the audience to form part of the comic society, would seem rather out of place at the end of a tragedy. The resolution of comedy comes, so to speak, from the audience's side of the stage; in a tragedy it comes from some mysterious world on the opposite side. (Frye 1973, p. 164)

Theatre history shows a shifting type of interaction between stage and audience. Direct address to the audience, particularly in the prologues and endings of the Renaissance comedies, echoes the intimacy of mediaeval theatre, when the stage was in the form of a raised platform completely encircled by spectators, who would move from one stage/scene to the next to follow the action. The Renaissance also saw the heyday of the soliloquy, that privileged speech vehicle which bound actor and audience together in an exclusive relationship. The use of the same sky for stage and auditorium further accentuated this closeness. It would also seem from contemporary accounts as well as the plays themselves, that the audience needed to be called to attention, in what appears to have been a 'struggle between stage illusion and the unperturbed sociability that reigned in the audience' (Marker 1977, p. 23). The play itself was only one of a series of spectacles which claimed audience attention, as will be seen in the next chapter. Also of considerable note was the preoccupation of members of the audience with each other. Because of this, the auditorium would remain well-lit during the actual performance.[38]

Some of the prologues indicate an expectation of audience inattentiveness. The prologue to *La mandragola* opens with a request to its 'benign listeners' to 'watch without making a noise', while that of *La cassaria* ends with the words 'let those watching be silent'. The first version of the prologue to *La Lena* introduces the players and then suggests that 'we quieten down a little and watch them'. This is clearly not yet the period of theatre history when actors relate only to each other, with the audience forming a fourth wall. The hierarchy of speech vehicles that interlinks with the gender hierarchy thus owes its characteristically wide range, and especially the prologue and soliloquy, to the type of stage–audience relationship still current in the Renaissance.

Speech hierarchy

Speech vehicles in Italian Renaissance comedy are organized along hierarchical lines in terms of both the degree of audience attention which they each command and their allocation according to the gender, age, class and social status of the characters. In addition to the particular phase of stage–audience relationship represented by the Renaissance period, the fact that the comedies are structured around intrigue, with the need for characters to be secretive and to communicate exclusively with an omniscient audience, would also have contributed significantly to the use of a wide variety of speech vehicles ranging beyond the dialogical to the monological. In the standard dialogical interchange between actors which has come to be regarded as the characteristic speech vehicle of drama, taking the form of the dialogue (involving two speakers) or the polylogue (involving three or more speakers), audience attention is divided between the actors, none of whom communicates exclusively with the audience (Pfister 1991, pp. 126–59). If the interchanges between the characters are very short, then the degree of equality which already exists between them can be seen to increase even further (Pfister 1991, p. 142). The monological speech vehicles are therefore of primary importance in ascertaining the participation of female characters in audience address in comparison with their male counterparts. The first observation to be made is that certain female characters, such as Clizia and Licinia, do not take part even in the relatively low-status communication represented by the dialogical speech forms.

The characteristic prologue which opens the Renaissance comedies (as it did their Roman predecessors) is the most exclusive dramatic speech vehicle of all, for a number of reasons. Its speaker, usually alone on the stage, addresses the audience in direct speech. The basic function of the prologue can be defined as the establishment and clarification of the position of the audience in the sign system of theatrical communication. In other words, when, for instance, the audience is told the name of the town where the play is set, what has been communicated is not the fact that the decor *is*, for example, Rome, but that it indicates that city. In short, 'The spectator admits intellectually the validity of the sign' (Molinari 1964, p. 69). In its detailing of the plot and its didactic commentary, the prologue also tells the audience exactly how to interpret what it is about to see, thereby allowing for only one possible interpretation of the events on stage. This highly influential speech vehicle is invariably spoken by a man, usually the producer, or, at times, the dramatist himself. In *La cortigiana*, the prologue exceptionally takes the form of a dialogue between two of the male characters, one of whom, Signor Parabolano, is at the top of the social scale depicted in the play. There is, exceptionally, an intriguing account of a performance of *I suppositi* which added a new dialogue introducing a female character who was to recite the prologue before a Princess in the audience. As a result of the Princess' objections to this, however, the play was performed without any prologue at all (D'Ancona 1966, II, p. 442). Occasionally a female character ends the performance with a direct address to the audience (Sofronia in *Clizia*, for example, says: 'And you, spectators, can go home).

The prologue of *La mandragola* reveals the crucial and insidious role of this speech vehicle in predetermining audience response to the characters and their actions. After describing the street scene, the young lover, Callimaco Guadagni, is introduced by name (his surname, from *guadagno*, meaning 'gain', already suggesting that he will be successful). The next lines introduce the anonymous object of the play's trick in the passive voice: 'a shrewd young woman was much loved by him and was thereby tricked, as you will hear'. A list of characters is then given, from which both Lucrezia and her mother are absent: 'A wily lover, a stupid doctor, a dissolute friar, a malicious parasite, will this day provide your entertainment.' Marginalization of female characters precedes the opening of the play in a variety of ways, thereby conditioning audience reaction from the outset. The prologue to *Clizia* is directed particularly at male spectators, who are told how much they will learn from the play. Female spectators, on the other hand, are addressed in terms of their modesty, thereby confining them, as ever, to the sexual realm, while also excluding them from the educational process.

Like the speaker of the prologue, the speaker of the soliloquy is alone on stage. However, this speech vehicle does not take the form of direct address, in that the speaker muses alone, thereby creating the illusion that the speech is overheard by, rather than directly aimed at, the audience. Nevertheless, the speaker claims the undivided attention of the audience with the soliloquy, which is therefore a privileged dramatic speech vehicle. The main purpose of the soliloquy, in the context of intrigue as a major feature, is that of character revelation. It is therefore opposed to dialogic speech, which aims at 'ostensive and deictic description' (Pietropaolo 1986, p. 48). Other functions served by the soliloquy, such as giving necessary plot information which is not enacted on stage (for instance, events preceding the opening of the play, or action that takes place off stage) can also be performed by other speech vehicles. In so far as Renaissance comedy deals at all with the inner state of the characters (this being more of a feature of tragedy and the pastoral), then the soliloquy is the means whereby the audience best receives this type of information. The other privileged monologic speech vehicle is the monologue, a lengthy speech spoken when other characters are present on stage.[39]

Before examining these two privileged dramatic vehicles in relation to the type of character who uses them, it is worth recalling that the dramatic importance of a character can be gauged by her/his stage presence in terms of both visibility and audibility. One might therefore expect to find that the soliloquy and the monologue, privileged speech vehicles in terms of both exclusive audience attention and often length, are invariably allocated to high-profile, but low-status, female characters, and high-profile male characters of both high and low social standing. In terms of the gender, age, class and social status of the characters who are given soliloquies and monologues, this is the case overall. The reason there can be no absolute correspondence between the hierarchy of speech vehicles and that of the characters is the complexity of the character–speech vehicle partnership. The function of neither can be said to be simplistic in itself, while the combination of the two at any given moment in the play fulfils more than one of a set of functional permutations.

As a general rule, however, the lack of participation by high-status female characters traced in setting the scene and plotting the trick appears, not surprisingly, to find a parallel as far as the use of speech vehicles is concerned. The female characters who are so high in status that they are effectively idealized out of all dramatic existence (Clizia and Licinia) have no access to speech whatsoever. Then there are female characters similarly high in status but who are allowed marginal participation (Polinesta's appearance in the doorway with her Nurse which opens *I suppositi*, and the lengthy dialogue in which she takes part before disappearing, never to be seen again). Next in line is a character such as Lucrezia in *La mandragola*, still young and beautiful but married, and thus slightly lower down the hierarchy. She is allowed participation in both the dialogue (II, 10) and the polylogue (II, 11; V, 5, 6). Female characters who are allowed soliloquies and monologues are mothers and wives (Sofronia in *Clizia*, Fulvia in *La Calandria*), servant women (Doria in *Clizia*) and procuresses (Lena in *La Lena*, Alvigia in *La cortigiana*). The only occasion when high-status female characters use these forms is, not surprisingly, when they are cross-dressed as men (Lelia in *Gli ingannati*, Santilla in *La Calandria*).

The last type of monologic speech vehicle is the aside, which can be regarded as a small soliloquy as far as the speaking character is concerned, if the character believes s/he is not being overheard. Once again, the aside results in an exclusive communication with the audience. Facilitated by the new perspectival stage, the three-dimensional scene allowed for the illusion of distance between groups of characters, thereby making credible the aside as a secret, self-addressed form of speech (Bjurström 1964, p. 79). As in the case of the soliloquy, the frequent use of the aside stems from the predominance of intrigue and the need for furtive behaviour. In line with this, only characters who participate actively in the trick, rather than those who wait in the wings as the prize to be won at the end, make use of asides. In the comedies examined, only low-status female characters, such as the ex-prostitute and procuress, Alvigia, and the wife turned temporary procuress, Lena, make use of this relatively privileged speech vehicle.

Speaking for women

Both the participation of female characters in onstage action and their use of high-status speech vehicles are limited in scope. However, this does not mean that the actual concept of 'woman', notably woman in her idealized form, is itself peripheral to the comedies. As the prize to be claimed when the trick to gain access to her has been successfully played out, she represents a much-desired goal. Yet, while the plays detail the scheming of the male characters as they attempt to get close to the female characters, the latter are distinctly marginalized in terms of both visible and audible stage presence. This finds a parallel in Renaissance writings extolling the virtue of silence in the ideal woman: 'Silence is as it has always been, the peak of dignity and the source of respect for a woman. Talking too much has been ever the habit and sign of a silly fool. So be glad to listen quietly and to talk less than you listen' (Alberti 1969, p. 217).

The silencing of the female voice, and female subjectivity itself, within patriarchy, has been the subject of discussion across a variety of disciplines (linguistics, psychoanalysis, semiotics and literary and film theory), and will be explored in relation to theatre in the final chapter.[40] In the particular context of the Renaissance comedies, one obvious dramatic method of marginalizing the female voice is its takeover, or ventriloquizing, by male characters. Female characters are often first introduced into the play through the mediation of male characters who talk about them, with the male hero opening the play with the narration of his desire for a particular female character who may or may not make an appearance later. *La mandragola*, for example, begins with Callimaco's account of his passion for Lucrezia, whom he has never seen, but whose reputation came to his notice in Paris; and after the trick has been executed, he gives a full account to Ligurio of Lucrezia's reaction (v, 4). As for her speaking part, it has been observed that 'Lucretia says very little – knowledge about her is generally gained from other characters' (Radcliff-Umstead 1969, p. 125). At the beginning of *Clizia*, Cleandro speaks to Palamede about his passion for Clizia, who will never appear on stage. Licinia in *La Lena* is another example of a female character who is talked about but who is never seen or heard. *Gli ingannati* opens with a discussion between Virginio and Gherardo about the projected marriage between Lelia, Virginio's daughter, and Gherardo, a scene that precedes her first appearance on stage. Exceptionally, Polinesta appears herself at the beginning of *I suppositi*, rather than having been talked about first by a male character. It is even she, rather than Erostrato, who acquaints the audience with their affair. However, she never reappears, and her subsequent actions and reactions, such as her distress when the affair becomes public knowledge, are only known through the words of her father.

As a result of entering the stage through the speech of a male character, these female characters are often to be found in the grammatical position of direct object pronoun. Clizia, for instance, is spoken about in the following manner:

PALAMEDE: What is it to you if it's Pirro who has *her* or Eustachio?
CLEANDRO: What do you mean, what is it to me? This Pirro is the biggest scoundrel in Florence: because, apart from sharing *her* with my father, he's always hated me; so much so that I'd rather the devil in hell had *her*. (1, 1, italics added)

At first sight, this commonplace grammatical detail may not in itself appear to be particularly remarkable. All the same, a female character who is never seen or heard to be the subject of an action, but is always its object, and who is talked about rather than speaking for herself, is relentlessly marginalized in terms of audience perception. This occurs not only in the grammatical aspect of language, but also in the area of semantics. Frequent references to the female character as 'thing' underline the dominant objectification of the ideal woman as property. In the case of Clizia, this even extends to her becoming an object to throw dice for. As Alberti notes, concerning the duties of the prospective father-in-law regarding his son's bride: 'He should act as do wise heads of families before they acquire some property – they like to look it over several times before they actually sign a contract' (Alberti 1969, p. 115).

A variety of differences between female characters informs the nature of their stage presence and the corresponding audience attention they command. While some female characters are more prominent than others, no female character dominates the stage to the extent of her male counterpart. The higher the status of the female character in these comedies, moreover, the greater the degree of marginalization and at times the complete silencing of that character. This is achieved in dramatic terms by mutually reinforcing conventions in the areas of time, place, plot and diction, in line with the contemporary socio-economic configuration of patriarchy defining and delimiting female presence in public/dramatic space. At the interface of sixteenth-century patriarchal and dramatic convention, the playing out of patriarchal fears and fantasies ultimately relegates female characters to the position of waiting in the wings.

CHAPTER TWO

Gender deceptions: cross-dressing in Italian Renaissance comedy

The adoption of male disguise by female characters in Italian Renaissance comedy and male characters cross-dressing to appear as women can be seen to have complex and interesting implications for definitions of gender and sexuality.[1] By playing with the relationship between biological and social gender categories (female vs male and feminine vs masculine) and toying also with questions of sexuality (heterosexuality, homoeroticism, lesbianism, homosexuality and narcissism), the plays raise a variety of issues to be explored in this chapter.

One key concern is whether cross-dressing opens up any possibilities for radical positions in relation to dominant patriarchal stereotypes of gender and sexuality, or whether it works ultimately to maintain and reinforce traditional definitions of sexuality; or indeed both, at different times. This question can only be adequately addressed by examining cross-dressing as a dramatic device interacting with a complex set of other factors. In addition to the dramatic texts themselves, the context within which the performance took place must also be considered. Of special interest are the dynamics of spectatorship involving the particular psychosocial processes which cross-dressing sets up in that performance context. Factors relevant to this discussion are available to us now only in the limited form of surviving contemporary accounts (treatises, letters etc.) and, of course, the dramatic texts themselves. From these sources it is possible to gather information regarding both the events taking place on the stage and the audience that watched them.

Of fundamental importance to the study of cross-dressing is the fact that a biological gender switch has already taken place before the play opens, in that female characters were usually played by male actors before the second half of the sixteenth century. This clearly adds another dimension to the onstage dynamics which result when a female character (in reality already a man) dresses as a male character,

Plate 2. Watching a performance of a Roman comedy in Venice in 1561.

in plays which foreground sexual themes. The composition of the audience is also relevant here; audience reception of the playing out of gender games would have varied at least to some degree in relation to the gender, class and age of its members. The social status of those who played the characters and those who watched them would undoubtedly also have fed into the actual dramatic text that provided the basis for the performance.

Not to be ignored is the fundamental fact that the erudite Renaissance comedies that have come down to us were written by men, a fact which would have coloured gender portrayal in general, and that of cross-dressing in particular. One dramatic area in which women writers of the Italian Renaissance were to be found is that of convent comedy.[2] Outside the all-female institution of the convent and in the public context of the court and the academy, male dramatists abounded. Interestingly, the speculations in the prologue of *La cortigiana* concerning the identity of its author do include references to two women writers as possibilities, namely the Marchesa di Pescara (Vittoria Colonna) and Veronica da Correggio (Vittoria Gambara). However, although these high-born women were known writers, they were famous for their poetry rather than for any plays they might have written. Moreover, their activity as writers was linked solely to their exceptional status as privileged members of the highest social order, and not to any occupation, such as that of courtier, diplomat, public official and scholar, usually performed by our male comic dramatists. In light of the female-authored convent comedies, which contain critiques of certain institutions, such as marriage, it is safe to assume that, while female writers do not of course inevitably deviate from the patriarchal mindset simply because they are female, there can be little doubt that the unreconstructed male writer would produce a patri-archally-oriented dramatic text.

It is in the dramatic text that other crucial factors relating to gender disguise are located. These concern the variety of functions served by this device in terms of the plot, and the link between gender-specific cross-dressing and other forms of disguise. It is important to bear in mind that disguise is not only a highly dramatic vehicle, but lies at the very heart of theatrical illusion. In the prologue to the first version of *La Lena*, the theatrical event itself is signalled by the presence of 'people disguised in a variety of garments' (with the term *travestite* used to denote disguise in general): 'But when I went into one of these rooms, and saw about sixteen people disguised in a variety of garments, speaking and replying to each other with certain verses, I realized that they wanted to do one of those nonsensical things, as they were wont to do, that they call comedies and think they do well.' Disguise was of course not limited to a change of sex, but also included other social areas such as class. Known also as impersonation and inversion, and, usually with a narrowing of reference in modern times to the adoption of a sexual disguise, as transvestism and cross-dressing, the gender switch has a long history both within theatre and outside it.

In the theatrical context, as well as featuring in the playing of female roles by male actors, disguise had always formed part of the standard dramatic theme of mistaken identity. The many Roman comedies which favoured deception as a central motif repeatedly used general impersonation to this end.[3] Outside theatre, the device of gender disguise appeared not only in the more learned narrative forms, such as the short story and the epic poem, but, along with other motifs of the Renaissance comedies, also featured in the ballads and folklore of popular culture.[4] It was particularly in that apotheosis of popular culture, namely the carnival, that cross-dressing was to be found. In its celebration of the topos of the world-upside-down, inversions of many different types, including that of gender, took shape.[5] Male cross-dressing is described during Carnival in Rome by an English observer:

> During the time of Shrovetide, there is in Rome kepte a verie great coyle, which they use to call *Carne-vale*. which endureth the space of three or foure dayes: all which time the pope keepeth himselfe out of Rome, so great is the noyse and hurlie-burlie. The gentlemen will attyre themselves in diverse formes of apparell, some like women, others like Turkes, and everye one almost in a contrarie order of disguising. (Taylor 1953, p. 142)

Carnival was significantly also often the occasion for the performance of the erudite comedies, so that the various levels of cross-dressing within the performance context of the plays would have resonated with its occurrence outside.[6]

In the context of real life, evidence of cross-dressing is sporadic and notoriously difficult to evaluate. Contemporary accounts chronicle instances of the donning of male clothes by prostitutes, by married and single women, and by nuns. City archives detailing the interrogation of prostitutes in Rome allude to punishment by whipping or imprisonment in cases of women caught wearing male clothes. In Venice, the large numbers of prostitutes using male attire in order to attract custom led to the passing of a decree by the Senate forbidding this fashion (Larivaille 1983, pp. 101–2). One particular motive for cross-dressing by female prostitutes appears to have been the competition they faced for male clients from male homosexuals (Brown 1989, p. 498). Transvestism is further associated with female prostitution in the custom of men dressing as women during Carnival in Rome, in that it seems to have been for the delectation of 'courtizanes' that male cross-dressing, along with other 'contrarie order[s] of disguising' took place at this time: 'And all this is done where the courtizanes be, to shew them delight and pastime: for they have coverlettes laid out at their windowes, whereon they stande leaning forth' (Taylor 1953, p. 142). In the case of non-prostitutes, transvestism has been suggested as perhaps originating in a 'general desire for the greater economic and political freedom of men', or, for women with lesbian tendencies, 'as a strategy for sexual and emotional expression' (Saslow 1989, p. 96). It has been argued, furthermore, that female transvestism was more prevalent in northern Europe (especially in England, the Netherlands and Germany), than in the south. This difference is attributed to factors such as the earlier age of marriage for women in the latter region, the context of greater protection combined with less freedom within which southern European women lived and the greater opportunities for employment as soldiers and sailors afforded by countries such as England and Holland. In terms of period, female transvestism appears to have been a feature more of the seventeenth and eighteenth centuries than of the sixteenth (Dekker and Van de Pol 1989, p. 102).[7]

As far as male cross-dressing in real life is concerned, sumptuary laws in Venice prohibited males dressing like women, which would seem to suggest that something akin to this actually took place. Contemporary accounts describe the open practice of homosexuality in the city which led to legislation regulating male attire: 'Young men made themselves look like women: they wore jewels; they perfumed themselves; and their clothes exposed most of their naked bodies. Parents did not dare to discipline their sons, but let them go their own ways. Again, the reason was that high officials, members of the Senate, were practitioners of this vice' (Gilbert 1973, p. 275). The decree issued by the *provveditori sopra le pompe* in 1512, which included the regulation of men's clothes, identified both dressing in a manner more appropriate to the opposite sex, and the baring of too much flesh: 'Men were forbidden attire which would increase physical attractiveness. Shirts should cover the entire upper part of the body and close neatly around the neck' (Gilbert 1973, p. 279). Incorrect dress of this type was judged 'a kind of sodomy', and late fifteenth and early sixteenth-century Venice saw the introduction of various laws attempting their prohibition (Brown 1989, p. 498).

Cross-dressing in the Renaissance comedies thus owes its existence to a variety of influences: erudite literary forms, popular narratives and festivals, Roman theatre and real life. In these different contexts, the duration of the gender switch is an important factor in terms of considering its radicalizing potential. The short-lived nature of the inversions of carnival is mirrored in the comedies, which portray cross-dressing as a means to a specific end, an unorthodox identity change regarded as abnormal and signalling trouble which must be righted by the play's *dénouement*. Yet, despite the fact that the device of cross-dressing is only ever temporary in the comedies, it cannot fail to raise questions because of its focus on the boundaries defining gender and sexuality. In the interstices of the conventionality of this topos, then, lie certain possibilities suggested by the positing of alternative ways of being as a gendered person. A space is opened up here for criticism of the stereotype, so that cross-dressing carries at its heart a critique of the fixity of boundaries. At the same time, however, these boundaries are in themselves being reinforced, if only by default.

Of crucial importance is the question of how the boundaries defining issues of gender and sexuality would have been viewed at the time
the comedies were written and performed. In order to historicize any
assessment of cross-dressing as a critique of the norm, it is necessary to
consider how this period in pre-modern Europe conceptualized sex-
related categories. In the case of biological and social gender definitions, the male sex was associated with a set of culturally determined
masculine attributes, and an opposing set attached to the female sex.[8]
The underlying system of binary opposites separating social genders
according to biology continues its ideological conflation of the social
with the natural in an unbroken trajectory from the Greeks through the
Renaissance until the present day, with some social gender attributes
receiving more or less emphasis in accordance with historical and
socioeconomic context.

The same continuity cannot be observed, however, in definitions
relating to sexuality. While the late nineteenth century saw the introduction of terminology which became used to define sexual identity
(such as 'lesbian' and 'homosexual'), sixteenth-century perceptions of
sexual behaviour focussed not on identity, but on acts. In other words,
sexual preference was not seen as defining identity, but as a series of
separate acts on the part of individuals who might engage in different
forms of sexual behaviour on different occasions. In both canon and
civil law, the notion of lust, or crimes against nature, could cover all
types of what is now referred to as 'sexuality' (masturbation, bestiality,
male and female same-sex acts, heterosexual and same-sex sodomy),
and it was believed possible to move from one to another (Brown 1989,
pp. 68–9). The concept of sexual behaviour was thus a more mobile
one than that implied by the current notion of 'sexuality' as fixed,
unchanging sexual preference. The fact that female prostitutes in
Venice dressed as men in order to win male clients away from male
homosexual competition clearly implies that the male clients were in
fact likely to choose between heterosexual and homosexual sex, rather
than *being* either 'heterosexual' or 'homosexual'. Writing about male
sexual behaviour in the Renaissance, Saslow draws attention to homosexual practice as 'only one element of what we would now call bisexuality', and notes that 'The prevalence and character of male bisexuality
reflect two important determinants of sexuality in this period: It was
often associated with a generalized permissiveness, even license, and it
is consistent with adult men's positions at the pinnacle of a social system that privileged patriarchy, age, and power' (Saslow 1989, pp. 91–2).

Within this phallocentric context, sex between women received little attention, with only occasional prosecutions on record compared with cases involving male same-sex acts. Various factors underlie what Brown refers to as 'an almost active willingness to *dis*believe' lesbian sexuality: the concept of sex as inevitably phallus-oriented, so that sexual activity between women, if possible at all, was regarded as practice for 'real' sex with a man, or as a form of (inferior) female emulation of (superior) male sexual behaviour; the dominance of male voices (legal, ecclesiastical, artistic) regarding sex between women, in a world where fewer women than men were literate; and the absence of a lesbian subculture (Brown 1989, pp. 68–71; Saslow 1989, pp. 94–5). The degree of urbanization was sufficient to provide both opportunity for contact and safety in anonymity for homosexual communities to develop in Renaissance Italy, but women's access to public space, and so to each other, remained limited (Saslow 1989, pp. 94–5). Only the insular community life of the convent provided conditions for the development of sexual relationships between women, but even within convent walls, all-female desire was translated into the heterosexual paradigm by women who could not yet perceive themselves as 'lesbian'.

While the modern term 'lesbianism' describes sexual acts between women, the extra dimension implied by this term of female same-sex activity as definitive of a woman's identity and of belonging to a distinct social group, would not have been understood in sixteenth-century Italy. On the other hand, there are indications that homosexuality was perceived as being linked to 'personality type' during this period (Saslow 1989, p. 104). The male-authored comedies elaborate quite openly on all-male sexual acts, often in great detail. However, while inevitably positing the possibility of all-female desire in their play on cross-dressing and mistaken identity, they do not investigate this sexual dynamic overtly. It is in the sphere of female cross-dressing that legislation concerning itself with lesbian sexuality appears to have been the most severely implemented in the few cases on record in premodern Europe. Women imitating men through transvestism, or by using phallic substitutes during sex with other women, received the death penalty, while the 'passive', and so conventionally feminine partner, incurred a lesser sentence (Brown 1989, p. 73).[9]

It is clear that female and male cross-dressing in the comedies must be considered very much in the legal and religious context of the sixteenth-century, as well as in relation to premodern conceptions and definitions of sexual practices. In its representation in cultural production of the period, cross-dressing appears as a convention, yet also as a device denoting the instability, and mobility, of gender-specific norms. At the heart of this paradox lies the construction of meanings and identities as a process, rather than as a given, even if, in the last resort, the traditional order, and indeed order itself, is reestablished and celebrated. Stallybrass concludes his discussion of the playing of female characters by boy actors in English Renaissance drama as follows: 'contradictory fetishisms (body parts, costumes, handkerchiefs, sheets) are staged not in the play of pure difference but in the play between indeterminacy and fixation' (Stallybrass 1992, p. 80). This dynamic, which is also apparent in the erudite Italian comedies (if in ways that are different in consonance with, for one thing, Italian staging conventions of the time), also has specific implications for definitions of femininity.

The key focus of this chapter, in terms of methodology, is the intersection in cross-dressing between the psychoanalytical, and so universal, process of sexual fetishism, and historically-specific material and social relations. As shown in the last chapter, social relations in early sixteenth-century Italy are informed by a fast-developing market capitalism, to produce a fetishism of commodities which extends to the female body. In the comedies the female body is particularly commodified as merchandise in its central role in the marriage market, especially as far as the merchant class is concerned. In relation to their Roman models, the Renaissance comedies show an increase in merchant characters (a development which reflects the difference in socioeconomic context between Roman and Renaissance periods). The intersection of these two types of fetishism in cross-dressing works in conjunction with the particular system of gender-differentiated spectatorship invoked by the performance context, to deny a femininity outside of its patriarchally circumscribing equation with a sexuality/reproductivity in the service of the dominant order.[10] The mechanism of fetishism is crucial here in setting up a dynamic that focusses on female sexuality while never quite 'getting there', let alone going beyond it to posit a more inclusive and 'whole' femininity. By 'coming to a halt half-way, as it were', the inherent fetishism of cross-dressing which incribes the playing of female roles by men in effect both freezes feminine identity at a sexually suggestive, but not replete, stage, as well as redirecting attention to masculine identity as the baseline.[11]

PERFORMANCE AND SPECTATORSHIP

The issue of who played the dramatic characters, and who watched them, adds a significant dimension to the dynamics of cross-dressing in the comedies. In the context of performance, a certain degree of suspension of disbelief is already obligatory from the start in an audience involved in a medium founded at a primary level on illusion. As a consequence, the real biological gender of the actor is simply part of this basic illusion of theatre which must be 'believed', in other words, discounted as irrelevant and without significance. However, there can be no doubt that an erotic frisson results from an adolescent male or boy actor playing a female character, particularly in plots centred, as they usually are, on gaining access to the female body. The erotic dynamic is increased in its complexity, moreover, when the persona on stage undergoes a further sexual transformation, as the 'female' character cross-dresses to appear as a male in what has been called triple-cross-dressing (Case 1988, p. 22). Another important element contributing to the construction of audience positions regarding the various levels of cross-dressing, is the reaction by other characters on the stage, particularly when these characters (but not of course the actors playing them) are unaware that cross-dressing is taking place.

The fundamental reason for the exclusion of women from the stage was the patriarchal association of the feminine with the sexual, a link defining femininity exclusively in sexual terms, and prioritizing the female body at the expense of all else. The equation of femininity with sexuality meant that female performers were seen as flaunting their bodies, and were thus automatically considered to be engaged in prostitution (an assumption already current in Greek and Roman times) (Case 1988, p. 20). With femininity not merely considered as embodying sexuality itself, but also held responsible for male sexual misdemeanours, women/female sexuality, had to be kept out of public view and particularly off the stage. It therefore follows that, even when a male actor plays a female role, the mere fact that 'femininity' is on stage means that the entire sexual arena has been opened. The theatre itself had long been regarded by that stronghold of patriarchal values, the Christian Church, as the site of immorality. This view was based not merely on the type of subject matter represented on stage, but on the grounds of theatre as the epitome of deception, as well as a source of distraction from spiritual concerns. Ecclesiastical censure of the theatre, and cultural activity generally, took more concrete form in Post-tridentine Italy, as the Counter Reformation took hold from the latter half of the sixteenth century (Andrews 1993, pp. 220–5). In 1558, Pope Sixtus issued a new edict forbidding women to appear on stage, a prohibition which was still current in the Papal states in the eighteenth century.

As regards the question of whether or not female parts in the erudite comedies were ever played by women, the situation is by no means straightforward. Some discussion is therefore necessary about whether females (and not just professional actresses), and indeed what males (other than professional actors), took part in performances. It is generally believed that in the first half of the sixteenth century, all parts were still played by males, both boys and men, with a few exceptions depending on the social context of the performance.[12] Unfortunately, unlike the case of English actresses, whose introduction can be firmly established as 1660, the year of the Restoration of Charles II to the throne, no such clarity exists as far as professional Italian actresses are concerned.

There is no doubt that the other important theatre form of the sixteenth century, the improvised *commedia dell'arte*, was performed by professional troupes and family companies including actresses from at least 1540, following the popular mediaeval tradition of the female *joculatrice* and *tornatrice* who sang, danced and joked in the market place (Gilder 1960, pp. 53, 56). It is also the case that women sang and danced in the *intermezzi* put on between plays and acts of plays. Indeed, the interludes of the first performance of Machiavelli's *Clizia* in 1525 featured a well-known singer, his mistress 'Barbara Fiorentina' (Andrews 1993, p. 55). This in itself is not unusual, in that women have always sung and danced, in conformity with the cultural prioritization of the female body as the hallmark of femininity (while masculinity has always been associated with intellect and reason). According to Gilder, 'the phenomenal rage for interludes increased the demand for women on the stage'; nevertheless, as she points out, 'the transition from singing and dancing, the arts of pure entertainment, to straight acting, came . . . very gradually' (Gilder 1960, pp. 51, 55).

Women also performed in the *sacre rappresentazioni*. Gian Lodovico Zuccone, in a letter dated 26 May 1534, reports on the performance of such a religious play, which took place not in an urban context, but in the countryside, and which contained twenty-five to thirty young women, aged thirteen to sixteen, who played the parts of virgins, martyrs and sybils. Commenting on these girls, Zuccone praises not merely their acting abilities, but focusses on the modesty of their comportment, which appears to have been even more significant than the performances of the men: 'they were truly even more worthy of praise than the men, because, together with modesty, they demonstrated great promptness, without any of them ever blushing' (D'Ancona 1966, II, pp. 433–4).[13]

As far as the erudite comedies are concerned, *commedia dell'arte* actresses of the calibre of Isabella Andreini were known to have taken part towards the end of the sixteenth century (although still depending mostly on their *commedia dell'arte* performances). It is also certain that, in the context of the court, women (but not professional actresses) played female parts in the erudite comedies. The importance of the private performance context in determining the participation of these upper-class women cannot be overemphasized. In 1539 Duke Ercole d'Este wrote to Cardinal Gonzaga about the acting abilities of his young daughter, Anna, cross-dressed as Pamphilo in Terence's *Andria*, a talent which he proudly wishes the Cardinal could become acquainted with, but strictly 'in private':

I wish you could see, *in private, however*, the performance of a comedy in which my first-born, Lady Anna, also acts; and even though it is in Latin, since it is Terence's *Andria*, I am certain you would not be displeased by a little girl of 7 years playing the part of Pamphilo. You will perhaps say that I am her father, and that I am crowing: this does not bother me. Suffice it to say that I hope to make you see that my offspring is spirited. (D'Ancona 1966, II, p. 137, italics added)

Another private context for female acting exploits was the all-female environment of the convent. Most commonly, however, the erudite comedies were performed by male academicians, courtiers and students.[14]

A further factor to be taken into account is the use of Latin in the performances of the Roman comedies which both preceded and continued alongside the new vernacular comedies. Latin was very much the province of the privileged classes, as a rule. D'Ancona cites an instance of Plautus' *Menaechmi* being recited, in Latin, at the Papal Court in 1511 by a cast also including 'a (male) servant and a woman'. D'Ancona's comment on this indicates the greater unlikelihood of a woman, rather than a man, knowing Latin, while he does not see fit to remark upon the unusual fact that a servant has this ability: 'it is noteworthy, given the severe conditions then prevailing in Rome, to see a woman act, and in Latin' (D'Ancona 1966, II, p. 80). That Latin was not understood by all those who came to see the comedies is shown in a letter to Don Ferrante by Ippolito Capilupi reporting on a performance of Plautus' *Captivi*, in which the costumes, together with some of the *intermezzi* giving summaries of the plot in the vernacular, ensured that the play 'did not end up boring men, or women, who did not understand Latin' (D'Ancona 1966, II, p. 440).[15] With the rise of the vernacular as celebrated in many of the erudite comedies, this genre was opened up not only to a wider audience, but also to a broader range of actor both in terms of class and gender.

While the professional actress began to appear during the latter half of the sixteenth century, her path was not without obstacles, particularly in view of the severity of the Post-tridentine climate. Nevertheless, the star status accorded the actress of the sixteenth century was growing.[16] One outcome of this was the fact that the history of the role became that of the actress who played it (Duchartre 1966, p. 264). In other words, the ideology of femininity as sexuality still predominated, so that the actress was perceived as merely playing herself as a woman, rather than as being engaged in the activity of acting.[17] That the notion of the actress inevitably playing herself as a woman was still current in late nineteenth-century Italy, is attested to by the index to D'Ancona's *Origini del teatro italiano* of 1891: while male actors are indexed under the entry *attori*, no independent entry exists under *attrici*, who are to be found as a sub-species of 'women' under *donne*.

In the case of actors, on the other hand, consideration of their amateur or professional status, educational standards and age, comes into play, while their bodies/sexuality remain unremarked upon (however, actors as well as actresses were denied burial in consecrated ground well into the seventeenth century) (Andrews 1993, p. 224). The urban-based erudite theatre of the mid-1500s in which they took part was about to receive a boost both from the building of permanent theatre buildings and from the organization of professional acting companies. The advent of the professional actor replaced the makeshift conditions which resulted from 'temporary actors gathered here and there', so that theatre became a constant, rather than an ephemeral, cultural activity, and acting itself 'a life's profession' (D'Ancona 1966, II, pp. 436–7).

In the first half of the sixteenth century, however, the erudite comedies were usually played by amateurs such as courtiers and academicians, as were the Roman comedies, which continued in popularity. In a letter to Duke Ercole, dated 13 February 1501, Sigismondo Cantelmo reports on a performance of Terence's *Adelphi*, 'performed by learned people' (D'Ancona 1966, II, p. 382).[18] Not only older academicians, but also young students, regularly took acting roles.[19] That the age of the actor was not ignored by the audience is shown by the comments of Castiglione on the odd effect of young boys playing the parts of older men. Writing about the performance of a play, written by the fourteen-year-old Guidobaldo Ruggiero, in 1513 at Urbino, he notes that 'most certainly they acted miraculously: and it really was extraordinary to see little old men a few feet high, keeping up that air of gravity, and those very severe, parasitical gestures' (Castiglione 1978, I, p. 1069). This would also suggest that the gender of the actor playing a female part would not go unnoticed, and consequently enter the dynamic of further onstage cross-dressing.

In terms of professional actors, and the advent of professional actresses, it appears that mid-sixteenth-century Italy saw a period of change. However, the most common scenario as far as performances of erudite comedies for the first part of the century are concerned, is still that of an all-male cast. In terms of the composition of the audience, women, and particularly those belonging to the nobility and upper middle classes, not only formed part of the audience watching the erudite comedies, but also featured as a major attraction in themselves. They therefore occupied the dual position of coming to enjoy the spectacle of the evening's entertainment (the play, the *intermezzi*, the dancing) and of providing it. These beautiful women had their own audience, not merely within the auditorium itself, but onstage in the form of the (male) actors whom they were to inspire. While male actors completely dominated the stage during the play itself, the *intermezzi* featured women performing songs and dances, in other words, a focus on the real female body on stage.

The provision of spectacle by the female body coincides with the spectacle of Renaissance comedy itself, and the visual pleasure it generated. Of relevance to any performance art, and especially to theatre and cinema, visual pleasure has been given special theoretical attention in relation to the latter in terms of the psychoanalytical concept of scopophilia, or pleasure in looking.[20] Writers of the Renaissance were already well aware of the significance of this effect of performance and of the need to fulfil the audience's desire for this type of pleasure. In a manner which goes beyond the general Horatian element of delight (*delectare*) as an essential ingredient of cultural production, Renaissance theorists of the stage specified how visual pleasure was to be quite literally built into the scenery. In his section on how to lay out the ground plan for scenery in his *Pratica di fabricar scene e machine ne' teatri* of 1638, a work summarizing Renaissance developments in staging, Sabbattini advises as follows:

Let the streets be as narrow as possible, so that the houses can be the wider and consequently give the greater space for doors, windows, archways, and booths: things that give both magnitude and depth to the scene and *pleasure to the spectators*. (Hewitt 1958, p. 52, italics added)

Likewise in his paragraph on how to place the highlights and shadows in painting the scene, he warns that unless these are well-managed:

the spectators will experience dissatisfaction since they will always have the impression that they are not seeing clearly, or *with pleasure*, the various parts of the scenery (Hewitt 1958, p. 56, italics added).

The use of the term 'spectators' (*spettatori*), both here, in contemporary accounts of performances and in the plays themselves, would seem to indicate that the primary zone of audience response to the stage was felt to be visual. A contemporary account of the performance of *La Calandria* in Urbino in 1513 outlines its visual, as well as auditory, pleasures, beginning with the most visual elements, the costumes and the *intermezzi*:

The costumes, the interludes, with the acting of the Urbinese whose tongue is much used to such things, together with the action, were so pleasing to the spectators, and likewise the music, heard at its own time, that I was there for many hours *looking* and listening. Yet at the end of the play it seemed to the spectators that little time had elapsed, and as a result of the *beautiful sights* and sweet sounds for the eyes and ears, when they left the hall they appeared exhausted but not satiated by the pleasure experienced. (Bonino 1977, p. 449, italics added)[21]

The prologue to *Gli ingannati* also discusses spectatorship in terms of seeing (*vedere*) and hearing (*udire*). While visual pleasure was thus an important element of the staging of Renaissance comedies, it was especially catered for in what took place between the acts and between performances of more than one play, namely the *intermezzi*.[22] These were elaborately staged entertainments, often based on classical myths, which included singing and dancing, and which specialized in a dazzling display of visual delights. This type of theatrical display typified contemporary taste, and extended beyond the confines of the performance of the comedies to festive occasions, such as banquets and weddings, with the former featuring table decorations and service in the form of scenes (Laver 1964, chapter 4). The *intermezzi* began in the context of court performances, court taste being more frivolous than that of the academy (Jacquot 1964, p. 477). On occasion these *intermezzi* even proved more successful with the audience than the plays themselves.[23] The degree of theatricalizing of the female body as sexual spectacle in the *intermezzi* can be ascertained from contemporary descriptions which focus on the classical costumes of the nymphs, with their revealingly short skirts (Newton 1975, pp. 204–5).

The matter of spectacle extended from the stage to the auditorium. The auditorium was carefully arranged in order to seat the spectators according to both gender and rank, with the women segregated from the men, and allowing also for spectators from the lower social orders. A contemporary account of the performance of *La Calandria* in Urbino in 1513 mentions the order in which spectators were seen to their seats, beginning with high-ranking women, and ending with 'the other inferiors': 'A beautiful, calm order was then maintained in introducing into the hall the duchesses, ladies, and all foreign and native gentlemen, and then the other inferiors' (Bonino 1977, p. 449).[24] In his *Il secondo libro d'architettura*, 1545, dealing with theatre design, Serlio lays out a ground plan for the auditorium, noting that:

The first tiers, which are marked G, are for the most noble ladies; the ladies of lesser rank are placed higher up. The broader levels marked H and I are passageways between which are tiers reserved for the noblemen. Men of lesser rank will sit on the tiers above. The large space marked K is for the common people and may vary in size according to the dimensions of the hall. (Hewitt 1958, pp. 22–3)

Unlike the men, the women were also positioned in relation to their beauty and age, as shown by the following extract from Sabbattini's *Pratica di fabricar scene e machine ne' teatri*, The opening lines of this section also reveal, once again, the potential danger of the female body, even to the ushers. The closing lines point out that this danger applies also to men in the audience, while the actors, by implication all male, can safely derive inspiration from these female bodies from the safe distance of the stage:

40. *How and in what order to accommodate the audience*

The accommodating of an audience is a matter of much importance and trouble. Yet, at these performances there is never a lack of willing helpers, especially those who seek the job of showing the ladies to their seats. Were the performances given daily, there would still be plenty of those. You must take care, however, to select for this purpose, persons of years of discretion, so that no suspicion or scandal arise The ladies are to be placed in the orchestra, or as we say, in the third of the hall nearest the stage, taking care to place the least important in the first rows nearest the parapet and proceeding in the other rows according to rank. Care should be taken always to place the most beautiful ladies in the middle so that those who are acting and striving to please, gaining inspiration from this lovely prospect, perform more gaily, with greater assurance, and with greater zest. The more elderly ladies should be seated in the last rows on account of the proximity of the men, so that every shadow of scandal may be avoided. (Hewitt 1958, pp. 22–3)

Contemporary accounts report the presence of beautiful women in the audience. The prologue to the first version of *La Lena* opens with the assumption that the audience will include 'beautiful young women': 'A little while ago, when I saw these gentlemen gather here, and so many beautiful young women, I was sure that they wanted to dance.' The prologue to *Gli ingannati* goes so far as to use the conceit that the male spectators will neither see nor hear the play because of the distracting presence in the audience of the most beautiful women in Siena: 'How do you then expect them to concentrate on looking at scenes or plays, or hear or see anything we do or say, with you before them? What more beautiful pastime, what more beautiful spectacle, what more pleasing or delightful sight is there to be seen, than yourselves?' The same conceit is used by Bibbiena in his prologue to *La Calandria*. Addressing the women in the audience, he says: 'these gentlemen are so intent on contemplating the beauties of you women, that they'll take little or no notice of the play', a comment that concludes a satirical account of the beauty preparations undertaken by women prior to attending the performance.

At a performance in 1542, fifty women were invited, but only 'the most beautiful and the most noble' (D'Ancona 1966, ii, p. 438). Kernodle, commenting on 'the importance of the ladies in the whole spectacle', quotes a contemporary description of the 'social spectacle' which preceded a performance of *L'Ermiona* in Padua in 1637:

Along the ground of the theatre were set up two banks on which were arrayed eighty Padovan ladies of surpassing beauty and majestic manners, who, because of the excellency of their noble bearing and the luxury of their adornments, seemed to be worthy of being invited to the wedding of a goddess. To the onlookers their eyes seemed more luminous than stars when they began a stately dance to the music of violins and viols. (Hewitt 1958, pp. 3–4)

The link made here, and by Sabbattini, between beauty and class, is significant in the relation of these audience considerations to the performance context as a whole, and especially to the dynamic created by cross-dressing on the stage. The close association between audience and dramatic text in terms of shared gender stereotyping is revealed by the definition of the ideal woman in the plays themselves, in a formula which similarly features beauty, class and often also wealth, as prerequisites. Ligurio praises Lucrezia in *La mandragola* in terms of beauty and upper-class potential: 'a beautiful woman, wise, dignified and fit to rule a kingdom' (I, 3).

In *La cortigiana*, the ideal woman whom Rosso promises to his master, Signor Parabolano, is again, above all, beautiful, as well as noble and rich: 'One of the most well-born, the most rich and the most beautiful (which is most important)' (II, 15). Beauty and wealth feature in the attempt of a female character, Pasquella, to persuade Fabrizio to court her mistress, Isabella, in *Gli ingannati*: 'of the likes of her, so rich and so beautiful, there are few on this earth' (III, 5). Later in the same play, the ideal feminine qualities noted earlier in descriptions of women in the audience, reappear in the dramatic text and on stage by means of their opposites, as Flamminio swears that he would marry the type of woman whom Clemenzia has just described to him: 'even if she were ugly, even if she were poor, even if she were not of noble birth' (v, 2). The repeated references to the female spectators in terms of their bodies also reiterate the exclusive definition of femininity as sexuality, and a dangerous sexuality at that (Sabbattini).

It is clear that the dynamic engendered by cross-dressing must be analysed not simply as it appears in the written, dramatic, text, but as part of the overall performance context with its own specific elements (male actors, an audience containing an arrangement of beautiful noblewomen, the spectacle of the women in the *intermezzi*, and of the female spectators). Contributing to the signification of the performance is a complex system of identifications, particularly through a system of looks. The women in the audience do not merely watch the play on stage. They themselves are watched by the actors, who return their look, as well as by the men in the audience. Even before the third stage of triple-cross-dressing takes place, as 'female' characters dress as men, the women in the audience are already in a complicated position as female spectators, a complexity which does not apply to their male counterparts.

The construction of audience positions by the performance context, in conjunction with audience interpretation, involves a process of fantasy work and identification with the characters/actors on stage. Theories of female spectatorship suggest that a type of psychological cross-dressing takes place during this identification. These theories show:

> a tendency to view the female spectator as the site of an oscillation between a feminine position and a masculine position, invoking the metaphor of the transvestite . . . the woman who identifies with a female character must adopt a passive or masochistic position, while identifying with the active hero necessarily entails an acceptance of what Laura Mulvey refers to as a certain 'masculinization' of spectatorship. (Doane 1991, p. 24)[25]

There is the further consideration that femininity, as defined by patriarchy, already in itself denotes a false, and hence merely assumed, identity: 'It is femininity itself which is constructed as a mask – as the decorative layer which conceals a non-identity' (Doane 1991, p. 25). This non-identity could be seen as epitomized by the absence of real women on the stage where, just as in the ideological workings of patriarchy beyond the stage, they are defined from a male-dominated perspective. But as Doane also points out, the very fact that femininity is culturally constructed as an image allows the female spectator to separate herself from the images presented to her. The cultural studies approach to cinematic spectatorship, which emphasizes meanings based on consumption rather than production, disputes the notion of a passive female spectator position constructed entirely by the text, in favour of active choice and fantasy work.[26] According to this model, the female spectator watching the Renaissance comedies could choose to suspend disbelief, 'believe' that the female characters on stage are female, and use the cross-dressing of these characters as fantasy material according to the specifics of her own lived sexuality.

The position of the women watching the all-male comedies, with their female impersonations, is further complicated by the various types of sexuality suggested by different scenarios of cross-dressing. It is important to bear in mind that it is not only heterosexuality which is brought into play by plots aiming at heterosexual intercourse. As males play both males and females in sexual plots, the dynamic of all-male desire, namely homoeroticism, is inevitably also introduced. This is the case even when all-female desire, in other words, what is known today as lesbianism, is intimated (for example, Isabella's desire for Fabio, who, as the audience knows and 'believes', is really Lelia, in *Gli ingannati*). Here the fact that both are played by males ineluctably returns the sexual dynamic to that of homoeroticism at the baseline (unless, of course, the female spectator chooses, instead, to 'believe' the first level of cross-dressing). Lesbian sexuality has always been subject to a tradition of being recuperated and subsumed by patriarchy into the masculine viewpoint, often, as here, by functioning to provide material for male voyeurism. As far as the female spectator is concerned, the depiction of female desire which is heterosexual (e.g. that of Lelia for Flamminio in *Gli ingannati*, and Fulvia for Lidio in *La Calandria*), narcissistic (Pasquella's account of Isabella masturbating in *Gli ingannati*) or has lesbian implications, in actual fact bypasses and excludes her, unless she suspends her disbelief, or 'masculinizes' her act of spectatorship by means of an internal cross-dressing to identify with the male actors.

The use of boys, particularly in female parts, is crucial in feeding directly into the predominating homoerotic dynamic, bearing in mind the classical stereotype of the homosexual boy–man pairing.[27] The intergenerational Greek model of pederasty continued to shape most, but not all, homosexual relations in the sixteenth century, the majority of which took place between boys or adolescents and men (Saslow 1989, pp. 91, 93). In all-male sex, the younger partner would take the passive, 'woman's' part on account of physical similarities with the female gender. As Saslow states: 'In an atmosphere of indiscriminate pleasure-seeking, boys were considered interchangeable with women because of the still-"feminine" physical characteristics of beardless, high-voiced, smooth-skinned adolescents.' In this context, moreover, 'boys are treated . . . as essentially unphallused, and tend to be assimilated to women' (Saslow 1989, pp. 92, 492). If the Scottish traveller Lithgow is to be believed, this practice was particularly prevalent in Italy:

for beastly Sodomy, it is rife here [Padua] as in Rome, Naples, Florence, Bologna, Venice, Ferrara, Genoa, Parma not being exempted, nor yet the smallest village of Italy: A monstrous filthinesse, and yet to them a pleasant pastime, making songs and singing Sonets of the beauty and pleasure of their Bardassi, or buggerd boyes. (Taylor 1953, p. 150)

The similarity of boys and women in terms of social position and relation to men is highly relevant to the theatrical context:

Boys, by virtue of their age, were cast in a social role similar to that of women – dependent on and inferior to the adult male. Women could be represented by boys on stage because they shared their social attributes. (Case 1988, p. 22)

For the female spectator, the situation was one of being confronted with female parts played by male actors who, not just because of their costumes, but also in their youth, were similar in appearance and gender status, but still different, to themselves. A degree of erotic ambivalence would also have suggested itself to male spectators – men, youths and boys – inclined to either homosexual or heterosexual preferences, or both. Modern critical evaluation of boys playing women's roles includes notions ranging from that of the practice as a manifestation of anxieties about the monstrously unstable self, to that of all-male actors as mere convention, the 'natural and unremarkable product of a culture whose conception of gender was "teleologically male"'; or indeed as deliberately providing homoerotic pleasure for male spectators.[28]

One undeniable implication of an all-male cast in plays containing female roles, then, is that all the eroticism in the performance of the comedies, both for the actors and the audience, is ultimately male-focussed. This is the case even if the plays appear to centre on the attractions and dangers of female sexuality, for these are not only defined by men working within patriarchal traditions (the playwrights), but are also played out by them (the male actors). Yet, at the same time, it is also abundantly clear that female sexuality is of central importance. Indeed, it appears to be so much emphasized as to acquire the status of a fetish. In the context of spectacle as the overriding feature of the performance context of the comedies, both the female spectator in the auditorium and her male impersonator on the stage are 'spectacularized' as a visually and erotically central but disturbing element. In some cases, the impersonation is left out as too overpowering and replaced by words and plots which revolve around it 'at a distance' (Clizia in *Clizia* and Licinia in *La Lena*).

Female sexuality functions in the comedies as a mask, a part of the spectacle which is donned by the male actor playing a female part, put on in play by the female spectator in her fantasy, or discarded by her if she masculinizes her response to certain of the stage events. Underneath the mask lies the lack of identity/subjectivity with which patriarchy marks femininity. For the male actor, on the other hand, his female masquerade thinly disguises his identity/subjectivity as member of the dominant set of all-male relations governing patriarchal society, a position which is also occupied by the major addressee of the comedies, the male spectator. Taking this argument one stage further, female sexuality as the repository of sexuality itself, both in the impersonated 'female' characters on stage in the plays, and in the women dancing and singing in the *intermezzi*, as well as in the women-as-spectacle in the auditorium, can be seen to function primarily to open up the licit sexual, and specifically heterosexual, arena for the depiction of illicit, underlying homo-erotic desires by an all-male cast for male spectators.

Bibbiena's prologue to *La Calandria*, and the prologue to *Gli ingannati*, both address the women in the audience. Within the latter play, one of the characters, Pasquella, even speaks directly to the female spectators in a soliloquy, with the words 'my dear women' (IV, 5). It is particularly interesting to consider whether a play such as *Gli ingannati*, written especially for women by a team of male playwrights, in fact offers an alternative dynamic to the one just outlined.[29] In other words, does the female spectator of this play need both to masculinize her spectator-ship as well as look through the mask of a patriarchally-defined female sexuality, or does the play, in spite of its performance by an all-male cast, truly address her?

FETISHISM AND COMMODIFICATION

It can be argued that both the playing of female parts by male actors and the arrangement of female (but not male) spectators centring on their sexual attributes, are necessarily predicated on the definition and place of femininity within patriarchy. That the particular historical formation of patriarchy is that of expanding capitalism in the early modern north Italian states is attested to by the commodification of the female body and by commodity fetishism itself, as discussed in the previous chapter. This section links commodity fetishism, notably in the form of commodification of the female body, with the process of sexual fetishism which takes place during cross-dressing, particularly in light of the fact that all the stages of cross-dressing in the comedies have as their starting point the male gender of the actor.

This link is encapsulated perfectly in the comment made by Fannio, a male character who is here dressed as a woman, to another male character, Ruffo, in *La Calandria*. He says 'Aren't I a nice bit of stuff?' (III, 21) ('buona robba'). First of all, this remark foregrounds the elliptical relations within commodity fetishism whereby, it will be recalled, people relate to each other through things, or commodities, which are accorded value beyond their material worth to signify in social currency (see chapter 1). *Robba* (or *roba*), the quintessential, generic Italian term for material things, is associated by Fannio with being female or,

rather, with the pretence of femaleness, a temporary identity donned
fetishistically *and jokingly* along with women's clothes (for, as will shortly
be seen, femaleness is far from being a desirable state).

The process of sexual fetishism, known mainly through the writings
of Freud, has been theorized in connection with the practice of transvestism both inside the theatrical context and outside it by Garber, and
directly associated with the use of boy actors in female roles by
Stallybrass.[30] A brief outline of this process will precede an exploration
of how the ultimately fetishistic and 'unreal' nature of the female characters on stage works to undermine the variety of alternative sexual
dynamics which the plays in fact posit, while at the same time high-
lighting them as actual possibilities which the spectators can choose to
identify with. In the first of three early essays on sexuality, entitled 'The
sexual aberrations' (1905), Freud defines 'fetishism' in terms of an
'unsuitable substitute for the sexual object', a substitution which is
dependent on 'the factor of sexual overvaluation' (Freud 1984, p. 65).
Among the unsuitable substitutes he mentions is one which is particularly relevant to the convention of male actors playing female parts,
namely 'some inanimate object which bears an assignable relation to
the person whom it replaces and preferably to that person's sexuality
(e.g. *a piece of clothing* or underlinen) (Freud 1984, p. 66, italics added).
His next sentence links psychosexual fetishism with the original use of
the concept of the fetish as appropriated by Marx for his critique of
what he called 'commodity fetishism': 'Such substitutes are with some
justice likened to the fetishes in which savages believe that their gods
are embodied.'

For Freud 'the situation only becomes pathological when the longing
for the fetish passes beyond the point of being merely a necessary
condition attached to the sexual object and actually *takes the place* of
the normal aim, and, further, when the fetish becomes the *sole* sexual
object' (Freud 1984, p. 67). Given the definition within patriarchy of
femininity exclusively in terms of sexuality, the wearing of women's
clothes by male actors can be seen to be a fetishized form, and replace-
ment, of femininity on the stage. Although it is of course the case that
these male actors are not necessarily working out their own psychosexual dynamics by donning female clothes, but are quite literally
'performing' this process, the coincidence between the two is too great
for fetishism to be ruled out, particularly for the spectators.

In a later work entitled 'Fetishism' (1927), Freud theorizes the causes
leading to this condition, locating them in the castration complex:

When now I announce that the fetish is a substitute for the penis, I shall certainly create disappointment; so I hasten to add that it is not a substitute for any chance penis, but for a particular and quite special penis that had been extremely important in early childhood but had later been lost. That is to say, it should normally have been given up, but the fetish is precisely designed to preserve it from extinction. To put it more plainly: the fetish is a substitute for the woman's (the mother's) penis that the little boy once believed in and ... does not want to give up. (Freud 1984, pp. 351–2)

Fetishism takes place as a result both of the boy's realization and of his disavowal of what he has realized. Freud continues: 'It is not true that, after the child has made his observation of the woman, he has preserved unaltered his belief that women have a phallus. He has retained that belief, but he has also given it up.' The process of fetishization is thus one of compromise, made up of contradictory components which, as it were, 'freeze' the traumatic memory of the moment of realization:

It seems ... that when the fetish is instituted some process occurs which reminds one of the stopping of memory in traumatic amnesia. As in this latter case, the subject's interest comes to a halt half-way, as it were; it is as though the last impression before the uncanny and traumatic one is retained as a fetish. (Freud 1984, p. 354)

This 'coming to a halt half-way' at the same time also serves not only to transfix femininity in its circumscribing sexuality, but provides visual evidence of a mere token sexuality, reduced as it is to a metonymic substitute of itself by the objectification process of the fetish.

Despite the phallocentrism and misogyny inherent in the processes of fetishism, attempts have been made recently to appropriate female fetishism for feminism.[31] One of these arguments, concerning female narcissism, is helpful in illuminating the portrayal of female masturbation in *Gli ingannati* in view of the predominance of male fetishism located at the first level of cross-dressing in the playing of female parts by male actors. Female narcissism is theorized as female fetishism predicated on a specifically female form of castration disavowal. Summarizing Grosz, Schor writes:

Female disavowal, whatever its form, differs, however, in one crucial respect from its masculine counterpart: the castration that is disavowed is not the mother's, but the daughter's. Women can, according to Grosz's reading of Freud, disavow their own castration through narcissism (the woman turns her own body into the phallus). (Schor 1992, p. 115)

Female narcissism, in the form of masturbation, enters the scene in *Gli ingannati* in the indirect form of an account by Pasquella, Isabella's maid, of her mistress's frustrated behaviour as the result of her un-requited passion for Fabio. Isabella appears to be 'always scratching her nether regions and always stroking her thighs' (II, 2), with the first phrase in the original Italian commonly interpreted as a direct refer-ence to masturbation. Through these actions, Isabella's sexual desire would appear to have become self-directed; she has, in Schor's words, turned her own body into the phallus. For a sixteenth-century audi-ence, masturbation would have been perceived as a form of illicit sexual activity classified under lust. Penance of varying lengths was advocated for this 'solitary vice'. For women, Theodore of Tarsus pre-scribed three years, while Borromeo recommended two years. For men, on the other hand, Borromeo stipulated only ten to thirty days' penance (Brown 1989, pp. 71–2, 497).

Pasquella's one line undoubtedly posits female narcissism as an alternative, female-centred sexual dynamic. There are, however, sev-eral problems with considering this an unmitigated alternative, not least the phallocentric, patriarchal framework within which female narcissism/female fetishism is theorized in its triumphant disavowal of castration. In the first place, Isabella's narcissism is triggered, and hence mediated by, her passion for Fabio, and so does not exist in its own right independent of a male fantasy object. The next important factor is that male fetishism in any case undercuts any possible female fetishism: Isabella, Fabio and Pasquella herself are all biologically male and, at least as far as the performance of the play in Siena in 1532 is concerned, even the identities of the actors playing Isabella and Fabio were known to the audience (Andrews 1993, p. 99). Furthermore, if Pasquella's brief reference to Isabella's masturbation is compared with Rosso's longer and more voyeuristic description in *La cortigiana* of Signor Parabolano's solitary bedtime activities, involving both verbal and physical fantasy, it seems that male masturbation provides a more comfortable topic which can be entered into with relish:

I put my ear to the door of my master's room, and in this position I heard him chattering away in his sleep, and, appearing to be at it hammer and tongs with his mistress, he was saying: Livia, I'm dying, Livia, I'm burning, Livia, I'm suf-fering agonies, and implored her crudely with a lengthy stream of nonsense. And then, changing tack, he'd say: o Luzio, how lucky you are to enjoy the most beautiful woman there is, and then going back to Livia, after telling her: my soul, my heart, dear blood, sweet hope etc., I heard the bed shaking loudly. (II, 4)

The element of voyeurism merely implicit in Pasquella's reference is much more pronounced in Rosso's account; a contrast which has the effect of moving sexual pleasure, whether directly experienced (Parabolano, Isabella) or vicarious (Rosso, Pasquella), into the male arena. Voyeurism by male characters is crucial to the unravelling of all the sexual possibilities present in the complex dynamics of the scene between Isabella and Fabio in *Gli ingannati* (Act II, scene 5). Unique in being 'the first staged love scene in Italian "regular" comedy', the portrayal of Isabella's passion for Fabio is in itself the exception rather than the rule for the erudite comedies (Andrews 1993, p. 99). For female desire to be represented actually in action on the stage would appear to give credence to the view that the play, written for female spectatorship, indeed addresses women as sexually-desiring subjects. On one level this is certainly the case: a fictional female character, Isabella, is involved in a passionate love scene on the stage with a fictional male character, Fabio. This is complemented by another fictional level, namely that the male character, Fabio, as the spectators, but not Isabella, are aware, is 'in reality' the fictional female character, Lelia, who is cross-dressed as a manservant to Flamminio, whom she loves. For female spectators, Isabella's onstage passion for Fabio/Lelia therefore introduces not only heterosexual female desire, but also the possibility of yet another all-female sexual dynamic in addition to Isabella's narcissism three scenes previously, namely that of lesbian sexuality. Isabella, then, would seem to be the fictional locus of an entire gamut of female desires: heterosexual, narcissistic and lesbian.

However, these alternative possibilities are drastically undermined from the start at the level not of fiction, but of reality, in that all these characters are played by male actors. Moreover, as if this were not enough to defuse these sexual possibilities, their undercutting is repeated at the fictional level by the introduction of *male* voyeurism which turns to blatant *male* sexual gratification. Two male servants, Scatizza and Crivello, observe the couple secretly from a doorway, issuing a running commentary all the while which intrudes on, and distracts audience attention from, the love scene. After a while Scatizza declares that he is becoming aroused. Scatizza's sexual gratification occurs at the expense of lesbian sexuality, in particular, as any all-female sexual dynamic suggested by the scene is appropriated for male pleasure (the classic way in which patriarchy recuperates lesbianism, a sexuality dangerously excluding male membership).[32] This process is aided by the device of dramatic irony, in that the presence of Scatizza and Crivello is known to the audience, with whom they are therefore in collusion, but not to Isabella and Fabio/Lelia, with the result that their comments and reactions take priority over those of the couple.

The scenario of an all-female desire appears particularly overt in *La Calandria*. Fulvia's request to Ruffo, the magician, that Lelio come to her *as a woman*, leads to her receiving a visit not from a male character in female disguise, but from Santilla, Lelio's twin sister, resulting in a (narrated) scene of sexual exploration as Fulvia gradually discovers that her lover is not 'whole' (IV, 2). However, unlike the comic treatment given to pederasty in the plays, in this play as in *Gli ingannati* there is no further exploration, comic or otherwise, of that unnamed, and unnameable, form of female desire, lesbian sexuality. *La Calandria* also includes a dialogue on hermaphroditism which includes a limited play on Fulvia's desire for a female Lidio (by which she meant Lidio dressed as a female for safety of passage). Hermaphroditism was the archetypal challenge, on both biological and social levels, to binary sexual categorization. The few instances which came under legal and medical scrutiny in the sixteenth century were 'resolved' by decreeing that the individual concerned should adopt one gender only, or incur the death penalty (Brown 1989, p. 498). In *La Calandria* Fannio convinces Ruffo that Lidio possesses both sexes, and 'will only use the female sex with Fulvia so that, having asked for him in female form, and finding him to be a woman, she will place so much faith in the spirit that she will adore you' (III, 17) (and, by implication, reward Ruffo handsomely). *La Calandria* thus plays with gender in a way that goes beyond the sexual signification of clothes in cross-dressing to involve the body itself.

However, the fictional level of the characters and the 'real' level of an all-male cast, with its attendant process of male fetishism of femininity, work together to defuse alternative and forbidden female desire, along with the heterosexual, narcissistic and lesbian sexualities posited temporarily as a means of expressing it. The dynamic of sexual desire is thus continually returned to the male domain, and particularly that of homoeroticism. This takes place through the implicit voyeurism inherent in the stage–auditorium relationship, as well as overt voyeurism of the type just described in *Gli ingannati*. This is clearly for the benefit not of the female spectators addressed in the prologue, unless they 'masculinize' their spectatorship, but for the exclusive delectation of male spectators. It is the male spectator as voyeur who identifies with the male voyeur on stage in a scene such as that between Isabella and Fabio/Lelia as watched by Scatizza and Crivello. At the same time, both the female presence on stage and the female spectators seated according to their sexual attributes serve as fetishized spectacle for male actor and male spectator alike.

The baseline of homoeroticism to which all sexual dynamics are returned is also portrayed in a more overt way. This takes place in the form of the narration of a homoerotic experience by one male character to another. At this point, a special bond is forged between these male characters on stage, a relationship that extends to include the male spectators in the audience (and excludes the female ones). In this context the device of cross-dressing between male identities, rather than between genders, plays its part both in the male bonding process and in that of vicarious sexual gratification. This process can be seen at work in *La mandragola*. A powerful homoerotic experience results for Nicia from the scheme to get Callimaco into Lucrezia's bed for the key fictional heterosexual encounter (fictional not just in the sense that the event is narrated, or even not actually the main objective, but because this can only ever be a homoerotic event, given that the actors are both male).

Nicia describes his experience of undressing the lute-player (Callimaco) to Ligurio as follows: 'He had a horrible nose, a twisted mouth; but you never saw more beautiful flesh! white, smooth, soft, and other things that you shouldn't ask me about' (v, 2). With his coy reference to 'other things' which he does not wish to be asked about, the male organ enters the scene, along with Nicia's pleasurable amazement at the colour and texture of Callimaco's body. His excitement intensifies as he describes his actions using *double entendre* metaphors of touch and penetration which reveal his ill-concealed desire for Callimaco: 'Once I'd got underway, I wanted to get to the bottom of it . . . I wanted to feel at first hand how things were going.' In this instance no second-stage cross-dressing by a male character as a female character appears necessary for homoerotic desires to be allowed to surface.

Connotations of homosexuality itself are also present in this episode as Nicia, an older man, describes the youth of Callimaco, thereby suggesting the classical stereotype of the homosexual old man–young man pair. That this stereotype was also current in Renaissance Italy is shown in a remark by Dulippo in *I suppositi*. He surmises that the older Cleandro may be suffering from 'a certain infirmity, which is helped by, and for which the appropriate remedy is, being with young boys just beginning to grow a beard' (ii, 3). A similarly negative view of homosexuality between men and boys is expressed by Stragualcia in *Gli ingannati.* In trying to persuade Fabrizio's tutor, the Pedante, to allow the group to take lodgings, Stragualcia entices him with the suggestion of possible pederasty: 'Master, I have seen the host's young son there, beautiful as an angel' (III 2). Pederasty was a typical element of antipedantic satire at the time. Saslow notes: 'Classical sources also familiarized Renaissance readers with *paiderastia*, the sexualized peda-gogic relationship between men and youths, which offered a precedent for genital expression of an emotional bond', and Lithgow's travel book mentions 'Schollers' in this context (Saslow 1989, p. 98; Taylor 1953, p. 150). While male same-sex acts, and particularly sodomy, were illegal, being considered to be 'against nature', their roots in classical tradition gave them some support. Works were also written in their favour, such as Della Casa's *De laudibus sodomiae seu pederastiae* (Taylor 1953, p. 150). However, pederasty is used as a source of comedy in the plays, which treat this form of sexual practice as a laughable weakness in older male characters.

An older, learned male character is also involved in antihomosexual satire in *La Calandria*. In this play, allusion is made both to misogynist and homosexual practices of the court, in which 'almost everybody is inimical to women' (I, 2), presumed to be a reference to the Papal court in Rome, where the play is set. When Lidio counters the misogynist remarks of Policlinico, his tutor, Fessenio comments that there is no need to go to any great lengths in praising women: 'Don't we all know that women are so worthy that there's no-one today who doesn't go round imitating them, and who wouldn't voluntarily, body and soul, become female?' (I, 2). This remark also suggests the use of cross-dress-ing by males for homosexual purposes. Homosexuality, in the form of pederasty, is linked to upper-class males in *La cortigiana*, where sodomy is intimated as the practice of 'signori' and 'grand'uomini' (V, 12). In *La mandragola*, however, homosexuality remains suppressed, appearing in the form of a homoeroticism in the service of heterosexuality, as Nicia checks out the body of his wife's future lover.

After his homoerotic thrill, Nicia proceeds to become a voyeur to a heterosexual experience, remaining in the room while Callimaco and Lucrezia have sexual intercourse. Lucrezia becomes the object of desire of several male characters at the level of narration, a process which leads to more male bonding and more vicarious sexual gratifi-cation. Further to Ligurio's alignment of his desires with those of Callimaco, Friar Timoteo, by disguising himself as Callimaco, also identifies with him. This process of identification is reiterated on a verbal level as Timoteo says to the audience at the end of Act IV: 'Callimaco and Lucrezia won't sleep, because I know that, if I were he, and you were she, we wouldn't sleep' (IV, 10). In the event, Timoteo does pass a sleepless night, the reason being his 'desire' to find out how Callimaco has fared. He opens the next act with a soliloquy beginning: 'I wasn't able to sleep a wink last night, so strong was my desire to hear how Callimaco and the others had got on.' It does not take much imagination to see that he has spent his night in a fantasy of vicarious sexual gratification as Callimaco.

The sexual act between Callimaco and Lucrezia has thus given vicarious sexual pleasure to three male characters: Nicia (who was present), Ligurio and Friar Timoteo. In the light of the ensuing male bonding, both between the male characters/actors and the male spectators, as well as the homoerotic episode between Nicia and Callimaco, it is arguable to what extent the ultimate aim of the play was genuinely heterosexual in inclination. The play could well be interpreted as a classic representation of the all-male relations which subtend patriarchy (Irigaray 1977, p. 168). Such a context would also help to account for the insidious misogyny, not just of the mass collusion that takes place against Lucrezia in a plan which might have led to her actual rape, but the fear and hatred of women which lies at the heart of the combination of folktales from which the plot derives. Radcliff-Umstead states:

Some folk legends enter into Machiavelli's plot, which is not derived from any particular ancient comedy or modern novella. The two major legends are those of the poisoner girl and of the medicinal virtues of the mandrake plant. An Arabian book of the twelfth century, the *Secretum secretorum*, tells of a girl who was nourished all her life on the venom of extremely poisonous serpents. Coming to adulthood, this beautiful girl was able to poison males in several different ways, *but especially in the sexual act*. This tale of the poisoner girl came down in several Italian renderings. (Radcliff-Umstead 1969, p. 120, italics added)

The notion of a man dying as a result of sex with a beautiful woman is rooted in the fear of women that haunts patriarchal ideology, most notably in connection with the castration complex as mythologized by the *vagina dentata* and elaborated upon by Freud in the context of fetishism.[33] The legend of the poisoner girl is linked in *La mandragola* to that of the mandrake plant, whose properties give its owner immense power (Radcliff-Umstead 1969, pp. 120–1). The effect of joining these two legends together is to feed into, and further reinforce, the dangers of female sexuality already inherent in one tale, by according it the extraordinary power which characterizes the second. That Lucrezia is potentially fatal to the first man who sleeps with her is of course introduced into the play as a blatant untruth, used by Callimaco as the lynch pin of his scheme to fool others (and not only the stupid Nicia, but also Lucrezia, who is described as shrewd). Nonetheless, patriarchal fears concerning female sexuality are brought into play here, as the audience is reminded of popular legends which act as their vehicle. The misogynistic undercurrent in the play would also serve to heighten the importance of the homosocial, and specifically homoerotic, elements.

In *Clizia* the main scheme also culminates in a narrated homoerotic scenario, as the young bride is substituted in bed with Nicomaco by Siro, a male servant. Again, much is made of both their reactions as dramatic attention leads to a focus on this scene as the *dénouement*. It could in fact be argued that this was not the only possible method of saving Clizia from rape, an argument which would make the bedscene between the two men gratuitous, and indicative of interest in a homoerotic agenda, rather than of essential importance to the plot. The scene centres on homoeroticism, but differs from that in *La mandragola* in several ways. The case of Nicomaco and Siro is based on a misunderstanding, as the former believes he is in bed with Clizia. After his initial arousal he is, however, alarmed rather than excited at what he believes to be a dagger pressing into his back (in reality, it is Siro's erect penis). Homoeroticism is thus present here in part by means of its negation, namely in Nicomaco's negative reaction once it becomes manifest. However, in the case of Siro, fully aware that he is in bed with another man, homosexual desire is clearly manifested.

As in *La mandragola*, disguise in *La cassaria* involves no gender switch, but still forms an integral part of dramatic gender relations. In this comedy, a class switch from servant to master is enacted. The master in question is Crisobolo, the wealthiest merchant in Metellino, and the disguise is achieved by the servant Trappola donning his clothes. Clothes were a prime indicator of status during the Renaissance, playing their part in commodity fetishism. The male characters in the play relate to each other by means of material goods, or, more precisely, by the surface appearance of material goods, with the female characters (the slave women Eulalia and Corisca) as the central commodities to be acquired by virtue of these false appearances. Of course both Eulalia and Corisca are also false appearances. As male actors in female clothes, the further dimension of psychosexual fetishism is apparent in these vestiges of femininity. Fetishization of commodities and of femi-

ninity-as-commodity link up very clearly here. For the female spectators present at the play's first court production during the carnival of
1508 the low status of the female characters, in conjunction with their
depiction essentially as 'chattel', would probably not have encouraged
any identification with them. In fact, the play incurred the disapproval
of Isabella d'Este, who considered it 'lascivious and immoral beyond
words' and actually barred her ladies from seeing it (Gilder 1960, p. 52).
Interestingly enough, this opinion was not universally held. According
to D'Ancona, the play was judged, presumably by male spectators, 'as
more elegant and more pleasing than any other, and highly com-
mended on all sides' (D'Ancona 1966, II, p. 136).

A comparison of the class switch in *La cassaria* and that in *I suppositi*
reveals an interesting correspondence, in that the well-born Polinesta,
daughter of a wealthy father, appears to be aligned with the low-status
Eulalia and Corisca in terms of the commodification system which
structures both plays. In *I suppositi*, master (Erostrato) and servant
(Dulippo) have exchanged roles so that Erostrato can have an affair
with Polinesta from the convenient vantage point of being a member of
her father's household. In order to subvert the efforts of Cleandro to
obtain Polinesta's hand in marriage, Dulippo persuades a visiting
Sienese gentleman to disguise himself as Erostrato's wealthy father, the
merchant Filogono, who can then compete in the negotiations. A list of
parallel relationships linking the two plays can now be drawn up. In the
context of financial negotiations for the female characters, the crux of
the plot in *I suppositi* involves il Sanese disguising himself as the wealthy
Filogono, just as that of *La cassaria* entails Trappola donning the clothes
of the wealthy Crisobolo; Erostrato, the son of Filogono and would-be
husband of Polinesta in *I suppositi*, corresponds to Erofilo, the son of
Crisobolo and hopeful lover of Eulalia in *La cassaria*; Damone,
Polinesta's wealthy father in *I suppositi*, is the equivalent of Lucrano,
procurer and owner of Eulalia in *La cassaria*; and, as this parallel listing
makes abundantly clear, Polinesta is structurally aligned with Eulalia,
in a pairing which differs from all the others in that these two female
characters are, on the surface at least, of greatly differing social status.
It would seem, then, that the plays work to evaluate them in fundamentally very similar ways. This is a result both of the fact that the women
are themselves commodified, and of the way that this process is
brought to a head in both cases, namely through male-to-male cross-
dressing that involves a class switch centring on all the dynamics of
commodity fetishism.

As regards cross-dressing which does include a gender exchange, a crucial difference emerges between male characters dressing as female characters and female characters dressing as male characters. Both a male character cross-dressing as a female character and a male actor cross-dressing to play a female role involve the conventional performance of fetishism whereby femininity does not exist in its own right and in complete form, but is only partially evoked. The partiality of such an evocation is due to the actual mechanism of power relations. According to this mechanism, the ongoing process of domination is inevitably countered by the equally ongoing process of insubordination, as a result of which the dominant fear the subordinate. Fetishizing the dual threat of femininity, a femininity which, it will be remembered, must, in the interests of patriarchal capitalism, continue to allow itself to be sexually commodified, permits partial reassurance. This entire dynamic does not apply, on the other hand, when women dress as men in the plays.

While both male and female cross-dressing were popular across a range of cultural forms, including theatre, where male cross-dressing was of course essential in the playing of female parts, as a practice in real life it was not generally countenanced. That female cross-dressing was regarded as a socially transgressive act is attested to by the rigorous, but unsuccessful, prohibition by the Church and local authorities (Larivaille 1983, p. 102). Clemenzia's initial reaction to Lelia's male attire in *Gli ingannati* indicates a negative attitude towards a form of female behaviour which was seen as a transgression of the social and sexual order. Clemenzia immediately links cross-dressing with prostitution. She asks Lelia: 'Surely you haven't turned into a loose woman?' and 'have you lost the name of virgin?'. Lelia replies that when she was in Rome she saw hundreds of women dressed as men, adding that Modena too has its fair share of women who circulate out of doors in male clothing, including the Sister at the Convent which she has just left. Clemenzia's reaction, however, is to make an immediate association between the presence of women out of doors and their sexual availability, an association upheld by the strict etiquette of the time forbidding 'respectable' women, particularly unchaperoned, to be seen in public places.

It is, of course, this very etiquette which prompted women to cross-dress in the first place. Moreover, the streets were particularly unsafe for women at certain times. Alvigia instructs Togna, in *La cortigiana*, to dress as a man 'because these stableboys get up to mad tricks at night'

(IV, 8), while Lelia comments on how unsafe she feels on the streets early in the morning, even, or especially, in her male disguise (*Gli ingannati*, I, 3). Since men had complete freedom of movement, they had no need to cross-dress in order to go about their business unhampered. When Arcolano dons his wife's clothes in order to look for her in *La cortigiana*, the reason he gives is that she has taken his clothes, and he does not want to 'follow her with nothing on' (v, 10). While Togna dresses as a man for greater safety on the streets, Arcolano's cross-dressing is a hasty act of expediency (although this is not how it is viewed by other characters, who consider him a source of ridicule). Cross-dressing by male characters as female characters in the plays is therefore perhaps even less of a reflection of reality than the portrayal of female characters who cross-dress as men.

For female characters, male attire gives them the freedom of the stage, and it is in this guise that laments on the restrictions faced by women are voiced. The common refrain is not, however, that these restrictions should be lifted, but, rather, that the female characters fervently wish they were indeed men. 'O God, why am I not a man, just as I appear to be in these clothes?' complains Togna (*La cortigiana*, v, 5). Santilla too regrets that she is a woman, wishing she could remain as she has appeared all her life, a man. Willing to sacrifice their female identity, these characters promote the dominant gender, a message which is all the more potent in that the characters who voice it on the stage are of course already male. For male characters who dress as women, the experience is portrayed as much less problematic. Unlike his twin sister Santilla, Lidio happily cross-dresses as a woman to facilitate his path to Fulvia's bed, and to trick Calandro, who is besotted with him in his female guise (Fessenio describes Lidio as awaiting the arrival of Calandro 'with glee' (III, 1)). For Fannio, his experience of dressing as a woman is a joke, while Siro's disguise as Clizia is the fount of endless mirth.

Cross-dressing in the comedies is thus the bearer of a complex set of sexual significations which go well beyond the traditional playing of female parts by young males, and the ensuing fetishizing of femininity at this first level of disguise. In particular, cross-dressing appears in the plays as a signifier for sexual desire itself. This can be identified, if not always in the purpose of female characters dressing as males, in the implications raised by their assumption of male attire. In the case of male characters dressing as females, the intent is invariably linked to a sexual project, either their own or that of others. Lelia's desire for Flamminio in *Gli ingannati* can be described as licit because her intentions are honourable (marriage is her goal). However, the method she adopts in order to achieve her aim, namely cross-dressing as Fabio and entering Flamminio's household as a servant, has illicit connotations, which she is quick to dispel. She does so not only in her first appearance on stage, but also at the end of the play, when she carefully clarifies, and almost, it might be said, overstates, her motives for having adopted male disguise, to Flamminio after his proposal of marriage to her: 'Flamminio, you are my lord, and you know well what I have done, and why I have done it; for I've never had any other desire than this' (v, 3). However, while her own desire may well have been licit, her cross-dressing lays her open to a variety of illicit desires.[34]

The first of these, pointed out by Clemenzia, is an association of female cross-dressing with prostitution that might lead her into dangerous situations, not least that of rape. Lelia, as Fabio, is also vulnerable to being asked to perform sexual favours by her master, Flamminio. Once again it is Clemenzia, her old nurse, who draws her attention to the possibility that he might experience what she calls 'that accursed temptation', in other words, homosexual desire. Having ascertained that Lelia serves Flamminio at table and in his room, and that she sleeps 'in one of his antechambers, alone' (i, 3), Clemenzia asks: 'If, one night, tempted by that accursed temptation, he called to you to sleep with him, how would that turn out?' (i, 3). It was not uncommon for a servant to share his master's bed. The anonymous, non-erudite play *La Veniexiana*, c. 1535, shows the sexual ramifications of a female householder sharing a bed with her female servant (i, 4). Bedsharing by strangers also appears to have been common practice. In Ariosto's *Satires* of 1525, a reference to the humanist penchant for pederasty states: 'the vulgar laugh when they hear of someone who possesses a vein of poetry, and they say "It is a great peril to turn your back if you sleep next to him"' (Saslow 1989, p. 98).

Bedsharing was a situation that clearly exposed a servant to the master's sexual whims, particularly if the servant was still a youth, at a time when it was apparently not uncommon for adult noblemen, for example, to have sexual relations with their pages (Saslow 1989, p. 92). In addition to the physical danger involved, any refusal to cooperate might lead to dismissal from service and consequent homelessness. Later in the play, Pasquella asks Fabio/Lelia, whether he sleeps with Flamminio, in order to establish whether Fabio would be free to visit her mistress, Isabella, at night. Lelia's ironic reply imbues the custom of bedsharing with the sexual innuendo of her own desire for Flamminio:

PASQUELLA: Do you perhaps sleep with him?
FABIO/LELIA: If only God wished me to be in his grace to that extent! I
    wouldn't be in the mess I'm in now. (II, 2)

As a young male servant, Fabio/Lelia is of course also vulnerable to the
sexual desire of Isabella (even though Isabella is not the mistress of the
household Fabio is serving, she is still the well-born daughter of the
master of another household).[35] In *I suppositi*, on the other hand,
Polinesta, the daughter of the house, has Erofilo willingly at her disposal in his disguise as a servant in her father's household.

Unlike Lelia in *Gli ingannati*, Santilla in *La Calandria* is an orphan
whose original reason for cross-dressing is not linked to sexual desire,
but is directly related to wartime conditions. The summary of the plot
preceding the play and outlining the antefact states that when the
Turks took Modena in 1500, in order to save Santilla, then still a child,
her nurse and servant dressed her as her brother, Lelio. Lelio had gone
missing in this war, just as, in *Gli ingannati*, Lelia's brother, Fabrizio, had
vanished during the Sack of Rome. Lelia cross-dresses solely in order to
enter the service of Flamminio. However, Santilla's continued disguise
has no similar amorous motive. She too is now in service, in the household of Perillo. However, her vulnerability as an orphaned female leads
her to continue to dress as a man. Santilla explains what would have
happened had she not appeared as a boy:

If in dress and in name, I had shown myself to be a woman, as in fact I am, the
Turk to whom we were enslaved would not have sold us, nor perhaps would
Perillo have redeemed us, had he known that I was female, and as a result we
would have had to remain in miserable slavery for ever. (II, 1)

The reason why Perillo, a Florentine merchant, might not have bought
a female child and her servants, is perhaps linked to the fact that female
servants were facing competition from male servants from the last
decade of the fifteenth century onwards (Klapisch-Zuber 1985, pp.
176–7). Another consideration could have been the eventual provision
of a dowry for a nubile female servant, which, it seems, was the responsibility of the employer (Klapisch-Zuber 1985, p. 173). As Lelio, Santilla
now risks exposure in that her faithful service to Perillo has won her the
hand of Verginia, his daughter. At this point, Santilla faces not simply
the possibility of the ill-founded desire of Verginia, but, more seriously,
she risks death as a result of her gender deception. As she explains to
Fannio: 'If I marry her, she will immediately realize that I'm female and

not male; and, deceived by me, the father, mother and daughter can have me put to death' (II, 8). Moreover, it seems that, even as Lelio, she does not have the option of refusing to marry the master's daughter, risking dismissal and all its consequences in so doing: 'I can't refuse to marry her; and even if I do refuse, they'll be annoyed and send me to the devil' (II, 8).

As if this were not enough, for Santilla there lurks the added danger of Calandro's illicit designs. He desires a certain female servant who is really Santilla's brother, Lidio, in female disguise. Since Lidio is Fulvia's lover, there is a coincidence of love-object, with Calandro appearing to desire his wife's desire. Castiglione's prologue explains that the play derives its name from Calandro and from the stupidity of this older man in not recognizing the true gender of the object of his desire. As in the case of Nicia in *Clizia*, Calandro is ridiculed for failing to distinguish correctly between the sexes. Deception through gender disguise is clearly central to *La Calandria*. It is not just the two identical twins who cross-dress, but also Fulvia, Calandro's wife, and Fannio, Santilla's servant. In Fulvia's case, cross-dressing plays an integral part in her adultery. Not only does Lelio visit her in female disguise, she also decides to cross-dress in order to find him. As her maid, Samia, intimates, Fulvia's disguise places her at risk: 'Unable to have her Lidio, she's going dressed as a man to look for him; without sparing a thought for all the ills that might befall her as a result, should she ever be found out' (III, 6).

Togna's use of cross-dressing in *La cortigiana* is particularly ironic, in that she dresses in her husband's clothes in order to carry out actions that would leave him cuckolded. As the traditional *malmaritata*, or ill-wedded woman, she feels compelled to use up the 'excess' sexual passion that her husband's inattentiveness leaves her with (a topos already present in Boccaccio's *Decameron*). The particular type of sexual danger she runs by being on the street in male disguise is made plain in the play. When Parabolano asks: 'what scandal can come of her being dressed as a man? (V, 12), Alvigia and Rosso mention the vice 'for which burning is the punishment', in other words, the illicit practice of sodomy. This serves as another indication that cross-dressing was considered to be directly linked to homosexual practices.

In the context of cross-dressing as signifier of sexual desire, a distinction must be made, on the one hand, between cross-dressing used as a means to fulfilling some form of illicit desire (Fulvia, Lidio, Lelia) and, on the other, to preventing its occurrence (Siro's disguise as Clizia,

Arcolano's disguise as his wife, and Fannio appearing as Santilla).
However, in attempting to prevent one form of transgression, such as
Nicomaco's adultery with Clizia, and presumably her rape, another
illicit dynamic is introduced, namely the homoerotic scenario that
ensues when Siro shares Nicomaco's bed. Similarly, Fannio's planned
substitution of Santilla in Fulvia's bed as Lelio safely returned to the
male sex, would have led to the sexual deception of Fulvia and, effectively, to her rape. Also in play are the dangerous forms of unwanted
desire to which the cross-dresser may be subjected in the street (Lelia,
Fulvia, Togna). The case of Santilla appears to be somewhat exceptional in relation to other cross-dressing female characters, in that her
disguise is never associated with any desire on her part. She is not
linked with any love interest in the play. Her betrothal to Fulvia's son,
Flaminio, at the end of the play, receives a mere passing comment from
her, while Lidio and Fessenio rejoice in the wealth and security which
the marriages of both the twins will bring.

The complex social and sexual signifying properties of cross-dressing must also be considered in the context of the Renaissance idealization of the body (deriving from humanism), and in the light of sumptuary laws concerning its decoration. Sumptuary laws are another sign of
the fetishizing of commodities, this time of clothes, which take on a
value beyond their material worth, to denote social value. In this sense
there is a link between sexual fetishism, which concerns the body, surface and clothes as indicators of gender, and commodity fetishism,
which relates to the female body in particular, and to certain clothes as
symbols of social status. Adornment of the body was aided in the sixteenth century, as in no other, by the unprecedented availability of
luxury materials in the form of rich textiles, embroideries, jewelry and
lace. The opening up in the late fifteenth century by Spain and
Portugal of new trade routes to the Americas and Asia, a blow to Venice
as a trading centre but a stimulus to the European market, prompted
the development of luxury industries and banking systems in Italy.
Towns like Venice, Florence and Genoa became wealthy centres of
consumption, exchange and distribution, with the production of silk in
Milan and lace in Venice helping to supply the new demand for luxury
clothing materials in court and urban circles (Boucher 1967, pp. 219,
221).

Clothing had been the target of regulation and sumptuary laws in
Italy since the middle ages (with Genoa introducing the first such law,
the *Breve della Campagna* of 1157, which forbade the use of certain furs)

(Hughes 1983, p. 72). As far as theatre was concerned, it seems that sumptuary laws, such as those relating to the wearing of farthingales, did not affect performances even in Papal territory. Plays were presented with increasing luxury, with the costumes of the actors taking over from those of the mummers and dancers in terms of interest expressed in eye-witness accounts in the early years of the sixteenth century (Newton 1975, p. 201). Andrews draws attention to the fact that costume design-ers, along with scene painters, choreographers and musicians, were pro-fessionals employed for the performance of the comedies, while the actors were all 'gentlemen and amateurs' (Andrews 1993, p. 33).

Sumptuary laws in Italy were initially aimed at excessive display on the part of the aristocracy, rather than at social climbers (Hughes 1983, p. 74). Economic considerations also played their part in these laws restricting expense on luxurious clothes and jewelry (in Venice, for instance, money spent on luxuries could not be taxed) (Gilbert 1973, p. 288). An indication of the high cost of luxury garments is the impor-tance given to Flavio's velvet cloak and hat by his servant, Corbolo, in *La Lena.* Flavio wants to sell these garments to finance his scheme to gain access to Licinia, but in so doing he risks severe punishment by his father, including the possibility of being disowned:

CORBOLO: How he'll make out, I don't know, if he doesn't manage to sell the clothes. But if they are sold (and I know that in the long run he won't be able to hide the fact from his father), the cries, the noise, the arguments, will be heard everywhere, and he runs the risk of being disowned. (III, 1)

During the Renaissance, money was spent particularly on clothes, as well as food, as frequent references to food, and the significance of the cloak and hat in La Lena would seem to indicate. In La cassaria, Erofilo talks about 'cloths, silks, wools, and gold and silver material, wine and grain'. Luxurious clothes appear to function as profit made visible in a developing capitalist system. In this context, it is significant that, under the influence of the Church, sumptuary laws by the fifteenth century increasingly concentrated their focus on women, and particularly on married women. This has been linked to the economic centrality of the dowry brought into a marriage by the bride, and fears of its dissipation, at her hands, on luxury items. While only minimal attention was paid to men's apparel, sumptuary laws laid down severe restrictions on the clothes of women (Hughes 1983, p. 85, fig. 1). These laws did not go unopposed, and in a famous oration Nicolosa Sanuti argued for their repeal. This oration is remarkable in the way that it expresses the process of fetishization to which femininity, unlike masculinity, was subjected. The oration ends as follows: 'Magistracies are not conceded to women; they do not strive for priesthoods, triumphs, the spoils of war, because these are considered the honours of men. Ornament and apparel, because they are our insignia of worth, we cannot suffer to be taken from us' (Hughes 1983, p. 87).36 In the words of Hughes, 'women deserved freedom of choice in clothes because it was to clothes that they had been reduced'.

The sumptuary laws would undoubtedly have been familiar to the female spectators of the comedies, even if, as high-ranking ladies, they were probably able to flout them. Importantly such an awareness of the social significance of clothes would have been highly relevant to the way in which they perceived female characters cross-dressing as men, as well as female clothing on male actors. Given that they them-selves were also part of the spectacle, the clothes which they wore to the performance would also have entered the equation. In conclusion, then, this aspect of commodity fetishism, together with the way in which the characters relate to each other only by means of roles denoted by materialistic tokens, ties in with the process of psychosexual fetishism inherent in the donning of female clothes by male actors. Intertwined with this is the central commodification of femininity. All these issues are brought into play in the interplay between actor and audience in ways that can be seen to differ radically for female and male spectators.

CHAPTER THREE

Artful women: morality and materialism in Goldoni

Female characters abound in Goldoni's comedies. This is in marked contrast to the erudite comedies of the sixteenth century examined in the previous two chapters. There are two important theatrical reasons for this proliferation of female characters. One is undoubtedly the progressively increasing opportunity for actresses by the eighteenth century. This situation had been set in motion by sixteenth-century *commedia dell'arte* actresses, who preceded other European women on to the public stage by almost three-quarters of a century.[1] The initial establishment of actresses in improvised theatre would in turn have fed over time into the writing of scripted plays, notably in terms of expanding the role of female characters. The other theatrical reason lies in the representation on stage of indoor scenes, a scenario uncommon to erudite Renaissance comedy, which continued the classical Greek and Roman tradition by depicting an exclusively outdoor setting.

The most obvious reason for the advent of the indoor scene might appear to be improvement in technology, which facilitated scene changes.[2] However, given that cultural production and socioeconomic factors go hand in hand, both these developments in stage practice, which allowed female characters significantly more stage space, can in fact be attributed in great part to the increasing complexity of market capitalism and, concomitantly, of social relations in a rising population and expanding urban centres.[3] There were undoubtedly positive implications for some women (such as those of the thriving, urban middle class) in this more advanced socioeconomic context. Nevertheless, the ideology of patriarchy still continued to subtend the materialist ethos of market capitalism and to inform gender relations accordingly.

As far as Goldoni's female characters are concerned, the indoor scene allowed those who were nubile and of middle-class or noble birth to appear on stage, since the stage in that form did not signify the forbidden zone of the street. At the same time, these female characters

Plate 3. Placida , the *prima donna*, discussing theatre with the director and another actor, in Goldoni's play about plays, *Il teatro comico*, 1750.

were still not allowed free access to street scenes, and continued to need a chaperon out of doors. This meant that the traditional patriarchal alignment of inside, private space with femininity, and outside, public space with masculinity, continued to be reinforced. Moreover, it is not always only middle- or upper-class female characters who have this inbuilt restriction, as one might perhaps expect. *La putta onorata* (1748) shows the 'modest' and 'chaste' lower-class Bettina justifying her presence alone on the roof terrace, where she is hanging out the washing, but where she is visible from the street (I, 5). She is subsequently scolded by Pasqualino for appearing in public view, when he catches sight of her from down below. Rooftops, balconies, doorways and even windows, are all classed as public space in Goldoni's plays, in that they are all visible from the street.

The street itself remains the crucial area of prohibition, not least because it provides access to other houses, which are forbidden territory if they contain men. When Lucietta enters the house where Orsola lives with her son, Zorzetto, she earns herself a blow across the face from Anzoletto in *Il campiello* (1756, v, 8). While in this play nubile girls from the lower class sometimes appear alone in public space, this does not always go unnoticed. On another occasion, Lucietta looks out for Anzoletto from her rooftop, and, in a different scene, Gasparina sits on her balcony in full view of the street. They do not justify appearing alone in the public eye, and even respond to the greeting of a male stranger, the Cavaliere below (I, 3, 5). However, when Anzoletto spots Lucietta, he, like Pasqualino in *La putta onorata*, is displeased, while Gasparina is constantly being ordered indoors by her uncle, Fabrizio. Although Fabrizio blames her conduct on the lower-class upbringing her mother provided, it would be erroneous to infer that the rules concerning public appearance were not observed by girls from this class. Gnese, for example, tells Lucietta that she never goes into the street without her mother, and even refuses to come outside to play a game with the other women unless her mother is present (III, 4). When Anzoletto later sees Lucietta in the street taking part in the game, his rebuke, 'Always in the street, playing games?' (III, 8) is one of several comments by male and female characters in the play revealing an awareness, on the part of the lower class, of social custom regarding women and public space.

Le baruffe chiozzotte (1762) is another play which shows nubile, lower-class girls out of doors, but they are always in the company of a married sister or sister-in-law. On the one occasion when Lucietta and Orsetta appear at their windows to talk to each other, Pasqua, Lucietta's sister-in-law, repeatedly summons her inside (III, 16). The situation regarding lower-class girls in this play, and in *Il campiello*, is not one of total restriction to private space, but neither can they be said to have completely free access to public space. What can be concluded is that public appearance by unaccompanied nubile girls in these two plays often provokes comment by other characters, but appears to be less of an issue than in *La putta onorata*. One reason might be that *Il campiello* and *Le baruffe chiozzotte*, unlike *La putta onorata*, are not so much about individual protagonists, as about groups and communities. This means that young girls, like other characters, are rarely on their own on stage anyway, so that the issue of 'indecorous' public appearance is less likely to arise.

From the point of view of the actresses, the stage itself was of course still classified as public space, and they were still prohibited in public theatres within Papal territories in the eighteenth century on the same grounds that unchaperoned nubile female characters were not allowed in outdoor scenes. From the patriarchal viewpoint of the Church, women/actresses continued to be equated with sexuality, and signified prostitution or sexual availability when in public space. As a result, women could not be permitted on stage bcause this would automatically expose the audience to 'immoral' influence. This meant that female parts continued to be played by beardless males in these regions. Goldoni as a youth himself played a female role in Gigli's *Sorellina di Don Pilone* (Kennard 1967, pp. 40, 69). He did not appear to relish one particular male performance of two of his own female characters from *La vedova scaltra* in Rome in 1758: 'They began: Donna Placida and Donna Luigia . . . were acted by two young Romans, an apprentice barber, and an apprentice carpenter! Good heavens! What awkward gestures, what extravagant declamations!' (Steele 1981, p. 105). Of the actresses whom he watched for the first time in Rimini, however, he said that they 'adorned the stage in a more stimulating way' than the actors playing female parts (Steele 1981, p. 105).[4]

Nonetheless, women were allowed to act in the Legations, and particularly in the seven theatres of Venice which had established this city as the theatrical centre of the Italian states during the preceding century.[5] Goldoni himself wrote parts with individual actresses in mind; for example, the part of Rosaura, the maid, in *La donna di garbo* was written for Anna Baccherini. In concentrating on the soubrette rather than the leading lady, he also greatly expanded the role of the lower-class female character (while the actual plot of a servant becoming mistress of the household through marriage was a traditional one) (Steele 1981, p. 82). In *La cameriera brillante* (1753), for instance, the maid Argentina is the main protagonist, while the lower-class Bettina likewise occupies a central position in *La putta onorata* and in *La buona moglie* (1749). His representation of female, and male, characters from all classes, often together in the same play, means that class interaction is a key component of gender relations in his comedies.

Goldoni's comedies are overtly moralizing, a factor which has distinct bearing on gender portrayal in his plays. In this context, some of the proliferating female characters in his comedies appear to be portrayed in a positive light. The play titles mentioned so far all use laudatory epithets to describe the main female character, as do titles such as *La donna di garbo* (1743), *La vedova scaltra* (1748), and *La donna prudente* (1751). On the other hand, play titles such as *Le femmine puntigliose* (1750) and *I pettegolezzi delle donne* (1750) contain pejorative terms. Given both the range of Goldoni's female characters, and his critical reputation as a playwright interested in and ostensibly knowledgeable about women, one major area that invites analysis is the extent to which any of these female characters can be considered to be subversive of the patriarchal status quo. Characters such as Bettina, and Pamela in *La Pamela* (1750), seem to fall into the category of 'good' women. However, for characters like Rosaura in *La donna di garbo* and Rosaura in *La vedova scaltra*, the situation is not quite so straightforward, despite the apparently positive epithets used to describe them. These characters are particularly interesting because they appear to occupy an ambiguous middle ground between 'good' and 'bad', in other words between the 'virtue' and 'vice' categories into which the plays polarize many of their characters. This raises a fundamental question of terminology, namely, what exactly is meant by 'good' and 'bad', 'virtue' and 'vice', in Goldoni's plays? Furthermore, do these evaluative terms remain constant in their application, or do they vary according to particular circumstances? What relationship do the plays set up between morality and patriarchy? In the case of Bettina and Pamela, for instance, 'goodness' means playing by patriarchal rules. But is it 'good' in the same way for Rosaura in *La vedova scaltra* to be artful (*scaltra*), or for her namesake in *La donna di garbo* to be courteous (*di garbo*)?

In order to clarify the portrayal of female characters in plays which are so overtly moralizing, it is first of all necessary to shift the definition of generic terms such as 'good' and 'bad', 'virtue' and 'vice', away from their essentialist and ahistorically ethical orientation, and clarify the hidden agenda of their ideological status in the socioeconomic context of eighteenth-century Venice. A first consideration is the fact that a moralizing tendency was a key feature of European cultural production during this century, with comedies of character and of manner predominating in the theatrical field. In this context, the use of binary oppositions, such as 'virtue' vs 'vice', in the moralizing process, not only continued the tradition of western reasoning and its inherent epistemological structures, but gave them special emphasis in an 'enlightening' Age of Reason. As far as eighteenth-century Venice was concerned, what was perceived by bourgeois opinion as a decline in moral standards meant that the moralistic tone of European culture was particularly suitable for Venetian cultural production. The powerful Council of Ten in Venice kept a vigilant eye on any activity that might endanger the morality of its citizens and encourage subversion. The findings of their *confidenti*, or spies, sometimes led to censorship of plays, and even of ballets (Andrieux 1972, pp. 45–52). The performance of Goldoni's own *La donna forte* was prohibited in 1758, and his departure from Venice in order to work in Rome can be attributed at least in part to such censorship (Steele 1981, p. 111).

Goldoni himself frequently writes in his address to the reader about his deliberate aim of representing 'virtue' and 'vice' in conflict in his plays. For example, concerning the composition of *La buona moglie*, he notes: 'whoever would like to examine the characters imitated by me in my comedy, would find by chance not only that I haven't pushed them beyond where nature takes them; but maybe that I've held them back. So that wherever *vice* or *virtue* is to be imitated, *virtuous* or *vicious* originals are at times to be found who exceed by far what is usually done as a rule' (Goldoni 1978, p. 10, italics added). Anselmo in *Il teatro comico* (1750) states that it is indeed the function of comedy to 'correct vice': 'Comedy was invented to correct vice and to ridicule bad customs' (II, 1). However, while Goldoni's moralizing is overt, the reinforcement of patriarchal values which underpin it takes place covertly. Patriarchal ideology is made to appear as a seamless, natural order which allows for neat, uncomplicated polarization into the binary opposition of 'good' vs 'bad'.

It is the purpose of this chapter to access the ideological subtext of these generic, moralistic polarities by redefining them in the eighteenth-century Venetian context of patriarchal values, materialist concerns and cultural specificities which inscribe the plays and, in particular, the construction of the female characters. Attention will focus on a comparison of two types of female character. The first is the so-called 'virtuous' female character, who will be designated as the angelic woman. She is perhaps best epitomized by Bettina in *La putta onorata* (1748) and *La buona moglie* (1749), and by Pamela in *La Pamela* (1750) and *Pamela maritata* (1759). The second type is the artful female character. She falls in the intermediate zone between 'virtue' and 'vice', and at first sight appears neither 'good' nor 'bad'. This type is represented by Rosaura in *La vedova scaltra*, Mirandolina in *La locandiera* and Rosaura in *La donna di garbo*. Both the angelic and the artful woman will be examined by taking a gender-specific look at how virtue and vice intersect with categories of class, wealth, age, work and family belonging.

ANGEL IN THE HOUSE

The most extreme version of the 'virtuous' female character in Goldoni's comedies displays all the features of the stereotype that has come to be known as the angel in the house.[6] She is deemed to be 'virtuous' not simply on abstract moral grounds of 'goodness', but because she is the embodiment of patriarchy's ideal woman. Her 'virtues' are none other than reflections of specific patriarchal values that work to circumscribe the role of women in society. These values mean, first, that she is identified predominantly in terms of her body. Her key 'virtues' of chastity and modesty, linked to her sexual and reproductive capacity, are defined in relation to men, and in a heterosexual context. These virtues are also informed by a system of social relations that continue to be shaped by market capitalism.[7] It is in the context of social relations modelled on the market that prospective husbands are also viewed in economic terms (for example, in *Il bugiardo*, 1750). However, just as male characters are not commodified *in their bodies*, so chastity is not a prerequisite for their entry into the marriage market.

Chastity signifies the highly-valued patriarchal commodity of virginity that must be preserved until the wedding night to guarantee the exclusive patrilineal rights of the husband. If the nubile woman does not keep this commodity intact, she no longer has exchange value in the marriage market.[8] After marriage, chastity no longer denotes virginity, but refers to the absence of extra-marital sex, and, under Catholicism, to a further prohibition, within marriage, of recreational in favour of exclusively procreational sexual activity. In terms of the market, once married she loses her exchange value and acquires use value. While chastity itself is never mentioned by name in the plays, it is constantly implied by, and subsumed euphemistically under, the virtue of modesty.

With chastity denoting *what* needs to be preserved, modesty may be defined as *how* to preserve it; or, more precisely, how to *appear* to preserve it. Chastity is a social definition and manipulation of a biological fact, and has relevance in a social, and so public, setting. The modest woman must appear chaste in the public eye, whether she is or not, and consequently her reputation is all-important. It has always been the Achilles heel of patriarchy that female sexuality, and specifically female reproductive power, cannot be policed with sufficient certainty for patrilineal purposes, and that the mere appearance of patriarchal control must often suffice. In an eighteenth-century context, female sexuality may subvert patriarchy from within by actually providing an appearance of modesty, while the reality may be quite the opposite. This accounts in great part for the way in which Goldoni's plays frequently align *finzione*, or pretence, with femininity in a pejorative way, as will be seen later.

In addition to possessing the sexually-defined virtues of chastity and modesty, patriarchy's ideal woman is confined to the private, domestic sphere of the home, where she is allowed to occupy a pseudo-powerful position and expected to exercise her third fundamental virtue, domesticity. She does this by acting as nurturing, moral guardian of her family, and in particular by civilizing the excesses of her husband, both economic and sexual. Her own thriftiness in the management of the household economy represents the important material side of domesticity, while she is also expected to be frugal in her own sexual desire. Patriarchy has always worked to provide an illusion of power for women within the home, while ensuring their exclusion from the public sphere and its opportunities for economic independence and consequent autonomy. Eighteenth-century Europe actually saw an unprecedented glorification of domesticity, with the woman as angel heralded as presiding over the private domain. The angelic comparison was characteristic of this era, gaining credence as the century wore on, and can be seen to inform Goldoni's construction of the 'virtuous' female character (Anderson and Zinsser 1988, II, pp. 121–2).

In addition to the European patriarchal inscription of 'virtue', and its significance in the context of a market model of social relations, there are some further elements to its portrayal in Goldoni's comedies. These elements are specific to the culture of eighteenth-century

Venice, and they determine the particular variant of 'virtue' vs 'vice' conflict in which the 'virtuous' female character takes part. This is especially the case in the Venetian *La putta onorata* and *La buona moglie*. While *La Pamela* and *Pamela maritata* are based on Samuel Richardson's novel *Pamela, or virtue rewarded* (1740–1), and are set in London, these plays also show signs of being informed by Venetian cultural values, most notably those concerning class. It is, furthermore, in the category of class that interesting differences are discernible between Bettina and Pamela as angels in the house in these two very different pairs of plays.

All three 'virtues' of chastity, modesty and domesticity are necessary for the angel in the house, who, strictly speaking, attains this position when she starts a new family unit by becoming a wife and mother. It is her role to promote the family and its values, armed with these ideal qualities, which she may at any time be called upon to prove. This is the position of Bettina in *La buona moglie*, while Pamela in *Pamela maritata* has become a wife, but not a mother. Before the angel may take over her new domestic realm, in other words, in order to deserve marriage in the first place, she must already be seen to possess chastity and modesty. It is in the defence of their chastity and in the pursuit of modesty that Bettina in *La putta onorata* and Pamela in *La Pamela* spend their time, as the plays elaborate idealized personifications of female virtue in both lower and upper classes. The virtue of domesticity becomes an added issue for Bettina in *La buona moglie*, while Pamela's task in *Pamela maritata* continues to concern the sexual virtues.

Chastity

Youth and virginity are prerequisites for the would-be angel in the house, and both Bettina in *La putta onorata* and Pamela in *La Pamela* are young virgins. Bettina is referred to as *putta* and *fanciulla*, both terms used for young girls. Pamela, who is just over twenty years of age, appears as *Pamela fanciulla* and *Pamela nubile* in two alternative titles for *La Pamela*, with *nubile* indicating the importance of her unmarried state.

In addition to youth, a particular status in terms of family and class is typical of the as-yet-unmarried angelic female character, who at this stage is usually alone and of a lower class, and therefore conveniently vulnerable. Bettina is an orphan from the poor lower class, with no parental protection and little work. She lives with her exploitative sister, Catte, a laundress, and her brother-in-law, Arlecchino, who attempt to alleviate their poverty by acting as pimps for wealthy admirers of Bettina's youth and beauty. The lower-class Bettina has to defend her chastity against the upper-class libertine, Ottavio, a married aristocrat who resorts to kidnapping her and who is still in hot pursuit during the course of *La buona moglie*. She is also at some risk from the middle-class Pantalone, the rich old merchant who has taken her under his paternal protection. He provides for her financially, and has promised to give her a dowry, but he abuses his position of power by attempting to pursue his own sexual interest in her (thereby recalling his earlier lascivious *commedia dell'arte* persona). Bettina's vulnerability in terms of gender is mirrored by her low status in class terms in relation to Ottavio and Pantalone. However, as a reward for successfully retaining her chastity, she moves up a class through marriage into the middle class, as her husband Pasqualino is discovered not to be the son of a gondolier, but of Pantalone himself.

Pamela is also without parental protection, and appears to come from an impoverished peasant background. Separated from her parents at the age of ten, she was taken into domestic service by Lord Bonfil's mother to live and work in her upper-class household as a maid. On her mistress' death, Pamela's chastity comes under increasing threat from Lord Bonfil, all the more so because live-in domestic service exposes her to particular risk from male members of the household. Rather than provide any form of autonomy, this type of work appears to place Pamela's chastity in even greater immediate danger than in Bettina's case. Bettina, of course, is also at risk from the pimping attempts of Catte and Arlecchino, who, despite her protestations, introduce Ottavio into the house and leave her alone with him. Bonfil's sister similarly exposes Pamela to the unwelcome attentions of her nephew, Ernold. In this situation, Pamela's only escape is to lock herself in her room, which is what she attempts to do when their arrival is announced (II, 10).

Certain class differences come to the fore in the configuration of these two angelic female characters. Unlike Bettina, Pamela has been brought up in an upper-class environment, and uses her literacy and access to the discourse of reason in order to promote her interests, refuting Bonfil's claims on her chastity by means of prolonged, reasoned speeches which leave him speechless.[9] In *Pamela maritata*, an ambiguously worded letter to Artur, Bonfil's friend, sets the seal on her husband's doubts regarding her chastity, but, given the opportunity by a state minister to vindicate herself, she is easily able to commentate the offending piece at length and to Bonfil's satisfaction. Pamela's upper-class upbringing of ten years here intervenes to shape the way in which she defends her chastity, while Bettina in *La putta onorata* is not equipped with similar powers of discourse, and at one crucial point she is forced to rely on the goodwill of others. When Ottavio has her kidnapped, and locked in his house, it is his wife, Beatrice, who comes to the rescue, thereby pre-empting Bettina's impending rape. However, in Pamela's case it is not simply education that has determined her behaviour. When it is revealed that she is not, after all, the daughter of a peasant, but of an aristocrat who fell out of favour with the king decades previously, the innate nature of class belonging is believed to have revealed itself, not only in her physiognomy, but in her chastity itself.

Even before he learns her true class, Bonfil says: 'Pamela was not born to weave, she was not born for lowly kitchen duties' (III, 6). He also comments on her fragility ('She is weak, she is delicate') and on her snow-white skin ('She has snow-white hands') (III, 6). These are all presented as indubitable signs of eighteenth-century upper-class femininity. While weakness and delicacy are put forward as positive feminine qualities, here given as biologically innate rather than socially determined, in reality they are indications of a culturally-constructed female vulnerability and dependency which allow for male strength and supremacy, necessary requirements for the maintenance of a patriarchal system in which political and economic power are male-dominated. Once informed that Pamela is of noble birth, Bonfil reprimands himself for not having been alerted to the fact previously by her resolute defence of her chastity: 'Ah, Pamela's virtue should have alerted me to the fact that she was not of lowly birth!' (III, 11). His equation of chastity with nobility serves to heighten the idealized status of this female virtue even further. It also continues the promotion of a rigid class ideology which holds that each class has its own specific values, and that these are irrevocably instilled at birth. With the discovery of Pamela's noble parentage, she becomes the embodiment of this class 'truth' as far as upper-class female characteristics are concerned.

Richardson's *Pamela*, however, receives no such upgrading in class terms. Venetian class ideology is responsible for this addition by Goldoni to the English novel on which he based his play. Goldoni's Pamela still needs to appear of a lower class than Lord Bonfil for most of *La Pamela* in order for her (lower) gender status to be matched by that of her class in relation to her more powerful male persecutor. The gender-specific battle for chastity is very often linked in Goldoni's comedies to class difference, and it is significant that neither Pamela nor Bettina is under threat from males of her own class (although Menego, Pasqualino's gondolier father, does make advances to Bettina on one occasion). Pamela even makes the point that the male servants of her household 'love me like brothers' (1, 17).

However, Pamela's class must be upgraded in the Venetian play if she is to be able to marry Bonfil, since a cross-class marriage between lower and upper classes would not have been feasible as a plot resolution according to Venetian custom. Marriage between the nobility and middle-class families of certain professions (such as medicine, spice merchanting and glass-manufacturing) was countenanced, and it was not uncommon for the offspring of impoverished upper-class families to marry into wealthy middle-class families eager for a title. However, a nobleman who married a woman from the lower classes would forfeit his title (Andrieux 1972, p. 68). In the case of *La Pamela*, then, an extra Venetian element is added to the construction of the idealized English angel in the house. Noble birth and upbringing in an upper-class household, with its particular features of literacy and powers of articulation, shape the way in which this angelic figure protects her chastity.

By contrast, the lower-class Venetian setting of which Bettina is a part in *La putta onorata* and *La buona moglie*, can be seen to determine her struggle to maintain her chastity in quite different ways. Her chastity has to be defended in the context of Venice as a pleasure centre and city of European renown for prostitution. This may help to account for the frequent references she makes to herself as a 'good girl' or an 'honourable girl'. Her chastity must also be considered in relation to the pressures of her impoverished condition (Andrieux 1972, pp. 153–60).[10] In market terms, she must resist entry into the 'illicit' market of 'use which is exchanged'.[11] She is further urged to take up prostitution by her parasitic sister and brother-in-law, who are keen to share in the wealth offered by Ottavio for Bettina's services, and who already share in what Pantalone gives her. In a similar vein, the lower-class Truffaldino in *L'uomo di mondo* only allows his sister, Smeraldina, to have male visitors who give him money, thereby capitalizing on the market value of a female sexuality that is in his charge.

While both Bonfil and Ernold also offer Pamela money in *La Pamela*, she at least has the option of returning to her parents, indicating that her economic need is not as great as that of the unemployed Bettina. For Pamela, the conflict is more simply that of female 'virtue' (chastity) against male 'vice' (lust). For Bettina, the task is much more complicated. This is because in addition to this male 'vice', she also has to contend with falling into what is presented as the specifically female 'vice' of prostitution. Although the function of prostitution has always been to satisfy male sexual drives, it is traditionally portrayed as a form of female permissiveness of which all women are capable. That access to the female body is always available, at a price, is an assumption expressed by Ottavio. When Bettina rejects Ottavio's offer to make her fortune in this way, she argues that foreigners in particular do not distinguish between 'good-time girls' in which, she says, Venice abounds, and women from 'honourable homes'. At the same time, her emphasis on her own 'unsullied' status reveals her alignment with the traditionally negative view of the prostitute:

What do you think I am? Some good-time girl? We're in Venice, you know. In Venice there's pleasure for whoever wants it, but you'll have to go down to the Piazza; you should go where there are blinds and cushions on the balconies, or in fact to those women in doorways; but you can't go looking for girls just like that in the honourable homes of Venice. You foreigners from other parts, when you talk about Venice in matters concerning women, you lump them all together; but, by the blood of Diana! things just aren't like that. (I, 13)

Despite Bettina's moralizing, the play continues to commodify the female body, both in the illicit context of prostitution, and in the licit sphere of marriage-as-market, much as the erudite comedies of the Renaissance had done. When Ottavio temporarily suspends his pursuit of Bettina, he comments: 'I really must be quite insane to go to so much trouble for one woman at a time when women are to be had *at bargain prices*' (III, 25, italics added). While Ottavio is not portrayed in a positive light, his comment is not out of place in relation to other signs of illicit female commodification, in this as in other of Goldoni's plays. When Momolo in *L'uomo di mondo* (1757) encounters Beatrice, the wife of Silvio who owes a gambling debt of thirty *zecchini*, he pays off the debt with an aside that places a precise value on the attractions she holds for him: 'Oh what a nice encounter that was! Even if the thirty *zecchini* were to be lost, this face is worth more than a hundred' (I, 10).

Bettina herself uses financial terms to express her view that a woman's chances on the marriage market are destroyed if her chastity is at all questionable, in which case 'she has lost credit' (I, 6). The market element in marriage is at its most obvious in discussions concerning the dowry that a bride brings to her new spouse. A dowry continued to be one form of increasing the family fortune, as can be seen in *La famiglia dell'antiquario* (1750), and its crucial role in closing a marriage contract cannot be underestimated. As Marionette says to the wealthy widow, Rosaura, in *La vedova scaltra*: 'But you won't lack suitors: you're young, you're beautiful, and, most important of all, you've a good dowry' (I, 4). In another example, when Florindo in *La donna di garbo* offers to guarantee Isabella's dowry of six thousand *scudi*, her prospective bridegroom, Lelio, comments: 'The deal's improving' (III, 7).

Wealthy sons are in a sense also commodified in the marriage market. Pantalone in *Il servitore di due padroni* (1745) says of Federigo: 'a rich, only son of this quality is hard to find' (II, 3). He is eager to marry him to his daughter, Clarice, despite the fact that she is happily betrothed to Silvio. Sons, however, are not commodified in their sexuality. Far from chastity being indispensable to the would-be husband, the pursuit by bachelors of pre-marital sex was an acknowledged pastime (for example, Momolo in *L'uomo di mondo*, and Florindo in *La donna di garbo*). The crucial importance of chastity as a female commodity in the marriage market is made clear by the eagerness of Pantalone, Bettina's protector, to pay for her to remain chaste so that he may one day marry her himself. 'I'll happily spend', he says, 'so that Bettina remains a good girl, and in the hope that one day she'll say yes to me' (II, 18). Bettina is quite prepared to accept his money in order to help her remain chaste and therefore marriageable.

Her battle for chastity, which places her on the side of 'virtue', or rather, licit female commodification, is also to be seen in the light of what was perceived as a decline in moral standards in eighteenth-century Venice. As far as the Council of Ten, meeting in 1776, was concerned, female sexual activity was responsible for the decline of Venice:

The way the times are going, together with the great and universal alteration in manners whose full effect is now with us, demonstrate, to our profound and justifiable grief, the inevitable result of the free and licentious life our women lead. This was, and ever will be, the chief cause of the decline and ruin of the Republic. (Andrieux 1972, p. 136)

Bettina also complains about contemporary morals. She sees herself as someone supporting the values of previous generations, rather than those of her own. In the time of her mother and grandmother, chastity was more highly esteemed than material wealth, and she bemoans the fact that the opposite is true in her day, with material interests predominating over traditional female virtue. She now sees two requirements for a woman to be able to marry, namely 'either plenty of money, or little reputation' (1, 10). The 'vice' against which she has to fight is therefore not simply in the form of one upper-class libertine, Ottavio, but, rather, an entire value-system ruled by materialism, which stigmatizes her poverty and undervalues her chastity. In a similar way, she herself speaks not as an individual female character, but on behalf of an idealized order, of which female chastity is the cornerstone. The method which this 'good girl' suggests for preserving this order is to follow the dictates of the second female virtue, namely that of modesty.

Modesty

Modesty is the public face of a female 'virtue' which must be kept private. A woman's chastity, whether in the form of pre-marital virginity or marital fidelity, was to be kept inviolate in Goldoni's plays. In particular, it was to be *seen* not to be violated; with chastity as social circumscription of female sexuality, a woman's reputation, namely public evidence of her chastity, was crucial. The first rule of modesty concerns women's visibility, which was to be very much restricted. With women identified purely in terms of the body, to the exclusion of features not related to their sexuality, their mere appearance denoted not just sexuality itself, but sexual availability. In stage terms, this translates into invisibility as far as street scenes are concerned. There are also implications for indoor scenes, as well as for the dress code of the female character.

Street appearances by unaccompanied nubile female characters were associated with loss of chastity, or reputation. As a result, any such appearance in public space that might occur due to the demands of the plot, was problematic and had to be justified. Cross-dressing by the female character as a male was one way out of the dilemma, recalling the Renaissance comedies, in which female parts were played by boys, but which still needed to conform to the rules of feminine decorum. In Goldoni's *Il servitore di due padroni*, Beatrice disguises herself as Florindo in order to have freedom of movement as she searches for him, even winning a swordfight in the process, and in *La donna di garbo*, the noble Isabella presents herself as Flaminio when she accompanies Florindo to his paternal home in the expectation of becoming his wife.

While *La Pamela* and *Pamela maritata* are both set entirely indoors, *La putta onorata* and *La buona moglie* have both indoor and outdoor scenes. As indicated previously, Bettina's opening speech in the first play justi-

fies her appearance on a roof top that is in the public eye. The only
other occasions on which she appears out of doors in her nubile state
are when she is kidnapped by Ottavio's servants, and when she is taken
to the theatre by his wife, Beatrice, at which point both women are
masked. Nearly thirty years after the first production of the play, the
Council of Ten would debate a proposal to ban women going to the
theatres masked, and in the same year, 1776, they forbade women to
enter coffee-houses. While such strictures had little effect (for instance,
a former law forbidding women to wear anything but black was
ignored and cancelled in 1732), they testify to the moral climate in
which Goldoni worked.

Other plays by Goldoni also observe the prohibition of street
appearances by nubile female characters embodying the patriarchal
virtues. In *I due gemelli veneziani* (1746), Rosaura only ever appears in
indoor scenes or at the window. She refuses Zanetto's request to come
outside by saying: 'I'd be doing a fine thing, coming into the street!' (III,
11), and on another occasion asks her father's permission to do so:
'Pardon me, father sir, if I come into the street' (III, 25). Flaminia's presence outside her father's country villa in *La cameriera brillante* (1753) is
similarly made an issue. Pantalone discovers her alone in the courtyard
with Ottavio, and orders her indoors. In this case, since the courtyard is
described as a 'cortile in casa', it is possible that Flaminia's presence
there is unseemly not only because she is in a public place, but because
she is speaking to Ottavio.

Even when taking part in indoor scenes, nubile female characters
face certain restrictions. As Bettina points out, women lose 'credit' if
they have 'drawn lovers into the house' (I, 6). Her own reputation is at
great risk when Ottavio is allowed into the house and she is left alone
with him in *La putta onorata*. The situation becomes even more dangerous when he sends out for food and drink; for her to speak to him without a chaperon is bad enough, but to be known to have shared food
would have been tantamount to having sexual intercourse. The rule
that women could not receive male company indoors unaccompanied
can be seen to apply also to married female characters. It is Pamela's
private conversation with Artur in her room in *Pamela maritata* that
allows Ernold to spread rumours about her infidelity to Bonfil. While
the real reason for receiving Artur alone was her determination to
maintain secrecy regarding her father's political situation, the primary
implication of this broken rule of modesty was of unchaste behaviour. It
is this 'indecorous' and ambiguous act on Pamela's part that sets the

plot in motion, as it arouses Bonfil's jealousy. In *I due gemelli veneziani*, prostitution is intimated when Tonino's easy access to Rosaura's chamber elicits his suspicion that he has found himself in a *bordello*, with Rosaura as prostitute and her father acting as a pimp.

Modest behaviour involves not only the space where the female character appears, and the other characters with whom she is allowed to speak, but also how she dresses. She must not aspire to excessive ornament, at least in part because this would draw attention once again to her body. Sumptuary laws existed, although somewhat ineffectually, in Venice during the eighteenth century, with the purpose of curbing lavish spending and maintaining class difference. Such laws proved difficult to uphold in a city that thrived on the income provided by pleasure-seeking visitors, who often lodged in the homes of wealthy citizens which could not appear too austere (Andrieux 1972, p. 51). The laws applied to both men and women (with upper-class men having to wear the *veste patrizia* instead of the more comfortable middle-class *tabarro*). However, it is notable that these rules only had sexual connotations as far as women, and homosexual men dressing as women, were concerned. While there is not much danger of the impoverished Bettina transgressing any rules against luxury, she is given the opportunity to do so by Ottavio's offers of money and jewelry. Her refusal to be tempted indicates another important facet to the virtue of modesty, namely that of having no material, or class, ambitions, and the angelic Bettina is once again exemplary here.

Despite her poverty, and in a context dominated by material concerns, Bettina rejects both the illicit earnings offered by Ottavio, and any financial support from Pantalone beyond what she considers licit payment for her subsistence and a dowry that will enable her to marry. When Pantalone offers her his Venetian house, she says: 'I don't want such grandeur. What you've promised me is enough' (I, 10). In the first of the *Pamela* plays, the fact that Bonfil is Pamela's employer creates a different context for his offer of money and jewelry, both of which she accepts, albeit reluctantly. Further justification might exist in the case of the ring he gives her, which belonged to his mother, Pamela's deceased mistress, while any money could be counted as payment for licit domestic service. However, it is a different matter when Ernold wants to give her six guineas, at which point her refusal to accept, with the retort 'Give them to the sort of person you're used to dealing with' (II, 12) indicates an illicit exchange in which she will not take part. Her modest lack of economic aspiration also shows itself in her preference to retreat to a simple rustic home rather than live in Bonfil's upper-class house as his mistress.

Material concerns dominate Goldoni's plays, ranging from detailed prices of food items to Brighella's discussion of banking in *La buona moglie* (II, 12). Money, jewelry and other gifts are used as bargaining counters for women's sexual favours or hand in marriage. While the same is true of Renaissance comedies from other northern Italian cities, it is perhaps worth bearing in mind that Venetian prosperity had originated in trade, and that even during this later period, the biggest group among the Venetian middle class was still made up of manufacturers and merchants (Andrieux 1972, p. 83). Goldoni himself could be considered as being involved in commodity production, in that it was from the performance and publication of his plays that he worked to earn a living. It has been argued that the Venetian theatrical market developed along capitalist lines from the 1660s, as the public theatre became the site of profit-making cultural consumption.[12] This would have had a direct influence on the ideological bias of the plays, which needed to tap into accepted, traditional value systems in order to please the ticket-buying audience who in effect controlled the theatrical market.

Material concerns can be seen to intersect with patriarchy's (self) interest in female sexuality in the realms of licit and illicit commodification of the female body. These forms of commodification can only work successfully in the absence of female autonomy, and, specifically, in the absence of desire. In order to allay the threat of this potentially transgressive force, the patriarchal virtues of modesty and chastity forbid both materialist and sexual desire. Pantalone expresses the fear of insatiable female consumerism in a comment that compares women to leeches draining men's material capacities. When Catte says: 'Love springs from utility', he responds: 'In this world everyone operates out of self-interest, and women especially are worse than leeches. They're never satisfied' (II, 18). Tonino's speech on marriage in *I due gemelli veneziani* pinpoints the dangers of the wife who is 'vice-ridden and insatiable' (II, 12). Indeed, one of the grounds for a husband to petition for separation at that time was that of 'frivolous habits' and 'extravagance' (Andrieux 1972, p. 147).

Several plays depict wives whose expensive taste in clothes severely depletes the family finances. In *La donna di garbo*, for example, the Dottore complains to Rosaura about the 'accursed ambition' of his daughter-in-law, Beatrice, which threatens to ruin his household. Rosaura obligingly agrees: 'There's nothing worse than the vanity of fashions', and suggests that: 'the inventors of fashion should be banished as fomentors of human ambition' (I, 4). She offers to help resuscitate Beatrice's modesty: 'I'm made for teaching women modesty.' In *Le femmine puntigliose*, it is the middle-class Rosaura's extravagant expenditure as she tries to buy entry into upper-class *conversazioni*, which, according to her merchant husband, Florindo, threatens to dissipate the dowry she has brought him, while Pantalone's *morale* against women's 'chit chat' causing the ruin of families, turns into a misogynist diatribe (II, 14). It is curious that *La famiglia dell'antiquario* (alternatively entitled *La suocera e la nuora*, translating as *The mother-in-law and daughter-in-law*), while portraying the ruinous squandering of the family fortune by its head, Anselmo, on worthless 'antiquities', focusses on the misdemeanours of the female members of the family to the extent of foregrounding them as the main cause of the family's problems. In his address to the reader, Goldoni even prioritizes the disagreement between the two women, who constitute the 'main action', over the costly fanaticism of Anselmo, which is ultimately problematized only because it distracts him from his real duty to the family, namely 'to correct wife and daughter-in-law in time'.

In addition to consumerist desires, class ambitions are also prohibited in the modest angel in the house. Bettina's modesty in the economic sphere is matched by her view of Pasqualino, at that point still thought to be the son of a gondolier, as the correct match for her: 'That man is on my level. I don't want to put on any airs and graces' (I, 11). His initial lower-class identity is due to the transgressive class aspirations of Pasqua, the mother of Lelio, whom Pantalone has brought up believing him to be his son. She exchanged the boys at birth, supposing this to be in Lelio's interest. When Pantalone finally discovers the deception, he accuses her not only of being mad, but of causing disorder (III, 23). Her disruption of the 'natural' social order is punished when she has to witness Lelio's life of vice, as the 'innate' qualities of his lower-class birth come to the fore with a vengeance. His corruption of the middle-class Pasqualino in *La buona moglie* provides one of the few pejorative portrayals of the lower class in Goldoni, who tended to aim his satire, albeit rather carefully, at the upper class.

Bettina, unlike Pasqua, supports the dominant order, living up to patriarchal expectations by being 'modest and without ambition' (I, 10). Her frugality in this respect indicates that she also possesses 'the good sense to know how to rule a household' (I, 10), in other words, the third female 'virtue' of domesticity.

Domesticity

Tonino's lengthy discourse on the benefits of marriage in *I due gemelli veneziani* includes a blueprint for the ideal wife, whose duties he sums up as follows: 'She tends to the everyday economy of the household, regulates the family, and gives orders to the servants' (II, 10). This concept was not new to the eighteenth century, with works such as Alberti's fifteenth-century *Libri della famiglia* already providing the basic rules. However, as has been noted, Goldoni's century particularly glorified this female virtue, which his plays situate on the 'good' side of the virtue vs vice dichotomy informing gender interplay. One important aspect of the domestic role was the management of household finances. Domestic economy was heralded as the province of the angel in the house, as if to accord her some sort of real power, but, as the word *piccola* in Tonino's definition implies, this really is small change in comparison with the finances handled in the public world of men. The angel's economic activities, together with those of 'regulating' and 'commanding', are strictly confined to the house.

La buona moglie shows Bettina now married to Pasqualino, but severely hampered in her attempts to fulfil her domestic role of wife and mother by his vices of gambling, prodigality and frequenting prostitutes. Instead of investing the 1,000 ducats which his merchant father, Pantalone, has given him for business purposes, Pasqualino spends it on gambling and footing the bill for a group of parasitic hangers-on he believes to be his friends, but who are only after a free lunch. Amongst these are two prostitutes, one of whom Pasqualino frequents. Like prostitution, gambling and prodigality were activities with which eighteenth-century Venice was particularly associated, and on which its economy in fact depended. Cards had been invented in Venice, while the city's carnival atmosphere lent it renown as a place of permissiveness and excess. Gambling could be regarded in some ways as an extension of the capitalist ethos dominating mercantile Venice, with its emphasis on profit above all else. In 1628 the State itself opened the Ridotto as a gambling house to provide another source of revenue, only to close it down in error in 1774. Furthermore, a theatre's economic survival was often dependent in great part on the profits of its own gambling room (Andrieux 1972, pp. 130–1, 184). It has also been argued that gambling was a positive market force in that it stimulated the circulation of money and goods.[13]

However, as far as Bettina is concerned, Pasqualino's gambling and prodigal spending mean that she is left with no domestic economy to manage. She and their child even go hungry, while his dissipation of their business capital goes against all mercantile principles. She now bemoans what she refers to as his vices, which he has acquired during their marriage: 'Pasqualino, who was so good, who didn't have a vice in the world, who treated me like a queen for the first year, now has all the vices' (1, 17).[14] The decline of morality in contemporary Venetian youth, which she had observed in *La putta onorata* in terms of 'gambling, wining and dining, and women' (1, 16), is now personified by her husband. What is more, he also bears out her earlier fears about domestic violence: 'and the wife, instead of bread, is dealt accursed blows' (1, 16). Gambling, excessive spending on drink and food, and frequenting prostitutes, are all in direct conflict with those virtues which Bettina herself is expected to embody, and which sustain family life: gambling and prodigality are counter to thrift, while frequenting prostitutes contravenes the rule of chastity.

The angel in the house was considered as the guardian of family morality, and in particular as the arbiter of excess (a role which the ideal wife and mother was already meant to fulfil in the fourteenth century).[15] The wayward Florindo in *La cameriera brillante* declares: 'I need a wife who helps and *rules me*' (1, 9, italics added). As well as depriving Bettina of housekeeping money, Pasqualino uses domestic violence to oppose her verbal attempts to 'regulate' his unruly behaviour. As far as Pamela is concerned, once married to Bonfil she is not seen taking charge of the household economy. Her domestic task is to civilize Bonfil's unfounded jealousy, in other words, to subdue and control man's excesses.

While all four plays have happy endings, with female 'virtue' eventually subduing male 'vice', it does seem that both angelic female characters undergo inordinate suffering beforehand. Moreover, despite the fact that in *La putta onorata* and *La Pamela*, the betrothed Bettina and Pamela appear to be rewarded for remaining chaste and modest, the successive marital plays indicate that their struggle is by no means over, as their attempts to fulfil their domestic functions are met with hostile reaction on the part of their respective spouses. With Pasqualino now proving to be a major obstacle to Bettina's domestic virtue in *La buona moglie*, and Bonfil continuing to afflict Pamela in her virtues of chastity and modesty by doubting her fidelity in *Pamela maritata*, the reward of marriage appears to have turned into somewhat of a punishment.

While in *La putta onorata*, the chaste and modest Bettina was already kidnapped by Ottavio, and the nubile Pamela locked in her room by Bonfil, after marriage Bettina undergoes domestic violence and desertion at the hands of Pasqualino, while Bonfil effectively abandons Pamela. It is notable that Tonino's speech in *I due gemelli veneziani* actually advocates wife-beating: 'There's one particular cure called the stick, which has the ability to make even mad women see sense' (II, 10), advice that is all the more potent and sinister in view of the fact that Tonino is otherwise portrayed as the likeable hero of the play. It is not surprising, then, that one of the typical accusations brought by a wife suing for separation before the Council of Ten was that of brutality (together with the squandering of her dowry) (Andrieux 1972, p. 147).

The angel-in-the-house formula would appear to be a recipe for female self-victimization, as the 'good wife' is expected to endure all forms of abuse from her husband as yet further proof of her ideal femininity. Thus Pamela not only forgives Bonfil, but reinforces the belief that suffering is the norm: 'a great good is not usually acquired without misfortunes, without worries' (III, 17).[16] Tolerance and submission will be rewarded, she argues, in a speech that attributes her trials and tribulations to fate, rather than to Bonfil and the patriarchal values he embodies. She concludes the play with these words, ending on a note of submission: 'Fate sometimes puts hearts to the test to try their constancy, but seconds toleration, and doesn't fail to reward virtue, innocence and submission' (III, 17). Once again, this female stereotype is not new to Goldoni's plays, but already existed, for example, in the absurdly long-suffering figure of Griselda with whom Boccaccio concludes Day 10 of the *Decameron*. However, the stereotype of the woman who is virtuous because she is a victim is, in Goldoni's plays, slotted into the specific virtue vs vice conflict which characterizes his particular Venetian brand of eighteenth-century gender portrayal.

Although the follow-up marital plays both end well, with Pasqualino seemingly a reformed character and Bonfil apparently cured of his jealousy, one would be justified in suspecting that the happily 'rewarded' state of the wives might only be temporary, as it was at the end of the plays depicting their struggle as nubile women. Female virtue, it seems, must continue to be tried and tested in patriarchal culture. In the fantasy world of the plays, the reiteration of this process appears ceaseless, a phenomenon which would seem to testify to the real impossibility faced by patriarchy of successfully maintaining control over a female sexuality which cannot, in effect, be contained.

The uncontrollable excess of femininity in relation to its patriarchal circumscription can be seen to surface at the end of *La putta onorata*. Bettina, patriarchy's ideal woman, concludes the play by producing a subversive comment which effectively deconstructs the idealization of femininity she has previously personified. While this entailed her criticism of Catte's *finzione*, or pretence, she now concludes her song to other girls who wish to be 'honoured', with the advice 'If you want to be honoured, you should *appear* good' (III, 30, italics added). This element of *finzione*, which threatens to destabilize the patriarchal order by substituting mere appearance for certainty, is a key feature of Goldoni's artful women.

ARTFUL WOMEN

Artfulness in Goldoni's female characters reveals itself in what may be defined as a spirit of enterprise. Characters like Rosaura in *La donna di garbo*, Mirandolina in *La locandiera*, Rosaura in *La vedova scaltra*, Argentina in *La cameriera brillante*, and Beatrice, 'a young woman of spirit, of courage' in *Il servitore di due padroni*, all behave in an unusual way by taking the initiative, thereby stepping outside their patriarchally-confined roles. The precise nature of their artfulness varies from one character to another, according to the type of enterprise they each undertake. The range extends from the intellectual Rosaura in *La donna di garbo*, who makes use of her extraordinary legal expertise, to the physically courageous Beatrice, who, cross-dressed as Federigo and reminiscent of the female warrior in the epics of Ariosto and Tasso, defeats Silvio in a swordfight in *Il servitore di due padroni*.

However, Goldoni's artful women all have one feature in common in the way in which they execute their artfulness, namely their use of *finzione*. *Finzione* carries ambiguous value in Goldoni's plays, and whether its appearance in the female character is extolled, tolerated or execrated depends entirely on her reasons for using it. Some male characters also use pretence to further their own ends, and are negatively portrayed in the process. For example, Pancrazio in *I due gemelli veneziani* lies and flatters his way into the Balanzoni household in the hope of winning Rosaura, and finally tricks his rival, Zanetto, into drinking poison. In *La bottega del caffè*, Don Marzio tells lies and ruins lives, until he is found out. In the same play, Flaminio takes on a false name, class and marital status, to prevent being discovered by his wife and so that he can win over Lisaura, a dancer.

Other plays produce a comic effect by showing male characters pretending to be richer than they really are (the Marchese di Forlipopoli in *La locandiera*, Ottavio in *La cameriera brillante*) so that they may marry the woman of their choice. Male *finzione* is even celebrated in *Il bugiardo*, with Lelio's destructive lies being passed off as 'spirited inventiveness' (III, 14). Another example of positive representation of male pretence occurs in the *Pamela* plays, which depict Pamela's aristocratic father creating a political deception by taking on peasant identity while awaiting a royal pardon. When female characters use *finzione*, however, the implications are quite different. Not surprisingly, this difference is located in their sexuality, and, more specifically, in the patriarchal virtue of chastity which they are expected to exhibit at all stages of womanhood. The problem for patriarchal ideology, as indicated above, is that the appearance of chastity may be just that, in other words, a subversive pretence that harbours actual female sexual autonomy.

Artful female characters in Goldoni are depicted at various stages of womanhood. However, many of those who are central protagonists are nubile or widowed. Their unmarried state clearly facilitates a popular type of plot centring on what might loosely be termed 'love interest'. More notably, it also allows for the potential of their recuperation through matrimony as a plot closure. These artful women all protest an unblemished chastity which is not to be bought by illicit means, thereby retaining the position of respectable central protagonists who cannot be easily dismissed as personifications of vice, and who therefore provide a legitimate focus for audience attention. At the same time, *finzione*, with all its potentially pejorative connotations, is still a major feature of their behaviour, thereby generating a dynamic of ambiguity and tension.

Finzione

Intertwined with *finzione* as a key aspect of Goldoni's artful women, is the basic definition of theatre itself as pretence. Real actresses and actors pretend to be who they are not, before an audience which pretends to be unaware of the fact. The association of theatre with carnival adds a further resonance. Theatres in Venice were only open during carnival, which by Goldoni's time had been brought forward to October and lasted until Ash Wednesday. Carnival involved masking, disguise, playing with identities and norms, namely pretending to be who one was not. The audience would wear masks both in the theatre and on the streets. *Finzione* thus ruled both inside the theatre, on stage and in the auditorium, and outside.

A further level of *finzione* appears on stage in the theatre-within-the-theatre device. This can take the form, quite simply, of a play staged by the characters as actors, such as Argentina's play in *La cameriera brillante*. She writes parts for all the members of her household and their guests, and performs in it herself; in one scene she takes a cross-class role as a noblewoman, and in another she cross-dresses as Pantalone, her master. Alternatively, characters take on different identities in everyday dealings that are not formalized as theatre-within-the-theatre scenarios. Under the cover of carnival, Rosaura in *La vedova scaltra* changes her identity and her nationality, pretending to be English, French or Italian, to further her schemes, while Arlecchino pretends to be an Armenian in *La famiglia dell'antiquario*. In *La locandiera*, the two actresses Ortensia and Dejanira take on a higher class identity by pretending to be ladies, thereby adding a further dimension to their act on stage: real actresses play the parts of fictional actresses, who in turn play leisured noblewomen.

Masking, disguise and cross-dressing are variants of physical *finzione* used by female characters to facilitate their intrigues and to allow them freedom of movement on the streets. Beatrice in *Il servitore di due padroni* and Isabella in *La donna di garbo* continue the Renaissance stage tradition in cross-dressing as men, an activity that may have been a civil offence in some Italian states, if Tognin della Doira, writing to Beatrice from Turin, is to be believed. He writes: 'The Court has discovered that you have fled dressed as a man, and will stop at nothing in tracing you in order to have you arrested' (I, 13). In *La putta onorata*, Beatrice masks both herself and Bettina for their visit to the theatre. Bettina wears Beatrice's mask in a double bluff that leads Ottavio to kidnap his own wife by mistake (a ruse which perhaps indicates that masks were not always much of a disguise). In *La bottega del caffè*, Vittoria masks herself in order to observe her husband, Eugenio, who is gambling away her dowry, and Placida disguises herself as a pilgrim in her search for her gambling, womanizing husband, Flaminio, who has deserted her and left her penniless.

Placida and Vittoria use disguise as a means to saving their marriages. However, much of the time *finzione* appears to represent the complete antithesis of bourgeois norms. Truth, sincerity, order and respectability are all necessary for capitalism to function, a factor of particular relevance in a country which reputedly saw the first flowering of both the bourgeois and the capitalist spirit.[17] Alternatively, it has been argued that *finzione* is the repressed Other of bourgeois morality, in the same way that gambling can be regarded as the excessive extension of the capitalist profit ethos. Alongside bourgeois morality and market capitalism, patriarchy too appears in opposition to the workings of *finzione*, which functions in particular as a sign for femininity, or patriarchy's repressed and subversive Other. This is emphasized by the repeated association, throughout Goldoni's plays, of *finzione* with femininity, an association that is presented as threatening to the patriarchal status quo.

The crucial significance of *finzione* lies in its relation to female chastity, or rather, the threat of its mere semblance. For this reason *finzione* is particularly problematized when it is used by a female character. When Bonfil discovers Pamela's letter to Artur in *Pamela maritata*, he says: 'Women have the ability to know how to pretend perfectly' (II, 3). He spells out the link between *finzione* and female chastity in the following speech: 'But those tremblings, those tears, those sweet words? . . . Eh, such ruses are not unusual in a woman. She is most capable who knows best how to pretend; but I'll know how to unmask the lie, punish deception and avenge unfaithfulness' (I, 15).

Perhaps to even greater dramatic effect, female characters themselves claim *finzione* as the special talent of women. In *La putta onorata*, Beatrice declares: 'This is our art. Pretending to our husbands that we love what we actually hate, and that we don't want all that we in fact desire' (I, 2). Marionette similarly believes that: 'women know the art of pretending' (II, 23) in *La vedova scaltra*. While these women use *finzione* against men, for Rosaura, in *La donna di garbo*, it is the means whereby she wins over both male and female members of the household she works for. Her analysis of *finzione* as a female trait appears to clarify its patriarchal origins: 'Man makes use of the authority he has usurped over us, and we of pretence, which is the most beautiful endowment of our sex' (I, 2). On the one hand, this can be read as feminist in its recognition of patriarchal dominance as usurpation. Moreover, Rosaura also 'pretends' very well. In her dialogue with other characters, her true intent is not always transparent even to the audience, which must rely on her asides for the 'truth'. In effect, she seems to make good use of this endowment. However, it is also true to say that her acceptance of *finzione* as woman's gift conforms to a reactive make-do-and-mend scenario which reinforces this patriarchal stereotype of femininity.

The perception of femininity as pretence can at the same time be read as an indication of femininity as a false identity which is assumed under patriarchy. When deconstructed in terms of femininity as deliberate masquerade, the subversive potential of femininity as *finzione* becomes clear.[18] Whether or not Goldoni's artful women appropriate their patriarchal asset of *finzione* for their own, rather than for patriarchal, ends, can only be assessed in the context of the type of undertaking in which these enterprising characters employ pretence.

Enterprise

The spirit of enterprise, which is a defining feature of Goldoni's artful women, shows itself in the form of plot intrigues which they devise and carry out. This is undoubtedly a positive development from the erudite comedies of the Renaissance, when the trick was predominantly the province of the male servant who schemed to gain access to women for his master. As shown in the opening chapter, the purpose of the trick was for both intellectual and material gain, with access to female bodies falling into the latter category of goods, or chattel. One use to which *finzione* is put in Goldoni's comedies on the most basic level is also that of enterprise in the material sense. As the impoverished, lower-class Smeraldina says in an aside when dealing with Momolo, her wealthy admirer in *L'uomo di mondo*, 'I must pretend in my own interest' (I, 15). Catte in *La putta onorata* flatters Pantalone into giving her money, a ploy to which Bettina reacts with 'O what a pretender!' (I, 9), while Columbina in *La famiglia dell'antiquario* earns extra money by telling lies to both her mistresses about each other.

Male servants who use pretence for material gain of course proliferate in Goldoni's comedies, as they did in those of the Renaissance. An exception to the male trickster scheming to further the sexual desires of his master in sixteenth-century comedy was a female character like Lelia in *Gli ingannati*, who devises an intrigue and ventures, cross-dressed as a man, outside the confines of respectable indoor territory to pursue her desires. While Beatrice similarly takes on male identity in Goldoni's *Il servitore di due padroni*, she, however, shares none of Lelia's fears about being out of doors. She also takes on a more central role as one of the *due padroni* of the title, a role which she carries out with great conviction.

However, the reason motivating Beatrice's spirit of enterprise, and her consequent *finzione* of cross-dressing, is no different from that of Lelia. Beatrice says: 'I'm leaving my homeland, abandoning relatives, dressing in male clothes, exposing myself to danger, risking life itself, *all that I do is for Florindo*' (III, 3, italics added). She later justifies the 'fine courage' and 'excess spirit', of which Pantalone and the Dottore accuse her, in terms of her love for Florindo: 'Love makes you do great things!' (III, 15). The male disguise she has adopted enables her to continue her search for Florindo unhampered, in that it gives her a freedom she does not have in her own right: 'If I reveal myself, I'll achieve nothing. Pantalone will start lecturing me; and they'll all annoy me, telling me that it's not a good thing to do, that it's not fitting, and all the rest. I want my freedom. It'll only last a short time, but there we are' (I, 5).

While correctly explaining the limits imposed on her by society, she accepts that her freedom can only be temporary, as her final remark shows. Like carnival, her play with norms and identities cannot last. It seems that she has shown signs before of feeling restricted by the demands of conventional femininity. Brighella describes how she used to behave when he knew her in Turin: 'A young woman of spirit, of courage; she used to dress like a man, and ride horseback' (I, 1). However, while on the one hand she is a powerful character who fear-lessly uses male identity to further her aims, her ultimate reason for doing so is a conventional one. Just as Lelia schemes to regain Flamminio's attentions and to become his wife, so Beatrice's enterprise is exclusively geared to marriage.

Rosaura, the central character in *La donna di garbo*, is an equally for-midable artful woman, this time in the intellectual sphere. Despite being female and lower class, Rosaura has acquired considerable knowledge of the law, together with more than adequate powers of articulation. While the education of girls, albeit for the purpose of training them in all the patriarchal virtues, was a preoccupation of eighteenth-century Europe, which saw a considerable rise in levels of female literacy, this remained the province of the middle and upper classes. Rosaura, previously a laundress at the University of Padua, is exceptional as a lower-class character who has acquired legal skills from her student lover, Florindo. It is precisely in the unusual nature of her achievement that much of the dramatic tension of the comedy lies.

Rosaura is fully aware of all the legalities involved in the betrothal process, particularly in the event of a prior claim, and while her prowess is the cause of comic consternation in the other characters, she nevertheless stuns her employer, the Dottore, with her skills. She also possesses a particular ability which is important for her purpose, namely that of endearing herself to people. To this end she learns about their passions (such as gambling, in the case of Ottavio), and seconds them, all the while dissembling the most profound interest. As Goldoni says of her in his address to the reader, she has both skill and, like the male tricksters in the Renaissance comedies, ingenuity (*ingegno*). However, the purpose to which all of this is put is, once again, the legitimate one of marriage, rather than the radical one of becoming Doctor of Law. Learned women did of course exist, as Goldoni is at pains to point out in his address to the reader that precedes the play. In 1678 a certain Elena Cornaro Piscopia became the first female Doctor of Philosophy at the University of Padua. However, such recognition of intellectual ability in women was exceptional; it was also closely linked to high-class status (Elena's father was a patrician) (Anderson and Zinsser 1988, II, p. 86).

Goldoni declares in his address to the reader that Rosaura has 'satisfied her *just* desire with skill and ingenuity' (italics added). It is in the pursuit of this 'just desire' that other artful women in his comedies can also be seen to use their individual type of *finzione*. In *La vedova scaltra* Rosaura switches nationality in order to help her assess each of her four suitors from England, Spain, France and Italy without being recognized, finally opting for the Italian count. Argentina's purpose in writing and performing a play with a moral in *La cameriera brillante* is so that Pantalone, her master, will be persuaded to marry her. Rosaura's feigned illness in *La finta ammalata* keeps away unwelcome suitors, while enabling her to see more of the young doctor whom she desires. Using her 'illness' as a lever with her father, who is reluctant for her to leave home, Rosaura finally manages to marry the man of her choice. While her sexual wishes do enter the scene, the play ultimately problematizes female desire by medicalizing it and tranforming it into a nervous disorder, or madness, thereby working to mask the daughter's actual lack of freedom in matters of marriage.

Enterprise for these artful women entails using *finzione* not merely to further their own marriage prospects, but often also those of other women. Rosaura in *La donna di garbo* persuades Lelio to marry her rival, Isabella degli Ardenti, the noblewoman whom Florindo had brought home, intending her to be his bride. In *La vedova scaltra* Rosaura uses her status as a widow to arrange her sister's marriage. Argentina in *La cameriera brillante* acknowledges the custom that she cannot marry her master, Pantalone, unless his daughters also marry. Along with her own marriage, then, she proceeds to engineer those of Flaminia and Clarice. Normally the privilege of arranging marriage belonged to the patriarch of the family, as in the vast majority of the Renaissance comedies. While the father retains this power in some of Goldoni's plays (*I due gemelli veneziani*, *Il servitore di due padroni*, *La finta ammalata*), in others this position is taken over by artful women. They may be from a variety of classes and in different marital phases, for instance, lower class and nubile (Argentina, Rosaura in *La donna di garbo*) or middle class and widowed (Rosaura in *La vedova scaltra*). Despite the fact that her father is still alive, Rosaura, as a wealthy widow, claims the right to arrange her sister's marriage on the basis that she is able to provide her with a dowry.

All of these artful women use *finzione* to further the 'just' enterprise of marriage. However, the case of Mirandolina in *La locandiera* is quite different. Goldoni says in his address to the reader: 'Indeed he'll say that I've not depicted a woman who is more flattering and more dangerous than this one anywhere else.' Mirandolina as arch-pretender goes on to assume mythical proportions: 'these flattering women, when they see their lovers caught in their snare, usually treat them harshly. I wanted to give an example of this barbarous cruelty . . . and make the character of the enchanting Sirens appear odious.' *La locandiera* also appears to be unique in that: 'Among all the comedies composed by me so far, I'd almost say that this is the most moral, the most useful, and the most instructive.'

It is in her dealings with the misogynist Cavaliere that Mirandolina's style of *finzione* takes shape:

CAVALIERE: Well done! I like your sincerity.
MIRANDOLINA: Oh, the only good thing about me is my sincerity.
CAVALIERE: But yet, with whoever pays court to you, you know how to pretend.
MIRANDOLINA: Me, pretend? May heaven protect me from doing so! (I, 15)

Her *finzione*, rather than depending on masks or disguises, lies in verbal play on her undisguised sexuality. The Cavaliere himself is not portrayed with much sympathy, being intended by Goldoni as an example of 'degrading presumption'. However, this does nothing to lessen the disapproval with which Mirandolina's *finzione* is depicted. Furthermore, her pretence would seem to backfire on her, in that she ultimately proves the Cavaliere's point, namely that women *are* insincere. However, this does not suffice as a plot closure, as it might have done. This is because the real issue lies elsewhere. In the plays discussed so far, artful women have been seen to use *finzione* in a variety of ways, yet none

are portrayed in so condemnatory a fashion. Mirandolina's real crime
lies not so much in the pretence she weaves around her sexuality, which
is already bad enough, but in the fact that she does not use this for the
purpose of marriage. On the contrary, she declares: 'I'm not even considering marriage; I don't need anybody; I live honestly, and I enjoy my
freedom. I have dealings with everyone, but I never fall in love with
anyone' (I, 9). In other words, her *finzione* is aimed at *playing with men*,
rather than *for a man*.

Mirandolina, in effect, does not have those feminine needs on which
patriarchal hegemony depends. The foundation of her independence
from men is, significantly, economic in nature. The *locandiera* has for the
last six months been running her own business, the inn which she inherited on the death of her father. Her resulting financial self-sufficiency
means not only that she herself can employ men, but also that she is not
to be bought with gifts, the currency with which her male admirers
attempt unsuccessfully to gain her sexual favours. Mirandolina, the
autonomous woman who does not need men for economic or other
reasons, and who is artful into the bargain, represents a dramatic reconstruction of one of patriarchy's worst nightmares. *La locandiera* plays out
this female threat couched in the discourse of morality, while the recuperative powers of marriage provide the 'happy' ending.

In a similarly moralistic vein, Rosaura, the artful widow, moves
toward re-marriage in *La vedova scaltra*. Once again, economic founda-
tions underlie the 'unseemliness' of the unmarried woman, expressed
by her father in terms of 'making a good impression': 'A widow living it
up doesn't make the best impression in the world' (II, 1). Rosaura's
wealth means that she is independent, and therefore does not need
to re-marry. Nor is she under the control of any male relation. As
Monsieur reminds Pantalone, her father-in-law: 'She's a widow; you
have no authority over her' (I, 13). When her sister Eleonora does not
dare to oppose her father's decision that she should marry Pantalone,
Rosaura is able to step in:

ELEONORA: If my father comes to entreat me, what do you suggest I reply?
ROSAURA: Tell him that in this matter you can't come to a decision without me.
ELEONORA: He'll say he's the father.
ROSAURA: Tell him that I'm the one who's giving you the dowry. (II, 10)

Rosaura has the power to free her sister from their father's control: 'I've
put into play the freedom that is appropriate for choosing one's state,
and of which I've declared myself the guarantor before the entire

world' (II, 10). A wealthy middle-class widow like Rosaura is a far remove from the impoverished, nubile, lower-class Bettina in *La putta onorata*, or even another middle-class character like Rosaura's sister. Wealth and a widow's status were at the time important empowering factors that helped to reinstate a woman's right to choose whether to marry or not, a right to which, in Rosaura's eyes, women are entitled.

Unfortunately, the refreshing freedom from patriarchal restraints that finds its climax for both sisters in this scene does not last. Having offended Pantalone, with whom she lives, by helping Eleonora escape from becoming his wife, Rosaura contemplates leaving his household. When Marionette points out that her mistress is not without her own property, Rosaura replies, echoing her father's words earlier in the same scene: 'Yes, but a widow on her own isn't seemly' (II, 13). Not wishing to return to her paternal home, which would be one way of regaining the respectability of being, once again, under patriarchal control, she selects the only other secular option open to her, and opts for re-marriage. It is at this point, in order to help her choose among her four suitors, that she makes use of *finzione*. Her artfulness (the *scaltrezza* implied by the play's title) is justified as it has moved her towards the recuperative plot closure both of her own remarriage, which will defuse the threat of her economic autonomy, and the marriage of her sister.

In the concluding speech of the play, she reiterates the legitimacy of her enterprise in classic patriarchal terms: 'Now all my designs are brought favourably to fruition. Now the state of a widow and of an unmarried girl, states that are equally dangerous, have been redressed.' Her uncertain vindication of, or rather apology for, her use of *finzione*, similarly reinforces traditional values and serves to negate the audacity of her previous actions: 'I confess I've been artful in my dealings, but since my artfulness has never gone against the maxims of honour or the laws of civil society, I hope I'll be, if not applauded, at least pitied, and, just possibly, envied' (III, 26). The artfulness of this female character thus tails off on a hesitant, confessional note, as, together with her other artful sisters, she is ultimately recuperated for patriarchy.

Goldoni's artful women can be seen to differ considerably from his angelic women. The former are proactive, plotting intrigues and using various forms of *finzione* to further their schemes. The angel in the house is mainly reactive. She offers only passive resistance to the actions of others, relying on her patriarchal virtues of chastity, modesty and domesticity, to see her through. While her artful sisters are no less chaste, they tend to transgress certain rules of modesty and decorum, for which they often apologize at the play's *dénouement*.

The two types of female character also provide different forms of theatricality. The angelic woman utters endless moral diatribes. Bettina in *La putta onorata* repeats variations of 'I'm a good/honourable girl' over a dozen times. However, she is also dramatically at risk of kidnapping, violence and rape, the first of which is depicted on stage, while the latter two are narrated and threatened, respectively. She unambiguously represents one side of the 'virtue' vs 'vice' conflict around which the drama develops. The artful woman provides pivotal theatrical interest in that it is her *finzione* that generates plot development. She is similarly at risk, partly because she is female, and also as a consequence of the situations in which her *finzione* places her. For example, Beatrice's cross-dressing in *Il servitore di due padroni* places her in danger of injury or death in combat, while Mirandolina has to hide behind a locked door when the Cavaliere seeks revenge for the trick she has played on him. While dramatic tension around the possible rape of a female character is clearly not as pronounced as it is in, say, English Restoration tragedy, there is no doubt that this dramatically exploitative sexual dynamic is present, even if mostly only in the form of innuendo.[19]

Female sexuality is a major focus for critical patriarchal scrutiny in Goldoni's comedies, which make use of the eighteenth-century discourse of morality to explore patriarchy's fears and fantasies concerning femininity. It is in this context that similarities underlying both the angelic and the artful female character can be detected. The angel in the house represents the repression of female autonomy as vice. She is the embodiment of an idealized femininity that presents no resistance, showing passivity even to the point of self-victimization. The construction of the artful female character, on the other hand, plays out the threat of an autonomous female sexuality, while resourcefulness combined with a spotless chastity allow for both ambivalence and possible recuperation. Subversion is taken to the brink of success, at which point recuperation is introduced to close the play. For both angelic and artful women, marriage beckons as moral/patriarchal order is finally restored.

CHAPTER FOUR

Masterful men: difference and fantasy in D'Annunzio

This chapter examines late nineteenth- and early twentieth-century portrayals of masterful masculinity in a variety of pre- and postcapitalist, urban and nonurban settings in the decadent plays of D'Annunzio. The patriarchal strategies underpinning his decadent theatre can be most clearly identified by tracing the differences and similarities with realist theatre, represented by the works of Verga. While Verga's realism and D'Annunzio's decadentism are obviously distinct from each other in many ways, they share a fundamental affiliation with patriarchal values. Verga's aim of authorial impersonality resulted in a realism which did not manage to represent a neutral, ideologically-void position. In mirroring the status quo as a reality corresponding to a 'natural' norm, his realism worked invisibly to uphold the patriarchal view. In other words, while purporting to merely reflect real social relations, Verga's realism actually reinforced an ideology that is not fixed and inevitable, but whose dominance necessitates a continuing process of subordination of other value systems. In the case of D'Annunzio's decadent production, on the other hand, a veil of dream, myth and ritual provides a camouflage for patriarchal strategies that find expression not in realist invisibility, but in unreal, or even surreal, projections of patriarchal fantasy. D'Annunzio's aim was not to represent reality, but to reproduce on stage what he called an 'ideal life' (*vita ideale*), an expression he used in a theatrical manifesto written as the result of the riotously unpopular reception of *Più che l'amore* in 1906 (D'Annunzio 1964, p. 1068).[1]

While sharing a common patriarchal standpoint, Verga's realism and D'Annunzio's decadentism thus differ in their representation of patriarchal values. Intertwined with their reinforcement of patriarchy are considerations of class. Verga's dramatic realism deals mainly with the Sicilian peasant class, thereby conforming to the tendency of realism to be associated with the lower rather than the middle or upper

Plate 4. 'For Eleonora Duse of the beautiful hands': mutilated femininity in D'Annunzio's *La Gioconda*, 1899.

classes.[2] D'Annunzio's *vita ideale*, by contrast, is predominantly peopled with regal and upper- or upper-middle-class protagonists (one major exception being the rustic *La figlia di Iorio*, 1904). The lower classes are given a place, with the occasional glorification of the peasant class (as in the case of Ruggiero Fiamma's peasant origins in *La gloria*). In the main, however, the lower classes and their activities exist merely to provide a counterpoint to the aspirations and actions of their social superiors (for example, the gardener at the beginning of *Sogno d'un mattino di primavera*, 1897, and the various slaves and servants in plays like *Sogno d'un tramonto d'autunno*, 1897, *La città morta*, 1898, and *Fedra*, 1909). The plays show a particular rejection of the middle class. In a historical period which saw the beginnings of massification of society and new forms of organization of labour, D'Annunzio's plays cling resolutely to the old, polarized class order.

Also contributing to both invisible realist and veiled decadent reinforcement of patriarchal ideology are the stage settings of the plays of Verga and D'Annunzio. These vary, in terms of time and place, in accordance with their class orientation, as well as with their realist or decadent style. Verga's *Cavalleria rusticana* and *La lupa* are set, in true realist mode, in contemporary peasant surroundings that also represent a place of work for their village and farm inhabitants (the folk scenes of *Cavalleria rusticana* are set in a village square, and *La lupa* opens in a farmyard). D'Annunzio's only rustic play, *La figlia di Iorio*, 1904, has a similarly rural setting, and shows lower-class characters involved in the work of harvesting, woodworking and tending flocks. However, the play diverges from any realist tendency in its temporal setting, which, rather than contemporary, is both historically unspecified and in the past ('many years ago'). The play's emphasis on primitive superstition and use of ritualistic dialogue distance the characters and their actions even further from any tangible social reality.

In terms of temporal setting, the majority (nine) of D'Annunzio's fifteen plays take place in the distant past. Only two plays have clearly contemporary settings (*La Gioconda*, 1899, and *Più che l'amore*, 1905), while another three could be contemporary but are not overtly stated to be so (*Sogno d'un mattino di primavera*, 1899, *La città morta*, 1898, and *Il ferro*, 1913). One major feature of D'Annunzio's plays is that temporal distance or aspecificity is frequently matched by isolation in terms of place. Upper-class country properties (villas, castles) are often the setting for the working out of familial or other dynamics in a context that appears both timeless and out of touch with the world beyond (*Sogno d'un mattino di primavera, La fiaccola sotto il moggio, Il ferro*). Even when not directly set in the fantasy context of mythical or distant historical periods (like *Fedra*, 1909, or *La Pisanelle*, 1913), the plays often have a dreamlike, fatalistic quality. These characteristics of dramatic decadence serve to *appear* to remove the plays from an ideologically and often historically specific position. However, patriarchal ideology nonetheless informs the pre-capitalist mythology of *Fedra*, the pre-capitalist rural economy of *La figlia di Iorio*, and the contemporary urban capitalism of *Più che l'amore*.

The upper- or upper-middle-class location of the country villa (*Sogno d'un mattino di primavera, La città morta, Il ferro*), the castle (*La fiaccola sotto il moggio*), or indeed the regal palace (*Fedra*), all denote the higher echelons of society in materialist as well as class terms. As far as materialist issues are concerned, these are usually sidestepped, with a few exceptions (one of these being *Più che l'amore*, whose main character, Corrado, commits murder for financial gain). Most major protagonists appear to use what is presumed to be inherited wealth to finance their activities and households of servants or slaves. In the *vita ideale* there are no economic problems. In the plays, wealth is mostly taken for granted, and property relations thereby rendered invisible, while in his political *Discorso della siepe* of 1897, D'Annunzio publicly exalted private property. Material considerations are made to take second place in his plays, as the characters frequently interact in seclusion from exchange of any sort, material or social, with the outside world.

This is in complete contrast with the very social, and sociable, plays of Goldoni examined in the previous chapter, with their close attention to materialist detail in terms of prices, precise sums of money, and a preponderance of middle-class professions (merchants, doctors, lawyers), but not to the exclusion of both lower- and upper-class protagonists. As far as audiences were concerned, Goldoni's plays also reached across the classes, from gondolier to aristocrat, in both public and private theatres, with his use of spoken language and dialect. D'Annunzio's audience, on the other hand, was restricted to the educated upper classes who could understand the many classical references and the highly ornate, literary language in which his plays were written, so that his theatre received relatively sparse diffusion. Verga's attempt to mirror popular language in his plays by constructing an artificial version that was spoken nowhere was no more successful in expanding the class-base of his audience. Both Verga and D'Annunzio represent high culture which was undergoing emargination in an

emerging modern, massified society. The lower middle class was
expanding, and 1897 saw the founding of the Partito Socialista Dei
Lavoratori Italiani, both factors which helped to destabilize traditional
social polarization in terms of class and wealth. Aristocratic and upper-
middle-class wealth is the accepted norm for D'Annunzio, a norm that
tacitly underpins the importance of hierarchical organization in his
plays.

When economic issues are foregrounded in D'Annunzio's plays, it is
usually in order to dismiss them as base, inferior and incidental to
higher concerns (for example, the quarrel about inheritance between
the two 'unheroic' brothers in *La fiaccola sotto il moggio* is contrasted with
the relentless quest for revenge on the part of the heroic Gigliola). The
apotheosis of this rejection of materialism is expressed in Corrado's
disdain for 'mercantile morality' in *Più che l'amore*. This scorn for the
petty, materialist view in favour of a higher, idealist perspective, results,
paradoxically, in robbery and murder in order to finance the ideal
heroic pursuit. D'Annunzio has been interpreted as attempting a subversion of social relations based on the market (Mutterle 1980, p. 16).
However, when he is not taking materialist issues for granted in portraying the upper social echelons in both pre-capitalist and capitalist
periods living on unacknowledged wealth, his 'superman' simply side-
steps the market through murder. Moreover, plays like *La Pisanelle* see
the continuation of the commodification of the female body present in
the Renaissance comedies.

This leads to the key question addressed by this chapter: how are
gender relations represented in the context of D'Annunzio's decadent
veiling of both patriarchal and materialist values through fantasy, a
fantasy enhanced by dramatic settings that are frequently distant in
terms of both time and place? How does this representation differ from
Verga's realist plays? In focussing on the portrayal of masculinity in
D'Annunzio's plays, one cannot fail to be struck by the powerful presence of female characters. There is no doubt that D'Annunzio's plays
continue a fascination with femininity already evident in his other writings, and perhaps fuelled by his professional and personal relationship
with the actress Eleonora Duse, for whom some of his plays were written. They met in 1894, and she is reputed to have inspired him for most
of his seventeen-year period as a dramatic writer (1897–1908) (Mutterle
1980, p. 5). What is certainly clear, is that D'Annunzio's masterful men
cannot be analysed without taking into account their relations with
femininity.

This is due to the fact that mastery, and especially masculine mastery of femininity, is central to gender relations in general, and the construction of masculinity in particular, in D'Annunzio's plays. Masculine mastery must also be considered in the historical context within which D'Annunzio was writing, namely that of Italy's imperialist efforts, which included the attempted mastery of Africa through colonization. Will to power is the driving force behind masculinity in D'Annunzio's plays, and nowhere more clearly than in his depiction of the master–slave dynamic inherent in decadent sexuality and its excesses. Some of his plays, most notably *La nave*, show the extremes of this dynamic in the form of sexualized sadomasochistic power games (an element of which is also present in Verga's *La lupa*). One particular arena for the playing out of gender dynamics in both realist and decadent drama is that of the family, with its various sexual taboos. Social categories of family and class intersect with those of gender in the various temporal, spatial and socioeconomic settings of the plays shaped by the specific historical context of their production.

DIFFERENCE AS DOMINANCE

The masterful man, from Verga's peasant to D'Annunzio's superman, is defined by his desire for domination. This accords with patriarchal gender stereotyping which polarizes masculinity and femininity into opposing sets of attributes. The oppositional and often antagonistic relationship between masculinity and femininity reproduces the epistemological tendency to work in terms of mutually exclusive binary opposites, a tendency explored earlier in its sixteenth- and eighteenth-century manifestations on the Italian stage. This patriarchal configuration of gender also interlocks with the dominant view of power as oppositional and inherently hostile, and hence to be understood as a hierarchical dynamic, namely that of power exercised *over* others. Alternative definitions of power are based on an epistemology of relational rather than oppositional structures, with a consequent emphasis on community rather than hierarchy. Power as competence thereby replaces power as dominance.[3] However, it is the traditional interpretation of power as dominance that informs stereotypical attributes of patriarchal masculinity, namely hostility, aggression and desire for conquest. These attributes are foregrounded by the plays of both D'Annunzio and Verga, plays whose hallmark is violence and death.

The masterful man's quest for dominance in D'Annunzio's plays takes three forms: combative, exploratory and creative. The goals of these different types of heroic quest are all achieved through action and conquest. D'Annunzio's depiction of masculine will to power through these means is part of a world view current in late nineteenth-century Europe which found particular expression in the philosophy of Nietzsche. Of special relevance are Nietzsche's ideas in *Also sprach Zarathrustra* (1883) on the *Übermensch*, or Zarathustrian superman, the first of a higher species of aristocratic super-race that would regenerate the bleak mediocrity of unheroic modern mass society. Also of importance are Nietzsche's *Der Wille zur Macht* (1888), and the earlier master–slave discourse of Hegel in *Phänomenologie des Geistes* (1807).

Informing all these philosophies is the traditional assumption of power as hierarchical and dominance oriented, accompanied by a firm belief in a rigid class system dominated by the upper classes, and opposed to democracy as a threat to authority and to established property relations. Nietzsche's superman is an aristocrat, a stereotype of ideal masculinity with its roots in the often regal hero of precapitalist mythology. The values embodied by the superman of the late nineteenth century, in other words of late romanticism or decadentism, are in direct opposition to those of the eighteenth-century bourgeois Enlightenment, with its emphasis on reason, virtue, happiness and materialism, values epitomized on the Italian stage by the comedies of Goldoni. In D'Annunzio's plays, reasonable, everyday, materialist, bourgeois man is replaced by passionate, heroic, tragic, upper-class superman, a man of will and action.

In the combative and often militaristic quest, domination is pursued through physical power. This was the time-honoured method of the classical hero in precapitalist Greek mythology, and is still current in the popular genre of the action film in today's context of high-technology capitalism. D'Annunzio's bellicose action men span various eras: Theseus and his son Ippolito, eager for war in the mythological play *Fedra*; Marco Gratico, ready for conquest in *La nave*, set in AD 552; Paolo Malatesta seeking solace in war in the mediaeval setting of *Francesca da Rimini*; and Corrado Brando's heroic need to fight in *Più che l'amore*, set in Rome in the third republic. This latter-day would-be hero is of particular interest because the contemporary setting of the play removes any possibility for escapism into a distant historical or mythological past that might serve to shroud the implications of heroic excesses in the requirements of a mythological genre. Nor is any attempt at allegory made by using a different historical period to signify contem-

porary time (as in *La nave*). On the contrary, Corrado Brando is presented straightforwardly as D'Annunzio's answer to the needs of his
present time. In an era of change which saw the beginnings of a demo-
cratic levelling out of society, D'Annunzio, like Nietzsche, believed in
the need to reassert traditional hierarchies and values. This was to be
achieved by reestablishing the primacy of individual excellence over
the mediocrity of the masses, made up of 'little men' from the expanding, indeterminate zone in between the upper and lower ends of the
class hierarchy, namely the lower middle classes. Corrado Brando is
one of D'Annunzio's embodiments of reaction against 'grey, everyday
democracy'.[4] His heroic masculinity is intended to signal the dawn of a
new *vita ideale* through stereotypically masculine action and conquest.

In order to distinguish himself from the masses, Corrado Brando
turns his back on urban society with the intention of pursuing an imperialist quest in Africa, as befits his warlike spirit and need for combat.
Virginio describes and affirms his friend's heroism in militaristic terms:
'contradiction and war are for your nature the most effective stimuli for
living and for loving life' (1). The centrality of militarism to an ideal
patriarchal masculinity that is also exalted in class terms has a longstanding currency in western thought, and finds one of its earliest
expressions in the *Dicta* of Heraclitus: 'War is the father of all and king
of all; and some he has made gods and some men, some slaves and some
free. To me one man is ten thousand if he be the best' (Bentley 1947,
p. 112).

The specifically imperialist version of militarism in *Più che l'amore* is
shaped by the historical context of Italy's colonial hopes in Africa.
While on the one hand rejecting contemporary social developments
and showing a decided preference for the tradition of a material base of
inherited wealth, the militaristic versions of masculinity portrayed in
D'Annunzio's plays reveal an enthusiastic response to an era in Italy's
political history characterized by a growing pro-interventionist tendency in general, and imperialist aspirations in particular. Increasing
disillusionment with a conservative foreign policy and hostility towards
French colonialism in Africa, accompanied by factors such as unstable
home politics and the agricultural crisis of the mid-1880s, contributed
to an intensification of Italian interest in Africa, an involvement which
had begun in 1869 with the activities of the Rubattino shipping company at Assab. By 1906, the year of *Più che l'amore*, an Italian protec-
torate had been established over Abyssinia in 1889, and lost seven years
later. Massawa and Assab had become the Italian colony of Eritrea in

1890, while Somalia, the scene of Corrado Brando's military heroism in the antefact to the play, officially became an Italian colony in 1906 itself. The loss of Abyssinia in 1896, with the deaths of 25,000 soldiers at the Battle of Adowa, was to be rectified by the establishment of the Italian colony of Libya in North Africa in 1912 (Clark 1984, pp. 99–101, 153–4).

When *Più che l'amore* opens, Corrado has been back for two years from Somalia, where he fought alongside 'his' Sudanese and 'his' Somali (i), and achieved the status of a white god among the natives of Olda (ii). His colonial discourse is characterized by western imperialist assumptions of racial superiority. This is echoed in his attitude to Rudu, his Sardinian servant, who is placed firmly in a subordinate position in terms of race, with Corrado in the dominant role. Not only is Corrado a hero himself, he is even capable of generating heroes in other 'non-heroic' races. He says to Rudu: 'I stir your entire race into action in you, with all its sleeping heroes' (ii).

Domination over other races takes on a gender dimension in Corrado's nationalist, imperialist speech to Virginio in one of the many man-to-man dialogues of the play:

I have my own ideas, indeed I have my empire, a Roman word to be made Italian: *I have you, Africa.* Ah, if you could understand! Ah, if you'd felt just once what I felt when we entered the unknown region from the other side of Ima, when we imprinted Latin footprints on the virgin land! (i)

Colonial discourse here typifies western imperialism in its equation of Africa with the feminine and virgin to be conquered by masculine, intrepid Rome. Corrado's emphasis on Africa as virgin land results in the traditional alignment of nature with femininity, to be subjugated, along with its people, by the culture and masculinity of the 'civilized' west. Similarly *La gloria*, set in the distant but unspecified past, shows Rome described in terms of a woman to be fertilized, as two male characters, Ruggero and Daniele, discuss how to exercise power over the city (iv, 1).

Heroic masculinity through military conquest is also depicted in *La nave*, set on a Venetian island in AD 552, but interpreted as an allegory for contemporary Rome, and written in the same year as *Più che l'amore*. *La nave*'s superman, Marco Gratico, is also eager to conquer new lands overseas. Stage directions state that 'the will to conquer flashes in his eyes' (i). The military quest, a crucial component of one type of D'Annunzian superman, is also to be found in his non-dramatic writings. He argued for intervention in the Great War in *Canti della guerra latina*, while his poem *Canzoni della gesta d'Oltramare* exalts Italy's colonial efforts in Africa, a political and ideological stance which he continued to maintain in 1936 with *Teneo te, Africa*. In a venture into film in 1914, he wrote the screenplay for the historical epic *Cabiria*, a glorification of the Punic Wars fought by the Romans in Africa. As well as following decadentism's dictum of art for art's sake in his attempt to create the ideal man for his theatrical *vita ideale*, D'Annunzio also lived his own life according to his art. In performing his military feats at Fiume, he was to live out the same patriarchal stereotype of heroic masculinity which, often pre-packaged in mytho-history, governed the construction of his onstage action supermen.

Other types of D'Annunzian superman pursue a different quest in order to attain the masculine ideal of patriarchy. Corrado's military fantasies find a parallel in the actions of Virginio, a hydraulic engineer who 'rules over' the world's water. Like Corrado, atavistic, primitive energy is transformed for Virginio into Nietzschean will to power, the need for action rather than contemplation and the desire not to embellish the world (which he later deems to be women's work) but to conquer it:

I feel my instinct reaching towards the appearance of a new beauty, because my approach doesn't change natural energy into human form, but imprints on it the motion of my will to transform it into a more varied and vast creation, a will destined not for contemplation but action, not for ornamenting the world but for conquering it. (1)

Virginio follows a non-militaristic path in his engineering work, which investigates new ways to control and master nature's laws. The investigative or exploratory quest in D'Annunzio's plays involves power as domination in that it is portrayed in terms of the exertion of power *over*, rather working in harmony and cooperation *with*, nature. The depiction of Virginio's perception of his controlling, dominating role as hydraulic engineer offers a brief glimpse into traditional scientific thought as structured by an ideology of power committed to dominance hierarchies. While Corrado explores and conquers virgin land in Africa according to patriarchal imperialist ideology, Virginio's quest is to 'tame' nature according to patriarchal scientific ideology (Bleier 1984, pp. 29, 164).

The exploratory quest of Leonardo in *La città morta* takes the form of archeological excavation. His goal in discovering the sepulchres of

Atrides is to allow him access to the 'ideal life' (I, 4) through the power of knowledge of the past. However, his archeological activities are not carried out simply for knowledge, but also for the sake of possession; the many finds, far from being donated to a museum, are kept, damaged, or turned into commodities to be given away as presents. Above all, his discoveries do not bring him the one crucial form of mastery that he seeks, namely knowledge about and control over femininity. Among the treasures he has unearthed are the bodies of Cassandra and Agammemnon, bodies that crumble away as he looks on. He dismisses that of Agammemnon briefly, but talks at length about Cassandra, telling Alessandro: 'You'll see her shell, touch her empty waistband' (I, 5).

Their discourse fetishizes the female form as mere surface that is insubstantial and must be eliminated, thereby foreshadowing Leonardo's murder of his sister, Bianca Maria, for whom he has developed incestuous desires. His need to 'know' his sister, like his need to know the past, results in destruction as his exploratory quest leads him to exercise his heroic masculine dominance. That this quest, with its patriarchal goal and power dynamics, is an all-male concern, is emphasized in performance in that he recounts his experience in discovering the sepulchres exclusively to Alessandro. Yet both Bianca Maria and Alessandro's wife, Anna, are also present on stage, while Bianca Maria has also supported him stoically in his excavations for two years (a fact which is made much of in a dialogue between the two women). However, as Leonardo repeats a dozen times, it is Alessandro and not Bianca Maria whom he wants by his side at the moment of discovery.

As in the case of Corrado and Virginio, male friends and main characters in *Più che l'amore*, Leonardo and Alessandro each represent different types of hero on a quest for ideal masculinity. Alessandro is associated with the third type of quest, namely that of creativity. Like the exploratory quest, the creative quest involves a less overt exertion of will to power over another gender, race or country in the realm of action, as was the case in the military quest. Nevertheless, conquest still enters the artistic process of will to power in the realm of ideas, as Alessandro declares that he must possess Bianca Maria sexually in order to release his creative powers. He argues: 'You belong to me as if you were my creature, formed by my hands, inhaling my breath' (II, I). He and Leonardo later drown Bianca Maria: having created a femininity that corresponds to his desires, but still proves to be unknowable and uncontainable, the writer Alessandro/D'Annunzio proceeds to destroy it. Lucio Settala in *La Gioconda* is a heroic creator/sculptor seeking mastery over the female form through the plastic arts. His quest proves to be endless, since his model, Gioconda/femininity itself, provides material for 'a thousand statues' (II, 1). Once again, femininity thwarts the masculine, as the latter attempts to recreate, know and contain the Other whose subordination is crucial for the patriarchal dominance hierarchy to be maintained.

Throughout the process of delineating patriarchal constructions of ideal masculinity as a heroic brotherhood of masterful men on military, exploratory and creative quests, the presence of the feminine has made itself felt. While femininity will be explored in the second part of this chapter, further discussion of the role of femininity in relation to the masculine quest is necessary at this point. Of particular interest is *where* heroic masculinity pursues its quest, and what is rejected in the process. The location of the heroic quest is public, outside space. In order to fulfil his masculinity, the masterful man must leave behind the private, domestic sphere of the household. In *Fedra*, for instance, Theseus and Ippolito are mostly absent from the stage, which represents the palace, a household made up predominantly of women and where most of the play is set. Theseus is away laying siege to Thebes, while Ippolito spends most of his time hunting and taming horses. The dichotomy between public, heroic, masculine space and domestic, feminine space, is also reflected in the stage settings of other plays. In *La città morta*, Leonardo pursues his archeological quest in the ruins outside, while Anna and Bianca Maria wait at home. *Sogno d'un tramonto d'autunno* opens with its female protagonist, Gradinega, caged within her luxury villa and gripping the iron bars of the gate like 'a beast caught in a net' (I, p. 52). She is restricted to the private sphere of her erstwhile pleasure palace, the *locus amoenus* of her powerful sexual attractions which are now waning and in the desperate contemplation of which she is also trapped. In *Sogno d'un mattino di primavera*, the 'demented' female does leave the home to wander in the forest, but this is only because she is deranged.

The private, domestic sphere is the domain of the feminine. Action man, however, must travel overseas, as Corrado has done in the antefact to *Più che l'amore*, and as he prepares to do during the course of the play. Non-heroic men stay in the home, like Tebaldo in *La fiaccola sotto il moggio*. Rejection of the domestic sphere is epitomized in *La Gioconda* by the hero-sculptor's turning away from his (asexual) wife and home in favour of his (sexual) model and studio, where he pursues his creative quest. When Silvia visits the studio to confront Gioconda, she feels out of place. The dichotomy between the domestic home and the heroic workplace is spelt out by Gioconda: 'This isn't a home. Family affections don't have their base here; domestic virtues aren't sanctified here' (III, 2). The stage directions at the beginning of Act III contrast the studio (the location of the sexual side of femininity) with the home (the location of the asexual side) as follows:

The feeling expressed by the appearance of the place is very different from that softening the rooms in the other house and its view of the mystic knoll. The choice and meaning of all the shapes here reveal an aspiration towards a life that is carnal, victorious, and creative. (III)

The gentle mysticism or asexual spirituality of the domestic sphere has been rejected in favour of a sexual physicality allowing for victorious, heroic creativity. This is the location of Lucio Settala's creative quest for mastery over the female form, for domination and control over a femininity whose thousand variations and constant mobility exceed patriarchal confines (it is not fortuitous that he is sculpting a statue of the sphinx, the archetypal symbol of the feminine enigma).

Jettisoned together with the domestic sphere by ideal masculinity is everyday necessity, an existence described by Virginio in *Più che l'amore* as mediocre. In his later clarification of the distinction between 'illustrious lives', in other words, the lives of heroic men, and the negative factors which shadow them, he includes domestic, everyday concerns:

Poverty, domestic misery, everyday irritations, demeaning, wearing necessities, sickness, injustice, ingratitude, derision: aren't these the shadows of so many illustrious lives whom we ask each day for a guiding light to lead us to what lies beyond? (I)

Implicit in this binary opposition is an alignment between domesticity, everyday necessity, the private sphere and femininity, as opposed to heroic activity outside the home, freedom from necessary but lowly tasks, public space and masculinity. Adaptation of this generic dichotomy to include the creative version of masculine heroism results in an alignment that specifies natural, procreative, domestic femininity both in opposition and inferior to cultural, creative, heroic masculinity. In the case of the military hero, nurturing, life-sustaining, domestic femininity is counterposed to death-dealing and even death-seeking heroic masculinity. At the same time, however, the private sphere, necessity, the body and labour or useful activity are of course preconditions for the public sphere, freedom, the mind and heroic action (Hartsock 1983, p. 212).

Familial ties located in the domestic sphere are also discarded in favour of the heroic quest abroad. In *Le Martyre de Saint Sébastien*, 1911, the heroic immortality sought by male martyrs is contrasted with life at the family hearth, the province of the feminine. Marc rejects his mother's pleas to denounce a god who destroys families (by drinking the blood of children and virgins) and to return to familial happiness instead of seeking suffering and death. Familial, life-preserving femininity and heroic, death-seeking masculinity are sharply polarized in this play through heroic rejection of the domestic sphere, a polarization that becomes all the more pointed when the mother suddenly male-identifies, turning her back on her five daughters and choosing martyrdom with the cry 'Goodbye, hearth' (1).

The rejection by heroic masculinity of the private, domestic, familial sphere results in one of the most characteristic features to be displayed by D'Annunzio's contemporary superman, Corrado, namely his solitary nature; or rather, what he believes to be the solitariness that accompanies his uniqueness. 'My solitude begins', he says, explaining that:

my destiny lies in continual detachment, in the need to be always abandoning something or someone: an idea, a shore, a person dear to me. In going about my task, I'm not searching so much for glory, as for distance. (1)

The hero of Greek mythology was also identified on the basis of his individual prowess, an individuation, or radical alterity, predicated on the assumption of a public sphere structured according to traditional power relations of hierarchy and concomitant hostility, rivalry and competition (Hartsock 1983, pp. 252, 262). Corrado's belief in solitariness also owes much to the emphasis on individual identity in both romanticism and decadentism.

Realism, on the other hand, concentrates more on the social fabric of a community clearly defined in class terms. Verga's peasant in *La lupa* is socialized and is part of a working team on the farm. Masterful male characters like Nanni in *La lupa* and Alfio in *Cavalleria rusticana* are not involved in solitary, individual quests. The position of patriarchal dominance they seek to maintain is informed, rather, by the archetypally social code of honour that finds its most extreme form in Sicily, where these plays of Verga, himself a Sicilian, are set. Honour is defined not so much according to the actions that subvert patriarchal gender rules, but by whether knowledge of these actions becomes public or not. (This distinction is particularly exemplified in the play of another Sicilian, Pirandello, namely *Il berretto a sonagli* of 1918.)

D'Annunzio's superman Corrado does not consider himself a part of society. As a result he does not, however, stand outside society in a manner that is simply asocial; on the contrary, he is virulently anti-social, anti-urban and opposed to notions of community. Heroism for him cannot be achieved within society, but involves 'the marvellous need for solitude' (II). Gherardo in *Il ferro* similarly describes heroism as 'the courage of a loner, the courage of an eagle' (III). Corrado conse-quently regrets his 'great deed' in Africa when he saved another man's life, because the action was for someone else's benefit and so without glory, an attitude that bears out Bentley's dichotomy of masculine heroism vs feminine charity (Bentley 1947, p. 71).

The anti-social nature of Corrado's solitary stance is a Nietzschean attempt to place himself beyond good and evil and, specifically, beyond the law, in other words, society's encoding of good and evil. However, Corrado's actual ability to stand outside the law shows that he is not in fact beyond good and evil. On the contrary, his description of heroism reveals an acknowledgement by default of his culture's definition of these terms: 'a warrior's soul, toughness, the search for what has not yet been attempted, the capacity even to do evil, to break through barriers, to put oneself beyond the law' (I). Lucio Settala in *La Gioconda* similarly believes that his creative quest places him in a heroic position outside the laws of ordinary men, and beyond the need to comply with what society defines as the Good: 'I am my own law, even if it is beyond the Good' (II, I).

The solitude required for Corrado's heroism to flourish is class-specific in that it signifies the absence of the fast-expanding urban pro-letariat and their homes, described in terms of disease as 'a huge cage riddled with holes for locking up the scrofula and epilepsy of proletar-ians' (I). The ideal city he would like to construct or discover, he says, would be founded on colonial, military, masculine conquest by a race of heroes who, by implication, are contrasted with the diseased and effeminate urban proletariat. Corrado's rejection of democracy finds its apotheosis in his murder of a usurer from the middle classes, whom he describes with images redolent of physical disgust for civil society: 'all *civil* filth in that sack of fat that sweats and stinks' (II, italics added). Yet despite his arguments against the 'mercantile morality' that epito-mizes the middle-class values he despises, Corrado considers himself to be 'a slave merchant who at a glance judges the quality of human flesh, even as it's disguised by the tailor' (II). His is the ultimate commodifi-cation of the human body in a society structured by the market, as he murders for material gain in order to finance his next heroic exploit (he has no inherited wealth at his disposal to finance his next expedition to Africa).

Although both he and Virginio are engineers by profession, their roots are in the impoverished lower middle class. D'Annunzio himself came from the middle classes, as did his hero Nietzsche, whose scorn for the 'little man' from the lower middle class he shared. For D'Annunzio, as for Nietzsche's *Übermensch*, the superman as epitome of ideal masculinity is associated with the upper classes, a link that has as its corollary a lower-class alignment for patriarchally-defined femininity. D'Annunzio's superman not only belongs, in his own mind at least, to a class beyond the middle and lower classes, but, following in the footsteps of Nietzsche's Zarathustra, he belongs to a new race of men. Once again, this entails a violent rejection of the urban masses, 'the square, the street, the blind houses, the tenacious dirt' (II), to which Corrado counterposes 'the rising up of new men' as he visualizes his own rebirth elsewhere, 'beyond the Ocean' (II).

The future of this new race is assured when Corrado learns that Maria, Virginio's sister, is carrying his child, at which point his interest in her reawakens. He is delighted that his heroism will be perpetuated; his heroic line is now assured, and his victorious existence will live on in flesh and blood. The sole purpose of motherhood here, in producing a child which it is assumed will be male, is to perpetuate heroic, ideal masculinity. All Corrado can see in Maria is his own heroic self. As a result, his momentous declaration that he will now renounce his solitude appears as a mere continuation of his belief in his own superior uniqueness. However, Corrado's actual, rather than his fantasized, status of asocial, solitary heroism, points towards relationality and interdependency, rather than singularity and mutual exclusiveness. Quite simply, for Corrado to be a hero, he must be recognized as such by others; indeed, by the very others whom he despises so much. The actions of a hero, he himself says, must attract public attention, 'so that at least the slaves in the square look up and remember' (II). Heroism, like honour, is defined by the community, whose existence is crucial to the hero for its role not only in recognizing but also in preserving the memory of his deeds.

Corrado's anti-democratic rejection of the masses, his nostalgia for Italy's Roman past, and his quest for ideal masculinity outside Italy, are all indicative of particular aspects of the politico-historical climate in Italy during the early years of the twentieth century. These facets of his characterization are also revealing of philosophical and decadent tendencies current in intellectual circles of the period. In addition, Corrado also shares several other key features of D'Annunzian super-masculinity with male characters in other plays set not in contemporary time, but in the mythical or historical past, Features such as physical courage, energy, will and a violent disposition are displayed by male characters ranging from the mythical past of *Fedra* and the mediaeval period of *La nave*, through to the contemporary *Più che l'amore*.[5] Corrado is thus placed at the end of a line of supermen through the ages, the descendant of a heroic, dramatic brotherhood stretching back to Theseus in *Fedra*.

While the hero may despise the masses and the middle classes, and adopt a position of heroic solitariness, he does develop a 'virile' brotherliness with other men who display the same type of behaviour, or who at least understand and appreciate his qualities. This leads at times to a militarization of male friendship, such as that between Gherardo and Mortella's dead father in *Il ferro*, described by the former as follows: 'Who had a more virile heart? At times our friendship was a militia' (III). D'Annunzio's brotherhood of supermen, moreover, also shares a predilection for violence towards others and towards the self, in a desire for suffering and even death. Violence and the death wish can be traced back to ancient, mythic heroism, while the influence of decadentism is discernible in the desire for suffering and in some forms of the death wish, particularly when sexualized. The mother of Saint Sébastien describes this heroic male condition in terms of desire and lust for pain, torture and death.

The decadent desire for sensation, for plenitude in suffering and even in death, is very much in evidence in D'Annunzio's plays. It stems from an uncontrollable passion, intellectual or physical, that is seen as elemental and heroic, and that results in the destruction of others and often also of the self. Leonardo's intellectual passion for archeological excavation intertwines with a growing sexual desire for his sister in *La città morta*, passions that begin by taking a toll on his health and culminate in his sister's murder. For Lucio in *La Gioconda*, attempted suicide is the outcome of an uncontrollable creative passion that is fuelled by an adulterous liaison with his model, while for his wife the result is mutilation. Corrado's violent instincts culminate in murder and thereby also, in civil terms, in self-annihilation.

In Corrado's case, violence is not linked to sexual passion, but to an urge for military conquest. On the other hand, for other male characters like Leonardo and Lucio, violence has sexual connotations. Paolo throws himself into battle in *Francesca da Rimini* when he cannot enter a sexual relationship with his sister-in-law, venting his sexual passion in combative aggression. In *La figlia di Iorio*, Aligi's desire for Mila leads him to commit patricide, the ultimate subversive act in a patriarchal context, and one which mirrors the primeval dynamic later described by Freud in *Totem and taboo*. The way in which the prevalence of violence in this rustic play is portrayed as an integral part of primitive agrarian life provides a point of comparison with Verga's earlier realist play *La lupa*. In both plays, agrarian work tools double as weapons, while in *La figlia di Iorio*, the routine task of harvesting becomes a ritual that incites male sexual desire and functions as a metaphor for the sexual act itself. In this way violence towards women (Mila in *La figlia di Iorio* and Pina in *La lupa*) is naturalized and normalized as an inevitable result of rustic mores, along with the machismo that accompanies it.

Together with a violently destructive disposition, some of D'Annunzio's masterful men also desire death. The death wish is a standard feature of the classical hero, for whom a gloriously violent death in battle meant immortality through enshrinement in communal memory. In its differentiation from everyday life, the heroic world can even be understood as a rejection of life itself (Hartsock 1983, p. 188). Marco states in *La nave*: 'the hour of my death will be the greatest' (III), and Ippolito declares in *Fedra*: 'I want to live . . . for a glorious death' (II). For the contemporary hero, Corrado, death is another continent which he cannot wait to explore. 'I'll go without hesitation, singing' (I), he says. When the death wish is linked with desire for suffering, eroticization of pain enters the scene. While Corrado's belief that 'living isn't only about suffering, but also about causing suffering' (I) has no sexual connotations, for other male characters, however, pain is sexualized and death is the ultimate orgasm. The foregrounding of sadomasochism combines with the classical heroism of violence and the death wish to produce a dynamic that situates the plays clearly in the decadent era of Italian and European culture. With the eroticization of pain on the part of male characters who place themselves on the submissive side of the sadomasochistic relationhip, a complex and fascinating dimension to D'Annunzio's depiction of masculinity comes into play.

The cultural gendering of sadomasochistic positions places males and masculinity on the dominant, sadistic side, and females and femininity on the submissive, masochistic side. While role-swapping commonly takes place in the playing out of the sadomasochist dynamic in contexts of both hetero- and homosexuality, patriarchal power divisions inform the gendering of the respective sides. Given the fact that sadomasochistic fantasies manifest the 'pure culture' of domination, it is of particular interest to examine why D'Annunzio's male characters can be found to occupy both dominant and submissive positions, and sometimes even alternate between them (Marco in *La nave*) (Benjamin 1993, p. 52).[6] On the one hand, instances of male characters taking up the dominant position in relation to female characters accord with the traditional heroic, masculine desire for (sexual) conquest (Marco in *La nave* and Ippolito in *Fedra*). Heterosexual male characters who, by contrast, opt for the submissive role (Ruggero in *La gloria* and Glauro in *La nave*) would appear to go counter to this traditional heroic drive. On the other hand, the interpretation of sadomasochism that gives overriding control to the submissive position empowers the masochistic male characters with a different type of heroism. This latter reading would tally with the particularly decadent type of male character who is enthralled by violent, elemental passions, a worthy enthralment that takes him beyond the sphere of everyday banality, beyond 'good' and 'evil' and into the higher realm of heroism. Yet while male characters in the dominant position of sadism are portrayed as heroic, not all those who submit to women are positively depicted.

Several questions arise in this regard. What are the implications for masculinity in switching from one position to another (Marco in *La nave*)? What is at stake when the sexuality involved is not heterosexuality, but homosexuality, or at the very least, homoeroticism (as in *Le Martyre de Saint Sébastien*)? And what does it mean when the crowd, an invariably male collective, places itself in the masochistic position (*La nave*)? One approach to this complex area is to begin by considering D'Annunzio's portrayal of various types of sadomasochism as an exploration of the basic process of differentiation and recognition-seeking in male subjects. The Hegelian master–slave dynamic, which represents a philosophical deliberation on the nature of the self, here links up with the psychic process of the differentiation of the subject to provide one possible set of explanations.

In the quest for differentiation and recognition as a subject with a biologically-male and culturally-masculine identity, the path of co-operative mutuality through intersubjectivity is rejected. The collapse of paradoxical tension between oneness and otherness resolves into the confrontational duality of polarized opposites. This binarism functions by means of the dichotomy (rather than mutuality) of self vs other, an opposition evaluated in terms of idealization vs devaluation.

According to this theory of subjectivity, the plays can be seen to explore masculine differentiation from its (devalued) Other, by a continuing process of exorcizing the threat of oneness with the original, maternal 'crucible of femininity' (Benjamin 1993, p. 77). However, the process is not successfully completed (unless the murder, martyrdom and mutilation of female characters are read as the destructive component that seals differentiation). It is perhaps a token of the continuing quest for the desired differentiation and recognition, that masculinity is shown in the plays to be 'trying out' the submissive role, as well as its traditional one of dominance.[7] The submissive role is culturally associated with femininity. The female child continues to mother-identify, remaining merged with her, rather than seeking differentiation from her, and adopts her position of submissiveness as a path to recognition. As Benjamin explains, the dominant partner both bestows and receives recognition from the submissive partner. In the process of granting recognition to the dominant position, the submissive, feminine position also gains recognition vicariously (Benjamin 1993, p. 79).

Both positions are adopted by male characters. However, any allocation of the dominant role to memorably powerful female characters (Basiliola, Elena, Fedra) carries with it the privileging of the dominant over the submissive position. This is achieved by continuing the connotation of dominance as the *masculine* difference which is then idealized. These female characters are positively portrayed *in their virility*, namely in their possession of the masculine power to dominate. Nonetheless, important differences emerge in the way in which male and female characters take up these positions. Male characters appear to 'genuinely' occupy one side or other of the sadomasochistic divide, submitting, heroically or otherwise, to primeval forces that induce them either to dominate or to be enthralled. The female characters, on the other hand, are rational, wilful, and controlling in their adoption of both dominant and submissive roles, which they assume, rather than occupy in any genuine fashion (thereby recalling the fear of the threat of feminine *finzione* at work in the artful female characters in Goldoni's comedies). On a specifically dramatic level, the feminine pretence of taking up these positions and the switching of positions that these female characters also undertake, both signal the ritualistic dynamic at work in sadomasochism itself as performance.

The binary opposites described earlier in relation to patriarchal definitions of power and the resulting differentiation through sadomasochism, are present in the master–slave relationship of which sadomasochism is a model. While this differentiation takes place by means of dichotomy and polarization, processes that problematize femininity, their opposites, mutuality and interdependence, are actually implicit in and necessary to the binary function. Interdependence is the context within which opposites relate to each other. In this sense, D'Annunzio's exploration of masculinity takes place not simply in differentiation from but, rather, in relation to, femininity. Marco's definition in *La nave* of elements crucial to his existence in terms of Basiliola's 'bare face' and 'a naked sword' combines the feminine (a woman's face) with the masculine (his unsheathed sword). His eroticized definition effects a gender differentiation in its symbolization of masculine difference in the phallus, with the unsheathed sword as the instrument of aggressive domination placed not simply in opposition to the feminine-as-body, but at the same time, significantly, *in conjunction with* femininity. Masculinity in D'Annunzio's plays is very much tied in with femininity and it is with femininity that the following section concerns itself.

FANTASTIC FEMININITY

D'Annunzio's predominant dramatic version of femininity is fantastic both in the sense of being incredible and because it is the product of patriarchal fantasy. The particular type of fantasy in question is part of a western tradition dating back at least as far as ancient Greece, whose cultural constructions of femininity are also in evidence in D'Annunzio's plays in the overt use of classical mythological elements in both characterization and plot. In the context of nineteenth-century patriarchal fantasy literature, his construction of femininity shares many of its features with that of the *femme fatale*, especially as portrayed in the works of Gautier, a writer much liked by D'Annunzio. The *femme fatale* came to dominate the *fin de siècle* patriarchal imagination, and was to become a focal point of *film noir*, the cinematic crime thriller genre of the 1940s.

The *femme fatale* sets in motion a psychosexual dynamic of fear and desire in the male subject.[8] Elena, for example, is introduced in the stage directions of *La gloria* as both fascinating and odious (I, I), while Ruggero's initial reaction of terror at her appearance is soon complemented by the recognition that she has the power to tempt as well as destroy him. In *La nave*, the male collective responds to Basiliola with 'love and hate, horror and desire, scorn and marvel' (II), all variants of the classic fear–desire paradox. This paradox shows clear parallels with sadomasochism, with the fearing yet desiring male (Ruggero, Marco, Glauro) in the submissive position in relation to the dominant *femme fatale* (Elena and Basiliola). The combination of dread and longing for the *femme fatale*, who is both threatening and exciting, is a response to a female sexuality which is perceived as powerful and dangerous. The adjective '*fatale*' indicates the danger that this type of female sexuality poses for the desiring male. In the sadomasochistic play *La nave*, Basiliola inflicts suffering and death on willing male characters, and in *La gloria*, Ruggero's masochistic dependence on Elena contributes to his desire for death at her hands, all deaths that are eroticized along sadomasochistic lines. The passion of both Aligi and his father for Mila in *La figlia di Iorio* leads Aligi to commit patricide. Although he does so in order to prevent Mila being raped by his father, the fact that it is Mila who pays with her life by claiming she killed Lazzaro indicates that it is her sexuality that is ultimately held responsible. Meanwhile Lazzaro's violent intentions towards her receive no comment.

Interestingly, *femmes fatales* like Basiliola and Elena seem to possess little sexual desire of their own, functioning, rather, to incite male sexual desire which they then exploit as a weakness in order to further their own ambition. Female desire is very much in evidence in *Fedra*, on the other hand, and it is Fedra's unrequited passion for Ippolito that results in his death as the result of her false accusation of rape. The powerful female sexuality represented by the *femme fatale*, whether herself desiring or not, usually leads to her own demise as well as to that of the male character whom she has ensnared. This transgressive female sexuality is punished at the closure of the *femme fatale* text, which almost invariably shows her death, whether, in particularly damning ways, by murder at the hands of other women (as in *La Pisanelle*) or as the result of internalized patriarchal values that lead to self-inflicted death (Basiliola and Mila leap into the flames and Fedra takes poison). One important exception is Elena, who survives at the end of *La gloria* (possibly because she functions as an allegory for glory).

A crucial feature in the construction of the *femme fatale* and of female characters in general in D'Annunzio's plays is uncertainty regarding the sincerity of their sexual desire. While male characters are transparent in their desires and ambitions, female characters are often represented as enigmatic. Indeed, one of the aims of the male characters is frequently that of penetrating and understanding the mystery of femininity. Do powerful characters like Basiliola and Elena really desire Marco and Ruggero, or is it all a pretence? Ruggero describes Elena's

behaviour as 'false, artificial, fictitious, and bewildering' (IV, I). Ema in
La nave is similarly accused of pretence, masquerade and falsehood in
the context of her religious, rather than sexual, behaviour. In accordance with their master/sadist role, the will of these dominant women is
ultimately unfathomable by male characters in the slave/masochist
position. As Ruggero prepares to die at Elena's hands, he asks: 'But
who are you? who are you? I've never known you. I'll die at your hands,
without knowing you . . . Who are you? Before you kill me, tell me your
secret.' To his repetition of the question at the end of the play ('who are
you?'), Elena replies by stabbing him.

From the first, Elena has been a woman of mystery, with her voice on
entering the stage for the first time seeming to 'ring out in the remotest
mystery of existence'. Basiliola is similarly threatening in her unknowability, an adversary whom Marco, like Ruggero, asks: 'Do you love
me? Do you hate me? What do you have in store for me? But your kiss,
whether it's one of love or hate, is worth the whole world' (I). Basiliola
escapes death at his hands by capitalizing on her awareness of his fascination with the mystery she holds for him: 'I haven't yet told you my
secret. You don't yet know my plan' (I). Fedra too shares this mysterious
quality, her face described twice as flashing with stellar mystery, while
in the same play, Ippolito regrets Ipponoe's death in a description that
focusses on her secrets: 'the secrets of the fates were in her large, unshut
eyes' (II). Feminine mystique and secrecy confound male characters in
D'Annunzio's plays. In *La Gioconda*, Lucio sculpts a statue of the sphinx
in an attempt to know, while this age-old symbol of feminine unknow-
ableness also appears in Corrado's description, in *Più che l'amore*, of
Maria as custodian of the truth, 'a sphinx who has revealed the enigma
to me' (II).

The veiling of the truth by a femininity that plays with pretence
raises the issue of femininity itself as a masquerade (a concept discussed
in the context of cross-dressing in chapter two above). Femininity as
defined by patriarchy is a fiction, rather than deriving from a lived reality and its donning, like a mask, by female characters in D'Annunzio's
plays, conjures up the spectre of a temporary masquerade that
betokens the actual artificiality and contingency of femininity as a
patriarchal construct. In *La gloria* Elena's face is portrayed as in-
scrutably mask-like: 'her bloodless face has the immobility of a mask'
(II, I), and her masquerade is later described as monstrous in its ferocity
and avidity. In *La fiaccola*, this variant of assumed feminine identity is
contrasted with a delicate and vulnerable form of femininity. While the

face of Angizia, the mistress, is 'hard as a bronze mask' and 'horrible like an incubus', that of Monica, the mother, is quite the opposite: 'that tender face of hers, with that slender neck that seemed almost bluish, with all its veins' (III, 3). These two forms of femininity are of course in alignment with patriarchy's splitting of femininity into polarized opposites. However, what is also in play here is the fear that the false pretence of a threatening version of femininity can simply be assumed at will, unlike its more reassuring opposite.

Patriarchal femininity, unlike masculinity, is primarily located in the body, in the surface, a fact which makes possible its mas(k)erade. This is borne out in *La città morta* by Anna, whose inability to see her body (she is blind) means that she is detached from femininity itself. She attempts to access this femininity like a mask:

And how many times do I also press my face with my palms – this way, as I do now – to capture the imprint with the senses in my hands. Ah, sometimes I really felt as if I carried, pressed into my hands, my true mask, just like the one taken from corpses with plaster of paris (I, I).

But her attempt is unsuccessful: 'but it's an inert mask', and she remains detached from her femininity (until, that is, the sacrifice of a virgin's life, in the form of Bianca Maria, miraculously restores her sight). Together with the notion of the mask discussed by characters in the plays, the quintessentially dramatic wearing of a veil also contributes to the image of feminine mystery and secrecy. When Gioconda appears on stage in *La Gioconda*, she is veiled. She remains so throughout the play, her face unseen and unknown (a device that was to be repeated in Pirandello's play on the relativity of truth – or the unknowability of femininity – *Cosí è (se vi pare)*). Elena also first enters the stage veiled in *La gloria*, while beneath her veil a metal helmet is discernible as yet another layer, with contrasting gender implications, to be penetrated before reaching the 'real' woman (the female character, played by yet another woman, the actress). While serving to cover up the truth/femininity, the veil also has an erotic function, as in the case of Basiliola, whose long hair acts as a veil.

With its secrecy, mystery and ultimate unknowability, femininity goes beyond patriarchal definition and control. This excess is particularly manifested in the symbolic process of naming whereby patriarchy attempts to fix feminine identity. Some of the most powerful and threatening female characters in D'Annunzio's plays significantly have multiple names. This practice continues the traditional western culture of stereotypical feminine mutability, multiplicity and, ultimately, duplicity. D'Annunzio's Gioconda echoes Ariosto's Armida, in her turn a reconfiguration of Virgil's Dido, in her apparent ability to take on a thousand different guises (while Armida and Dido also had the power not just to emasculate, but to dehumanize by transforming men into beasts). For Lucio the sculptor, Gioconda's endless mutability is a mystery he will spend a lifetime trying to fathom, a mystery that is located in her body/femininity: 'A thousand statues, not one! She's always different, like a cloud that appears to you to change from one moment to the next without you seeing her change. Each movement of her body destroys one harmony only to create another one of even greater beauty' (II, I).

Like Gioconda, Elena in *La gloria* also has a literary precedent in the form of Helen of Troy, spurring men on with her deceptive, excessive desire that appears to push 'ever further, beyond all limits'. In *La nave*, Basiliola's multiple identities take the form of her supposed reincarnation of a list of notoriously sexual mytho-historical women (Bibli, Mirra, Pasife, Delilah, Jezebel, Hogla), a feminine lineage that defies patriarchal control:

> There's something in her, certainly, that is eternal
> and beyond fate and death
> and cannot be ruled by
> man. You believe you have struck at her lineage!
> She's in another league. (I)

Basiliola's identity poses problems for Marco, who cannot understand why she is also called Diona, a name that is constantly repeated in association with betrayal in the phrase 'Diona betrays all' chanted by the anti-Christians. For the Christian zealots, she has yet other names (Priscilla and Massimilla). Another *femme fatale*, the 'woman sinner' in *La Pisanelle*, is given a variety of names, while *La figlia di Iorio* attempts to contain Mila by identifying her with her father's name and restricting her to an exclusively filial capacity. The fact that Iorio is not even a character in the play, having died prior to its beginning, would seem to indicate control and containment to be the prime motive for this method of labelling Mila. While these types of naming betoken a fear of femininity as excessive and indomitable, they also represent an attempt to pin femininity down in the symbolic. That this method is insufficient is illustrated by the final containment of femininity through death in many of the plays.

While femininity is given much stage time by D'Annunzio, the nature of its representation requires close scrutiny. The plays undoubtedly fantasize about a powerfully excessive and unknowable femininity which is both threatening and desirable. However, there is also a focus on stereotypically feminine 'problems' such as ageing and sterility that is rather more straightforwardly hostile, while certain references to menstruation are overtly misogynist. Further clarification of D'Annunzio's fantastic portrayal of femininity requires attention to the basic patriarchal strategies of circumscription and control that inform his dramatic representations. These strategies can be identified in the fragmentation of femininity leading to false idealization and false problematization. It is important to bear in mind that these processes of idealization and problematization are false in the ideological sense of leading to false consciousness.[9] The fragmentation of femininity mirrors the polarizing of gender into dichotomous opposites imbued with value assumptions that idealize one side and problematize the other. The same pattern is repeated in the splitting of femininity into opposites, one superior and the other inferior. This splitting has great dramatic potential, in that each side of the dichotomy can be portrayed on stage in the form of a female character. The plays feature such opposites (madonna vs whore, angel vs monster) in confrontation with each other, like Silvia and Gioconda in *La Gioconda* and, representing a different variant of the dichotomy, Anna and Bianca Maria in *La città morta*. No such pairing exists as far as the male characters are concerned, where the relation tends to be that of contiguity in the form of bonding, rather than, in the case of femininity/the female characters, opposition shown as conflict.

Fragmentation of femininity has a long history, while its study as an ideological and cultural device is relatively recent. One of the oldest formulations is to be found in Christianity, with the Mary–Eve, or madonna–whore pairing. Female sexuality is the issue at stake in this division of femininity. The madonna represents the spiritual, non-sexual yet reproductive side (e.g. Silvia in *La Gioconda*). The whore epitomizes the carnal, sexual side (whether expressive of desire or 'instigating' desire in men), which is recreational and nonprocreational (Gioconda). Although the Mary–Eve pair forms the model for this enduring cultural dichotomy, it is of course the case in Christianity that Eve was the first mother, and that her original sin was that of desiring knowledge, not sex. Nevertheless, the Mary–Eve dichotomy continues to resound in the more familiar madonna–whore variant, and nowhere more loudly than in D'Annunzio's plays.

The madonna–whore split is fundamental to his dramatic fantasies of femininity, and forms the basis for his arrangement of attributes on opposite sides of the divide. Associated with the madonna side are spirituality, motherhood, domesticity and nurturing (Silvia, Maria), in opposition to the carnality, sterility and destructiveness of the whore (Gioconda, Gradinega, Basiliola, Elena, Pisanelle). While the former side is idealized and the latter problematized, it is the sexual side of femininity that attracts most attention in the plays, inspiring feelings of fear and desire in male characters. Linked to recurrent images of the Medusa, this *femme fatale* is in direct contrast with the nurturing, life-giving madonna, in that she is all-destroying, death-dealing, and of course has tremendous dramatic potential.

Idealization of femininity takes various forms, of which perhaps the most enduring is that of the essentialist, transhistorical Woman, a mother-earth figure associated with nature. Virginio describes his sister Maria in *Più che l'amore* as the human embodiment of earth's graces, an elevated position to which Maria objects. Her objection is not, however, to the idealization itself. Her brother's exaltation of her as his elemental 'water sister', and of her fresh, delicate simplicity signifying purity and harmony, embarrasses Maria because she is pregnant out of wedlock. Furthermore, behind the apparently high status endowed by idealization lies yet another fantasy, namely that of feminine powerlessness. The description in the stage directions of Maria as a victim shows how failure to comply with patriarchal law generates a discourse of female victimization through which patriarchy seeks to contain an errant femininity. At the same time, Maria is also moved from the positively-valued side of the essentialist Woman, with her nurturing, familial, domestic and above all, non-sexual, role, and over to the negatively-valued, sexual side. On the other hand, for Corrado, father of her illegitimate child rather than her male guardian, Maria retains her ideality, now taking on the significance of a divinity with all the powers of nature epitomized by her impending maternity. He tells Virginio, who has been rudely awakened from his fraternal fantasy of feminine domesticity, that a grander enterprise is now underway for Maria.

Idealization of the spiritual, angelic, madonna side of the dichotomy appears in *La Gioconda* in the form of religious mysticism, with Silvia described as being in a state of grace. As a result her husband, Lucio, 'holds in his hands a life of flame, an infinite force' (I, I). In other words, this idealization also serves a man's purpose. Silvia's religious fervour is matched both by her poor self-image regarding her femininity and by her self-abasement before Lucio. A prostrate image of the humble, domestic, maternal feminine, Silvia considers herself to be worthless; her idealized status is ultimately one of powerlessness. She may be the ideal spiritual madonna, but this does her no favours. In a grotesque scene of double female dismemberment, the statue of Gioconda falls on her, losing its arms and shearing off Silvia's hands in the process. She also fails to win back Lucio, who continues his liaison with the unideal, but compellingly sexual Gioconda.

Feminine powerlessness is disguised in the plays when female characters are placed in positions of apparent power. In *Più che l'amore*, Corrado says to Maria's brother: 'Neither I, with all the violence of my war, nor you with all your will to do good, can equal her power' (II). Despite this, however, Maria knows her place, and all the talk about her new-found potency through reproduction does not change the relations of power between herself and Corrado, as she herself tells him: 'It's I who belong to you; you don't belong to me. This is the agreement – I know. I accept it' (II). The dominant position into which she is apparently idealized is not that of power in her own right, but, rather, that of power behind the throne, as Corrado makes clear: 'You show me, in yourself, the greatness to which I was born' (II).

Elena, on the negative side of the feminine dichotomy in *La gloria*, also has the appearance of power. However, she too is not powerful in her own right, but manipulates men in positions of power. She is described as the arrow in Ruggero's bow, an instrument to be used by 'two virile hands', 'a formidable, shining weapon asking to be brandished in a fearless fist' (I, 3). Like Silvia and Maria, who are at the opposite patriarchal pole of femininity, Elena and Basiliola are used to draw out male masterfulness, while Basiliola's boast that women in her lineage create emperors begs the question 'why not empresses?'. Basiliola throws herself into the flames to escape a humiliating death, Silvia is mutilated, and Maria takes up a passive position in relation to Corrado. With Elena as the only one of these four superficially empowered female characters to escape some form of containment (possibly, as speculated earlier, because she is an allegory for glory), it appears that idealization carries with it few benefits.

Another false idealization that undermines femininity is to be observed in female characters who are positively portrayed on account of their virility. The masculinization of femininity as a route to patriarchal approval lays bare the workings of patriarchy that posit masculinity as the superior gender, with femininity as its (inferior) Other. In this way, femininity is idealized if it is a mirror-image of its opposite. In D'Annunzio's plays, this virile element is often described as discernible in the 'iron-like' appearance of the eye of the female character. Virginio tells Maria in *Più che l'amore*:

And that tiny constellation of iron in the iris gave me a sort of sense of security, as if it were a *virile* sign of your yielding grace . . . I sensed what was loyal, straight and faithful in you, what was *masculine* about the shape of your closed mouth. (I, italics added)

Mortella too is masculinized to heroic stature in *Il ferro*. She tells her brother: 'Whoever put me on this earth made a mistake! You're the one with the girl's spirit, and I have a *masculine* heart' (II, italics added). Her language is that of combat and recalls Marco's phallic 'naked sword' in *La nave*: 'But my thought is straighter than a naked blade, sharper than a knife' (II). She too is characterized by iron-like irises. Parisina is another female character who illustrates this self-reflective masculinity in her desire for combat. And, like Mortella, Basiliola's masculinity has emasculated the men in her family, who have been reduced to beggars. However, for a male character to be described as feminine is highly derogatory, as on the occasion when Tibaldo is accused of biting like a woman in *La fiaccola sotto il moggio*.

If femininity is undermined in an insidious fashion by the various processes of idealization, or apparent empowerment, attempts at disempowering the feminine are particularly evident in the way it is systematically problematized. Problematization, like idealization, is a false ideological process, in that it imbues natural, biological phenomena with sociocultural significance and values. The primary focus of negative evaluation on the sexual side of the feminine split is the female body itself. No longer idealized as the fecund embodiment of nature and as some sort of eternal essence, it is now the ageing decay of the female body and its sterility that are transformed into problems to be dwelt upon. In D'Annunzio's plays the sexual side of femininity is brought into line by the age-old *carpe diem* reminder that physical beauty is only temporary. Female sterility is represented as a particular failing (while male impotence remains unspoken).

Anna in *La città morta* tells the young Bianca Maria about a dream she has had in which her body ages suddenly. Her graphic description recounts each stage of this decomposition, and also works to ensure that she, as a female character, 'owns' the problem of ageing:

A sudden old age took over all my limbs; I felt the furrows of wrinkles all over my body; I felt my hair drop out and into my lap in great clumps, and my fingers caught up in them as in unravelled skeins; my gums emptied themselves and my damp lips stuck to them; and all of me became shapeless and wretched. (I, 1)

Gradinega looks anxiously in the mirror for signs of ageing in *Sogno d'un tramonto d'autunno*, a play that, like *La città morta* and *Fedra*, places older women in competition with younger women for men (Gradinega's rival is the young Pantea, for Anna it is the virginal Bianca Maria, and for Fedra it is Ipponoe). Mythology and ageism combine to produce a misogynist image of Elena's mother as a decrepit harpy (III, 3) in *La gloria*. Elena is accused of inciting a massacre of peasants in order to finance her mother's cosmetics and lovers. The link between ageism and sterility is made by Ruggero, who responds to Elena's remark that she would have liked to have borne him a son, with the taunt: 'you're sterile . . . you're sterile . . . you're sterile. All the old age in the world is in your womb. All you can produce is death' (v). On the whore/monster side of the madonna–whore, angel–monster division of femininity, the sexual woman whom Ruggero has desired cannot be associated with reproduction. The same patriarchal problematization of infertility is applied to Basiliola in *La nave*, while in *La città morta* sterility is classified by Anna together with blindness as an actual disability ('But the same Judge made me blind and sterile; in punishment for what crime, nurse?' III, 1).

As far as the tradition of the *femme fatale* is concerned, this fictitious female rarely produces children. More often than not, she is without any family at all, acting, if anything, as the destroyer of the family unit. In the stories of Gautier, characters like Arria Marcella and Clarimonde have no children. In the case of Clarimonde in *La Morte amoureuse* of 1834, her male lover interestingly becomes the child, as Clarimonde dresses Romuald and makes him dependent on her. As a vampire, she is also the mother who devours her child/lover. In this story, female desire is made to coincide with maternity in a way that plays out patriarchy's taboo on incest. This is mirrored by D'Annunzio's depiction of maternal sexuality in *Sogno d'un tramonto d'autunno*. Gradinega's desire is portrayed as threateningly vampiric, cannibalistic and predatory, as the following address to her absent young lover reveals:

Ah, what endless thirst and hunger I bore in all my veins for you, for your freshness! In my dreams I drank and ate your life, like one drinks wine and eats honey. I'd open up your living heart deep in your breast without making you suffer, and the drops of your blood were like pomegranate seeds to me. The taste of your blood was on your face when I kissed you in the dark, feeling the breath of death on the nape of my neck. (p.57)

It is portrayed as all the more alarming because her lover is younger than she is. However, it seems that this was a symbiotic relationship in which the lover fed from Gradinega, like a baby feeding from its mother. She continues: 'You nourished yourself on me as on a bunch of grapes; you satiated yourself on my sweetness up to the neck, up to the eyes' (p. 59). The fact that the young lover remains unnamed, and is thus fixed in an infantile, pre-symbolic state, further heightens his child-like nature. The type of symbiosis suggested by this episode provides the basis for recent theories of maternal sexuality (Hartsock 1983, p. 256). Indeed, Gradinega's description of this two-way nurturing sexual experience would seem to sit well with recent notions of breast-feeding as a 'reciprocal or symmetrical erotic activity that does not involve the infant alone, but also the mother' (Hartsock 1983, p. 257).

While this erotic interaction between mother and child is considered a positive experience for both individuals, it clearly comes uncomfortably close to violating patriarchy's incest taboo, as well as transgressing the stereotypical association of motherhood with asexuality.[10] In *Sogno d'un tramonto d'autunno*, it is this transgressive and threatening element that is foregrounded, with Gradinega's desire portrayed as terrifying in a play totally taken up with the portrayal of an ageing yet sexual femininity. At the root of the threat posed by maternal sexuality there is perhaps also the fear of the maternal 'prototype of the undifferentiated object' from which the male spends his life separating and distancing himself (Benjamin 1993, p. 77).

Other indications of patriarchal fears regarding not only the mother's desire, but female desire generally, make their appearance in D'Annunzio's plays in traditional, mythologized forms. The figure of the Medusa, for example, recurs as a symbol of destructive female desire. Once a beautiful goddess, Medusa was dehumanized and transformed by a jealous goddess into a gorgon, with snakes instead of hair and the power to turn to stone any man who beheld her. Many female characters in the plays are referred to as Medusa or as gorgon-like in their monstrous, destructive power: Elena in *La gloria*, Mortella in *Il ferro*, Fedra in *Fedra*, Angizia in *La fiaccola sotto il moggio*, Basiliola in *La nave*, and the animated statue of Venus in *La Pisanelle*. Another mythologized version of patriarchal fantasies of female sexuality that ensnares and destroys men is the Siren (Pantea in *Sogno d'un tramonto d'autunno*, Basiliola in *La nave* and, according to Goldoni in his address to the reader, Mirandolina in *La locandiera*).

Male characters become the prey of destructive female desire embodied in female characters such as Elena, who captured Ruggero in her 'snare'. Cosimo remarks that Lucio needs defending from Gioconda as from the enemy in *La Gioconda*, while another female character reinforces this imagery: 'But don't think that the enemy has laid down her arms. She won't abandon the field' (I, 2). While military imagery is also a topos of Petrarchan love poetry, in this play it is devoid of any positive amorous intent, with the stage directions describing Gioconda as bestial and homicidal. While Gioconda has 'armed' herself with charm, Basiliola's face becomes a weapon in *La nave* (II). Her dance with a naked sword in the same act resembles a Pyrrhic dance in the warlike intention it expresses, a violent, pagan, female sexuality that is counterposed to Mary's chant.

The violent destructiveness of female desire also disrupts and destroys the family and its domestic idyll. Maria's sexual act in *Più che l'amore* is fatal to the domestic sanctity of her brother's household, while the effect that Gioconda has on the Settala family in *La Gioconda* goes beyond simply luring away its male head, Lucio. As a result of the violent interchange between the two female characters, during which Silvia loses her hands, Gioconda is effectively held responsible for incapacitating Silvia in her maternal function. Much dramatic mileage is obtained from Silvia's despair at not being able to hold her young daughter, and the split between motherhood and female desire is starkly reinforced. When Mila, a type of rustic *femme fatale*, appears on the scene in *La figlia di Iorio*, she disrupts the wedding taking place between Aligi and Vienda. In the context of religious superstition, bad luck will befall the couple on account of the interruption, and because the wedding guests have not been able to unload their baskets of presents. Mila, in flight from a group of harvesters who want to rape her, finally makes her escape with Aligi. By taking the bridegroom with her, she prevents the formation of a new family unit. She is also portrayed as being responsible for the further destruction of Aligi's family, in that Aligi kills his father, the head of the family. With Aligi's arrest and imminent execution for patricide, his family (his mother and sisters) face destitution. In effect, Mila's arrival will have resulted not only in the prevention of the formation of a new family, but also in the destruction of the main family through the deaths of both its male members.

However, she takes Aligi's place to atone for Lazzaro's death and the family is saved. She has paid the price for the destructive effect not just of her own desire, but also for the desire she is held responsible for having elicited in other characters, who are exculpated.

In *La città morta*, it is the virginal Bianca Maria who comes between husband and wife. Bianca Maria is held responsible for both Alessandro's extra-marital passion for her, and for her brother's incestuous desires. Female responsibility is dramatized, as so often in D'Annunzio's plays, by a female death. Her murder at the hands of her brother functions, in his eyes, to preserve the sanctity of their particular family unit. At the same time, it restores to Anna both her sight and her husband. Bianca Maria's demise thus ensures, in very different ways, the survival of two different types of family. While Bianca Maria's sexual desire is still in its formative stages, it is described in terms of power as an imperious force. At the same time, it is also contained by the traditional feminine function of giving, rather than receiving, pleasure ('you're made to give pleasure') (I, 3).

Elsewhere in the plays, female desire is represented as carrying a high price, to the point when it is even criminalized. Ruggero tells Elena in *La gloria* that he has had to commit many crimes in order to be close to her. Her desire is excessive, going beyond all limits, involving murder and destruction along the lines of the whorish Sadeian woman.[11] Insatiability is a key feature in D'Annunzio's dramatic portrayal of female desire. Basiliola in *La nave* is described as monstrous libidinal matter with human eyes, while Fedra is afraid to kiss Ippolito for fear of destroying him in her insatiability: 'I don't dare kiss you for fear that my mouth will destroy you and still not be satiated' (II).

Often interlinked with female sexual desire is female material desire, once again a characteristic of the whore-side of Sade's split femininity. The *femme fatale* does not nurture, procreate and (re)produce, but, on the contrary, consumes. She functions as a metaphor for consumption in ways that are portrayed as parasitic, individualistic and depleting, and that place her in direct contrast with her nurturing, selfless, community-oriented, Madonna-like opposite. The *femme fatale* tempts men with material as well as sexual desires. Just as Gautier's Clarimonde lures Romuald, a young priest unaccustomed to luxury, to a (night)life of pleasures both sexual and material, so Basiliola incites Marco's desire for conquest and predatorial avidity with the same sort of combat imagery used to characterize sexual desire (I). The materialist temptations of characters like Basiliola, Elena, Fedra, and Pisanelle all work to reinforce the classic dichotomy between spirit and matter, a pair of opposites with gender associations that link masculinity with the superiority of the spirit, while femininity is linked to the baser, matter side of the divide.

Wealth and ornament are of course important theatrically, in that they provide dramatic pleasure of a visual nature in plays like *La nave*, *La gloria*, *Fedra* and *Sogno d'un tramonto d'autunno*, all featuring *femmes fatales* whose intense sexual desires are matched by high social status. Basiliola is a princess, Elena an empress, Fedra a queen, and Gradinega a *dogeressa*. The spectacle of their luxurious costumes and jewelry is, however, only part of the story. It is the female body itself that is the real source of dramatic spectacle, both on stage and by means of narration.[12] Of all D'Annunzio's female characters, Basiliola is the most exhibitionist actually on stage, notably in the second episode of *La nave*. Revealingly clad and with her breasts bejewelled, she brandishes a two-edged sword. Doubly dangerous as she performs her voluptuous, warlike dance, she embodies the dual patriarchal fantasy of fear and desire regarding female sexuality. The same fantasy lies behind the depiction of Mélisine in *La Pisanelle*. As a creature with a woman's naked torso and a writhing serpent's tail, she provides court entertainment in terms of the plot and, in terms of performance, spectacle for the theatre audience.

The female body reappears as spectacle in the following act, as Pisanelle is taken as booty from a captured pirate ship and displayed on the quay. Almost naked, and bound, she crouches on the ground, surrounded by jewels, coins, spices and precious cloth. The fact of being bound is not, however, sufficient to contain the power of female sexuality. If anything, she encapsulates the confident, controlling position of the masochist in an erotic patriarchal fantasy of domination and submission. She remains unmoved at her plight, not uttering a word and smiling to herself. The Prince's prostitutes deduce that she has not even shed a tear, as her eye makeup is still intact. In true *femme fatale* style, Pisanelle 'lures' men into trouble: as she crouches, bound and silent, a riot starts as the merchants take up weapons and fight for her possession. Fetishized fragmentation of the female body is added to spectacle in the lingering, head-to-toe description of Pisanelle by the Prince, who has arrived to quell the riot. He draws the attention of the onstage audience of merchants and the audience in the auditorium to the spectacle of bound female sexuality. In this way, the visual, theatrical spectacle of the female body is reinforced by reiteration on a verbal, narrative level.

The Prince's narrative accompaniment to the spectacle of the female body points to the high proportion of actual narration in the plays. (This in itself is perhaps not surprising when one remembers that D'Annunzio was primarily a writer of poetry and prose, rather than a playwright. Only one of his plays, *La figlia di Iorio*, ever became a theatrical success.) The Prince's narration also serves to illustrate the spectacularization of the female body in the plays not only in the direct, onstage form of exhibitionism, but also through the narration of exhibitionism that has taken place off stage. In this way, it enters the stage at one remove, as it were, and so with voyeuristic implications. In *Sogno d'un tramonto d'autunno*, Orseola narrates the erotic dance of Pantea at length to Gradinega and, of course, to the audience, which both listens to the narration and watches Gradinega's tortured, jealous reaction. In the description of Pantea's exhibitionism, female voyeurism enters the picture through Orseola as the narrator who has seen Pantea dance, and who is paid to tell what she saw: 'She showed herself to all those men, she threw herself before all those eyes as if into the flames, wearing only two little bejewelled wings' (p. 67). Unlike Basiliola, who dances on stage, Pantea's off-stage gyrations can be performed naked, thereby intensifying the voyeuristic eroticism of Orseola's account and her audience's vicarious experience of the event. Like Basiliola, Pantea also wears jewels, making her an embodiment of (female) sexual and material desire. The dynamic of female exhibitionism and voyeurism is set in the context of a play in which all characters are female, and which includes the fleeting staging of a lesbian relationship between two minor characters (Nerissa and Iacobella).

While male voyeurism is regarded as complementary to female exhibitionism, the latter is not, however, always performed deliberately for spectatorship, in the way that Basiliola and Pantea display their bodies both onstage, and offstage via narration. Ipponoe's naked dance on the sands in Ippolito's account in *Fedra* is motivated by female narcissism. The implication is that she dances for herself, believing herself to be alone and unobserved. However, hidden eyes are watching her, recuperating the female body for male desires only, in a true act of voyeurism. Basiliola, on the other hand, is in a position of complete control as regards her male spectators on stage, who begin a sexually masochistic dialogue that places her in the role of sadist. Her onstage exhibitionism involves the theatre audience directly as voyeuristic spectators in the sense that, as a theatrical character in the tradition of realism, Basiliola is 'unaware' of the audience as fourth wall. The actress playing Basiliola is, of course, aware of the audience, which is therefore not completely voyeuristic in relation to her. A double level of exhibitionism is also at work in that the actress-as-woman displays her own body as well as that of the character she is playing.

It is, notably, not only the female body that is involved in this dynamic of exhibitionism and voyeurism in D'Annunzio's plays. In *Fedra*, male nudity is described to a spellbound male onstage audience as Aedo gives an account of Ippolito's god-like body. He also recounts the reactions of the onlookers, while the Thebans, with 'burning eyes' and 'pale faces', watch him narrate. Ippolito is not dancing an erotic dance at this point, but is preparing to go into battle with his stallion in an episode denoting homoeroticism. Homoeroticism is also fore-grounded in *Le Martyre de Saint Sébastien*. In his martyrdom, Sébastien exposes his body on stage to his archers, placing himself in a masochis-tic position in relation to them: 'He who wounds me the deepest, loves me the deepest' (IV).[13] This contrasts with Basiliola, whose position is mostly aligned with that of the sadist, and who kills at the request of the desiring masochist. Sébastien is addressed by his archers as: 'Chief with the beautiful hair, your archers love you . . . You're beautiful, you're as beautiful as Adonis' (I). The reference to hair is a topos traditionally associated with female sexual beauty, and also occurs in the case of female characters, who are described as having flowing hair that is usu-ally red (Basiliola, Pantea, Fedra).[14] The female body, in effect, remains the main provider of spectacle on the D'Annunzian stage.

The focus of audience attention on female sexuality continues in a different, more indirect guise, when it takes the form of fetishization, as argued earlier in this chapter.[15] For Leonardo in *La città morta*, the larva of Cassandra has fetishistic importance, signalling the vestiges of a fem-ininity to which he simultaneously does, and does not, have access. Like the Wife in Pirandello's *L'uomo dal fiore in bocca*, femininity appears as a mere trace in *La gloria*. Of Elena's mother, Anna Comnena, only a face and a hand emerge between the curtains, an ageist parody of the fully visible, and also bejewelled, erotic Basiliola legitimately displaying her young body in *La nave*. In *La gloria*, on the contrary, the emphasis is on not seeing the female body, which is monstrous because it is ageing but still has desires:

One cannot see, between the red folds, anything other than her enormous, swollen, untidy face, beneath a sort of blondish wig; *One cannot see*, between the folds, anything other than a fat, pale hand with sparkling rings. (II, I, italics added)

Femininity is fetishized in the original anthropological sense by a female character in *Sogno d'un tramonto d'autunno*, as Gradinega is desperate to acquire a part of Pantea for the purposes of a spell that will destroy her younger rival:

> All my riches for a lock of your hair,
> for the hem of your vest, for a little part of you,
> for the slightest thing of yours, for a nail, a thread!
> All my gold, all my lands, all my houses for
> the person who brings me today a thread from your neckband! (p. 60)

The fetishization of femininity that takes place in D'Annunzio's plays can be aligned with the fear-and-desire reponse of male characters to female sexuality. The fetish is traditionally a sign of power which is not just revered, but also feared, and it is in this sense that it forms part of a representation of femininity in plays showing the female body at fault.

The strategy of patriarchy at this point is to bring various forms of containment to bear on femininity. This strategy is put into play by tactics of control through objectification, appropriation and, in the last resort, physical mutilation and annihilation. Objectification is particularly evident in two key areas. The first is that of the man-made woman, namely the woman-as-statue. The second takes the form of commodification of the female body, the workings of which were examined in chapter one. It could be argued that these types of objectification indicate both idealization and high evaluation of femininity respectively. However, neither of these does femininity any favours, at the very least interfering with its subjectivity and denying its autonomy.

The motif of the man-made woman has a longstanding tradition, and is encapsulated by the myth of Pygmalion in which the ivory replica of a statue of Venus is brought to life for a legendary king of Cyprus, for whom she epitomizes the ideal woman.[16] Patriarchal authorship of feminine identity is written into mainstream cultural production, and D'Annunzio's plays are no exception. Following the trajectory of author–sculptor–writer of femininity, the plays dramatize the man-made-woman. This is epitomized by Ruggero's quasi-rhetorical question to Elena in *La gloria*: 'Or have I myself made you and you are me?' (v). In *Il ferro* Mortella says to her mother about her father: 'he thought of you . . . as *his work* and his prize' (III, italics added), and *La Pisanelle* opens with the narration of a story about a statue of Venus that came to life.

The main play to concern itself with this form of objectification is *La*

Gioconda, which shows the sculptor, Lucio, attempting to master the secret of feminine sexuality in stone. His statue of the sphinx is based on his mistress, Gioconda, whose name recalls Da Vinci's enigmatic female portrait. When the statue falls on Silvia, she loses her hands, and the statue of Gioconda its arms, in a merging of woman and statue as a function of masculine creativity. The idea of the man-made woman is reinforced at the level of the props, which also include Verrocchio's statue of *La donna dal mazzolino*, with whose beautiful hands those of Silvia have been portentously compared by another sculptor, Lorenzo, in the opening scene of the play. At the beginning of the final act, the integrity of Verrocchio's statue is emphasized: the statue's beautiful hands are 'still intact' (p. 316), while Silvia's are not. This misogynist mutilation of femininity is extended, by implication, from the stage to real life, in the dedication of the play to 'Eleonora Duse of the beautiful hands'.

The woman-statue motif does not always, however, signify the idealization of femininity as perfected male creativity. There is a suggestion of alarming uncanniness in the resemblance between (animate) woman and (inanimate) statue in *La Pisanelle*, as Sire Huguet listens with a mixture of fear and delight to the story of the statue of Venus, goddess of love, come to life. The epitome of female sexuality, it/she kills Rinier's asexual wife (the latter is described as 'a bit simple and without breasts' (p. 613), and approaches him with vampiric intent: 'I want to gorge myself/on you, beautiful Pisan,/on your beautiful youth/and on your young blood' (p. 615)). With this particularly uncanny transition from the inanimate to the animate, the woman-statue variant of the objectification of female sexuality takes to an extreme the fearful side of the male fear-and-desire response to female sexuality. In its alignment with the uncanny, female sexuality is equated with the horrific on account of its sheer *Unheimlichkeit*, or unfamiliarity. In other words, what should be familiar (Woman), acquires extra features which make it appear the opposite; in addition, what should have remained secret (female desire) has been brought alarmingly to light (Freud 1962).

Objectification of femininity through the strategy of woman-as-statue slides into that of (racist) commodification of the female body, as a young black girl is discussed along with statues and other objects to be brought back to Italy by Cosimo as souvenirs in *La Gioconda*. Woman-as-gift features in *Fedra*, as a regal Theban virgin captured in battle is included in the presents offered to Fedra. In *La città morta*, Leonardo places the sister he has drowned among the artefacts he has excavated, where she will lie 'in glory' as one of his treasures. She is now idealized, objectified, commodified – and dead. The commodification of Bianca Maria's perfect/virgin body as a treasure is echoed in other plays, as female characters, both virginal and otherwise, are referred to, and treated as, merchandise.

Pisanelle's naked body becomes an object of barter, together with 'other' articles of booty in *La Pisanelle*, while Fedra describes her own 'thingness' as one of the war spoils captured by Theseus and placed with other objects: 'Not Theseus' woman,/but the despoiler's *thing* I was, placed/in the hold along with the tripods and the goatskin bottles' (II, italics added). Similarly, in *La gloria*, Elena tells of the shame of her own treatment as merchandise during the war, to which Cesare responds in the language of exchange: 'you've sold yourself once again, you've been . . . infected merchandise, a thing of gain' (II, I). In the plays, the female body is commodified in its recreational function through prostitution, and its reproductive capacity also appropriated. In *Più che l'amore*, Corrado's exultation in Maria's pregnancy expresses itself in his satisfaction that she now houses *his* spirit, *his* heroism and *his* victory. Maria's body is the bearer, the custodian, of Corrado's future. Motherhood, exalted and idealized, is commandeered into the service of patriarchal concerns.

Further to all these strategies of control, a more final solution is also played out. Death and mutilation of both female and male characters are much in evidence in the plays, in part because of the sadomasochistic tendencies of decadence and its fascination with aberrance in general. As has been shown, mutilation and fragmentation of the female body is fetishized, both as antefact (Anna's blindness in *La città morta*, the deaf-and-dumb women in *Le Martyre de Saint Sébastien*), or during the course of the play and actually on stage (Silvia's hands/the statue's arms, in *La Gioconda*). It is also brought on to the stage through narration, as in Leonardo's comment on Alessandro's liking for the deaf and dumb, and so powerless, Cassandra of myth. While mutilation of male characters also occurs, it does so for different reasons, and in a non-fetishistic manner. (In *La nave*, the motive is political, rather than sexual. Orso is blinded, according to Byzantine custom, as a punishment for treachery and for acting against the freedom of the people, while his sons are blinded as well as having their tongues taken out. In the same play Senza Pollice has acquired his nickname (Thumbless) after he has struck off his own thumb in an act of heroism.) Also of significance is the immediate cause of death. Of particular note is the fact that female, but not male, characters, die by fire in four plays.[17] Fire was the traditional method of dealing with what was portrayed as witchcraft, a variant of misogyny that translated the fear of female sexuality into religious dogma, and that receives overt mention in *Sogno d'un tramonto d'autunno* and *La figlia di Iorio*.

In the former play, Gradinega brings about Pantea's death by fire through spells, making use of a lock of Pantea's hair. The death of one female character at the hands of another raises the key issue of female collusion. Female collusion with patriarchy can be defined as the internalization of values that support the needs of a male-dominated society, even when these values go counter to the interests and well-being of women. One of the most insidious ways of reinforcing these values in theatre is to portray them as embodied by female characters on stage, whether directly, through word and deed, or indirectly through the narration of events that take place in the antefact or offstage. It is Gradinega who plans Pantea's death by fire; Fedra who stabs Ipponoe with a pin; the Queen who orders her female Nubian slaves to suffocate Pisanelle with roses while she is dancing; Gioconda whose collusion with Lucio culminates in Silvia being disabled; Ornella who abets Mila's suicide, in the full knowledge that it was her brother, and not Mila, who killed Lazzaro; and Angizia who murders Gigliola's mother, and whose murder is in turn plotted by Gigliola. This dynamic is particularly insidious in *La città morta*, when the murder of Bianca Maria has the 'miraculous' effect of restoring Anna's eyesight/femininity. The portrayal of one female character gaining at the expense of another strikes at the heart of female cooperation crucial to the successful countering of patriarchal strategies. It is the destruction of such cooperation that is, significantly, played out in this fantasy.

In the light of the plethora of female deaths, mutilation and fragmentation, how masterful can D'Annunzio's heroes be considered to be in relation to fantastic femininity? It is certainly the case that they employ strategies of dominance, containment and control, and play their part in maintaining a hierarchy in which masculinity predominates at the expense of femininity. Yet some male characters also appear to be engaged in inner conflict, while others are flawed by a physical or nervous disorder. While the patriarchal fantasy of femininity is explored and errant versions are ultimately either recuperated or destroyed, it cannot, however, be said that masculinity is portrayed as a monolith of dominant heroic fortitude and achievement. The tendency of D'Annunzio's plays (and novels) to portray male characters who desire heroic status but fail to achieve it may stem primarily from the fundamental fact that patriarchy itself is flawed. Just as femininity cannot be fully circumscribed and contained by a value system alien to its interests, so masculinity can never completely fulfil the role with which patriarchy seeks to identify it. Decadentism in many respects embodies this failed and unrealistic expectation of patriarchy. Characterized by a desire for plenitude that is never satisfied, decadence captures the fantasy world of the Imaginary, which not only cannot, but must not, be made Real. These hallmarks of decadentism play a crucial role in the particular inflection of patriarchy inscribing the portrayal of masterful masculinity and fantastic femininity in D'Annunzio's plays.

CHAPTER FIVE

Patriarchs and prodigals: the generation gap in Pirandello

One of the ways in which patriarchy problematizes femininity is through ageism in relation to the female body, a strategy evident in some of D'Annunzio's plays and noted in the previous chapter. While age as a male issue occasionally enters the D'Annunzian stage (Elena in *La gloria*, for instance, comments negatively on her ex-lover's advancing years), there is no particular emphasis on relations between older and younger male characters. There is, if anything, a recurrence of older female characters competing for men with younger female characters. In many of Pirandello's plays, on the other hand, relations between older and younger male characters provide a basis for the plot as well as a dynamic from which female characters are in one sense excluded, while in another sense they are vital to its maintenance. In contrast to femininity and ageism, with its focus on the ideally nubile, pre-menopausal body, cultural encoding of the link between heterosexual masculinity with age, while certainly not excluding sexual factors such as potency and attractiveness to women, is primarily based on considerations of economic power and concomitant social status.

The importance placed on economic and social factors in Pirandello's plays undoubtedly stems from the middle-class settings that tend to characterize them, in line with middle-class theatre and literature's perennial preoccupation with materialism. (There are some exceptions to this middle-class context, like the upper-class *Enrico IV* and a few peasant plays, although even in these plays socioeconomic factors play their part).[1] D'Annunzio's plays, on the other hand, either exclude or execrate the middle classes. His theatre plays out decadent fantasies in class settings that tend to be regal or upper-class, and in which wealth and private property are taken for granted as the norm. In terms of period, his settings are often mythic, historically-distanced, or even timeless. Such features of late nineteenth-century decadentism are not apparent in Pirandello's plays, although written roughly over the same period. In

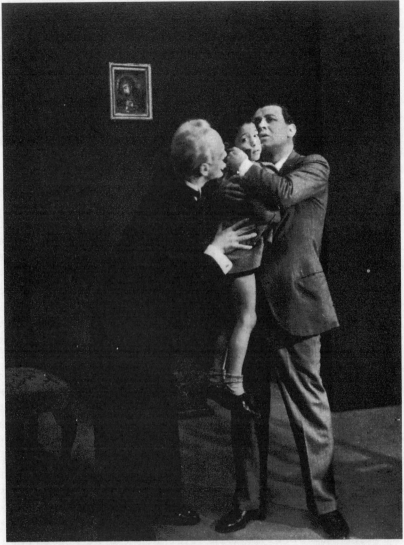

Plate 5. Masculine generations in Pirandello's *Pensaci, Giacomino*, 1935.

Pirandello a continuation of *verismo* can be perceived, with its emphasis on contemporary, everyday reality rather than the atemporal fantasies of the Imaginary in D'Annunzio's *vita ideale*.

This chapter focusses initially on age as a male issue, as revealed in the dynamics between older and younger male characters, and in relation to the socioeconomic context that informs them. This generation gap, with its associations of material wealth and sexuality, plays itself out in the arena of female sexuality in its specific relevance to patriarchal concerns. This is followed by a comparison of portrayals of the male and female generation gap. The terms 'patriarchs' and 'prodigals' are derived from the biblical topos signalling male generational difference. The fact that they signify much more than a mere age disparity already highlights the fact that cultural importance attached to age in men goes well beyond physical considerations, while the very word 'patriarchs' signals the high status accorded to older men within the ideology whose name they share. Some of Pirandello's plays underline the significance of male generational difference in that traditional associations of this difference inform the behaviour of his characters and the way the plot turns out.

One major factor determining the pattern of these social relations is the historical and cultural variant of patriarchy within which the plays were written. Pirandello's lifespan (1867–1936), with his first play written at the age of thirty-three and many of his plays based on earlier short stories, situates him more in the last century than in the current one. Importantly, the late nineteenth- and early twentieth-century Sicilian context with which he was familiar prioritized the age-old code of honour. This takes the form of a set of extreme and rigidly observed patriarchal rules defining relations between men as mediated by female sexuality and in terms of the institution of the family. The family, with the *pater familias* at the head of a hierarchy structured according to gender, age and concomitant access to economic resources, has long been the cornerstone of patriarchy, and nowhere more so than in Sicily. As Sciascia was to write in his novel *Il giorno della civetta* of 1960: 'The only institution in the Sicilian conscience that really counts, is the family . . . The family is the Sicilian state' (Sciascia 1987, p. 95). This family-based code of honour, and the predominance it accords to relations between men over those between men and women, is revealed as the primary concern of the cuckolded husband in Pirandello's first play, *La morsa*. Andrea believes that his wife's lover has stolen his honour, and makes him responsible for his wife's death when she commits suicide. In *L'innesto*, Giorgio's concern when his wife has been raped is with the insult carried out to his honour by the rapist: 'I am the husband . . . not even she can feel this horror more atrociously and more keenly . . . Do you know that my name is at stake here?' (I, 9; III, 4). He even considers killing her in order to obliterate the stain on his name.

This type of patriarchal preference for relations between men over those between men and women typifies what Sedgwick calls the process of 'homosociality': 'in any male-dominated society, there is a special relationship between male homosocial (*including* homosexual) desire and the structures for maintaining and transmitting patriarchal power' (Sedgwick 1985, p. 25). One of several indicators of the importance of relations between men within patriarchy is the emphasis on paternity, in other words, on *which* man is the father of the child (a child that, in Pirandello's plays, is always presumed prior to birth to be male). Similarly, Irigaray's term 'hom(m)osexuality' (spelt with a single 'm' to denote relations between men that are sexual, and with a double 'm' to denote those that are not), describes the relations that, while operating via heterosexuality, organize society according to the male perspective and to the exclusion of a genuine female one (Irigaray 1977, p. 168). One may wonder, in this context, where the dynamics of the male generation gap place female characters like Lillina in *Pensaci, Giacomino* and Melina in *O di uno o di nessuno*, both, significantly, unmarried mothers, and so particularly denied patriarchal legitimacy by their extra-familial maternity. In terms of the reproduction by one generation of the next, how important are maternity and motherhood in comparison with paternity and fatherhood in the plays? Does the thesis that patriarchal society allows for only one gendered voice, that of hom(m)osexuality or homosociality, open up new readings of these plays? How central is the interplay between older and younger male characters to the plot?

In this examination of relations between older and younger male characters, use of the term *generation gap* is extended beyond the area usually signified in sociological theory, which tends to treat intergenerational relationships of the kinship variety, namely familial relationships founded primarily on biological links. In this study it also includes relations that are not biological, but purely social (for example, Toti's social fatherhood in relation to Nini, the illegitimate child of Lillina, who becomes his wife in *Pensaci, Giacomino*). The term *generation gap* is also used to denote the interaction between non-related older and younger male characters (such as the older Toti and the younger Giacomino, Nini's biological father).

The point of studying the generation gap in this way is to shed light on gender as a social category with specific reference to that of age, and particularly to inter-age relations, as represented in Pirandello's plays. Like gender, age is a social category in that 'the significance of age is socially constructed . . . chronological age on its own is not deterministic; it is subject to social and cultural intervention at different times and different places' (Pilcher 1995, p. 3). Pilcher points out that even the method of measuring age is culturally specific:

In Western societies, the dating system and the numerical counting of age on which it is based, depend upon literacy, numeracy, and the techniques of science (Fortes 1984), and should be recognized as merely one way of conceptualizing time and of measuring age. In itself, then, counting age by reference to a numerical dating system is a social construction. It is a practice linked to specific conceptions of clock and calendar time in Western society, which came to be of increasing importance with the development of capitalism. (Pilcher 1995, p. 3)

Gender portrayal cannot be considered in isolation from that of age, a social category that is crucial in its inflection of other categories such as those of class and ethnicity, as well as that of gender. Interestingly, age is in some senses an even more complex category than that of gender by virtue of its inherent mutability. Pilcher comments on age as follows:

a further source of complexity is its transience as a social category (Babad, Birnbaum, and Benne, 1983). Every person ages, in both physiological and social terms. Moreover, these processes take place in societies where historical time marches on relentlessly. Other dimensions of social selves, such as 'race', sex, or even social class, remain much more constant throughout an individual's life. (Pilcher 1995, pp. 5–6)

Age clearly plays a crucial social role, and is frequently mentioned as an important factor in gender criticism. However, all too often there is no further development of this issue. Even as far as the sociological study of age is concerned, it is only over the last decade that attention has been focussed on this area to any significant degree.[2]

Of cardinal interest in this chapter is the playing out of generational difference in what has become known as the generation gap. The term *generation* is used in two ways. First, it denotes the cultural association of certain stereotypical characteristics and roles with particular stages in the life course. Second, it is also meant to imply historical and experiential difference between sets, or cohorts, of characters at different stages in the life course. A particular concern here is whether generational difference is portrayed by Pirandello in terms of conflict and/or cooperation. I have argued elsewhere that both conflict and cooperation are integral to male relationships in Pirandello's plays.[3] This chapter develops further those inter-male relationships that are also differentiated by generation, in the light of mounting theoretical interest in age as a social category.

Generational difference, or the generation gap, is of particular interest precisely because the dynamic of conflict is often assumed to be inherent, and is emphasized at the expense of cooperation. Mead's definition of the generation gap, for instance, assumes that relations between different generations are necessarily characterized by a difference in power, a hierarchizing of difference that implies conflict. This traditional, masculinist interpretation of power as necessarily conflictual, in that difference in power is made to tie in with, and signify, a difference in authority and interests, has been identified as only one of several possible interpretations. Power, as discussed in the previous chapter, can also be made to signify 'empowerment', or 'power with', rather than hierarchical 'power over', other social groups or individuals. In Mead's terms, this fixed, masculinist what might be termed 'imbalance of power', is taken to be a norm that becomes dislodged during a time of crisis (such as that experienced in the 1960s). She defines such dislodgement as follows:

a profound disturbance occurring in the relationship between the strong and the weak, the possessors and the dispossessed, the elder and the younger, and those who have knowledge and skill and those who lack them. The secure belief that those who knew had authority over those who did not has been shaken. (Mead 1978, p. 5)

This disturbance of the status quo of intergenerational power relations is to be seen in the light of what she defines as the 'small' generation gap that is a recurring feature in these relations mostly at points of change in circumstances. Examples she cites are the gap between rural parents and urban children, and that between 'the comfortable, pre-World War I, complacent world' and the post-war generation (Mead 1978, p. xvii). Intergenerational relations, she argues, are least disturbed in their imbalance of power when conditions are stable, and in cultures which are 'characteristically linked to their habitat', or which are able to transpose their traditions successfully to a different location if necessary (Mead 1978, p. 16). In these cultures, which Mead calls *postfigurative*, 'the children are reared so that the life of the parents and grandparents postfigures the course of their own lives. So reared, it is almost impossible to break away; a break means, inwardly as well as outwardly, such a change in the sense of identity and continuity that it is like a rebirth – rebirth into a new culture' (Mead 1978, pp. 22–3). She notes, moreover, that postfigurative culture is 'peculiarly generational' in that it 'depends upon the actual presence of three generations' (Mead 1978, p. 17). Some of Pirandello's plays appear to fit this postfigurative model, not least because of the presence of characters spanning three generations.[4] These plays will be dealt with in the next section.

Bearing in mind Mead's model, this chapter investigates whether the assumption of an intergenerational imbalance of power is reproduced in Pirandello's plays, and looks for indications of stability or disturbance in this power differential. Throughout this process, it is important to remain clear on the point of Pirandello's reproduction of the value assumptions of his culture in this regard, and not to be drawn into what Pilcher calls a 'necessarily asymmetrical approach' towards intergenerational relations, by automatically using the concept of generation in a divisive sense (namely, by opposing one generation, or cohort with the same life experience, against another) (Pilcher 1995, p. 133). Pilcher warns against ignoring 'the ways in which the apparent value consensus as to this state of affairs may reflect the interests of powerful and dominant groups within society, who find it advantageous to have age relations organised in such a way' (Pilcher 1995, p. 26). One might add that in patriarchal society it is assumed to be in the interests of the dominant male gender to exercise control over the means of production and reproduction, and, furthermore, that such control carries with it age-specific implications which differ in the case of each gender. Keeping this proviso in view, attention will focus on any imbalance of power, and how its stability or disturbance is defined in terms of age and gender, taking into account also the categories of class and family belonging. Of special importance are issues such as the centrality of the generation gap in relation both to the plot and to theatricality, and how generational difference is portrayed (overtly or covertly, as conflictual or cooperational).

In accordance with the interests of dominant power groups and in a western patriarchal, socioeconomic and cultural context, what all the intersecting categories of age, gender, class and ethnicity have in common is a socially-ordained hierarchical structure that dictates degrees of access to, or complete exclusion from, economic resources and corresponding social status. The degree of access is further determined by historical and political context, together with topographical factors such as a rural or urban location, and demographic features such as emigration, and stasis or mobility regarding habitat. These considerations provide the context for Pirandello's dramatic production, as well as for the dramatic, onstage scenario within which his characters are made to interact (for example, the nineteenth-century rural Sicilian location in which three generations of characters continue to live and work in *Liolà*, or, by contrast, which Maragrazia's son has abandoned for a new life in America in *L'altro figlio*).

The power differential that cuts across the categories of age, gender, class and ethnicity, given the predominance of the hierarchical 'power over', rather than the non-hierarchical 'empowerment with', interpretation and manifestation of power in social relations, can be distinguished on two levels. The first is that of structural, institutional inequalities within these intertwining, hierarchical categories, in terms of access to education, employment, citizenship and legal rights. The second is the cultural encoding of the age hierarchy in ways specific to the historical, political and topographical context, and in relation to the other social categories of gender, class and ethnicity. While elements from the first level enter the scene (for instance, the State-led withdrawal of access to employment and economic means in the case of Toti, the retired school-teacher in *Pensaci, Giacomino*), this study deals primarily with the second level, that of cultural production, in that the plays examined are a response to the meanings attributed to the age hierarchy by the play-wright's socioeconomic and cultural context.[5] This response is of course inflected by the particular genre (theatre) and mode (realism) used, and also involves the age-related topoi that are part of Pirandello's literary, dramatic and biblical heritage. The tradition of the age-specific love tri-angle consisting of the older husband, his younger wife and her younger lover, is reproduced in the *novelle* of Boccaccio and in the Renaissance comedies, while the biblical context offers the classic topos of the patri-arch and the prodigal.

Implicit in this pair of contrasting yet contiguous terms is, first, the hierarchical, or 'power over', familial relationship of father and son, with connotations of wisdom and foolishness, or conventionality and subver-siveness. Curtius outlines the classical old man–young man topos in terms of wisdom (Curtius 1973, pp. 98–101). However, the notion of prodigality traditionally associated with youth (as in the biblical story of the prodigal son) links the male generation gap with material concerns. In other words, the thrifty use and accumulation of wealth characterizes the older man, while its squandering and misuse is associated with youth. This hierarchical situation, in which the older man dominates in terms of wisdom and material wealth, is reversed in the context of the commonplace concern-ing difference in sexual potency. Old men are stereotypically perceived as dogged by impotence (Zio Simone), while a young man like Liolà fathers (male) children here, there and everywhere. Unfortunately for the patri-archs, the accumulation of wealth is accompanied by diminishing sexual returns; for young men, potency is not a problem, while finances fre-quently are. Sometimes, however, another variation of this stereotype emerges, in which the young man is not only the sexually dominant one, but is also wealthier than his older rival (this is the case in *Il berretto a sonagli* and *Ma non è una cosa seria*).

Regarding the relationship between patriarchs and prodigals, differ-ence within a hierarchical context may at first sight appear more conducive to competition than to cooperation. However, older and younger men are involved in a closed-circuit, all-male dynamic with each other. This dynamic, which some see as the defining feature of a patriarchally-ordered society, is predicated on material concerns and played out in the heterosexual arena. The relationship between patriarchs and prodigals is one of contrast and opposition in the context of an overriding bond of masculinity. It is this bond, which unifies despite internal conflict, that is patriarchy's strength. Patriarchy, the ideology reinforcing the hegemony of masculinity and males in society, rests on a fundamentally unified view of masculinity that, while admitting of certain differentials, such as that of the patriarch versus the prodigal, does not do so at the expense of the bond. What both older and younger men share is greater access to socio-economic power. This power is based on a series of interlocking factors: material wealth and control of the means of production, distribution and exchange, control of the means of reproduction through the ideological and cultural appropriation of women's bodies, access to education and its socially-privileged forms of knowledge, access to the professions and to political and legal decision-making, all reinforced, and indeed made possible, by the ideological underpinning of patriarchy.

The hold of patriarchy is contingent on its continued control, not only of the means of (re)production, but of the way in which femininity is defined, understood, and thence lived, in relation to the dominant gender. The splitting of femininity by variations of the madonna–whore dichotomy is a longstanding patriarchal strategy which, as shown in the previous two chapters, continues to inform western culture as an arche-typal stereotype. Splitting female images is categorized by Kleinian psycho-analysis as childlike behaviour in response to the mother (Press 1991, p. 209). However, Press (drawing on Irigaray) points out that 'the notion of splitting the mother-image into two dichotomous, good/bad parts has its origin in our cultural representations of women as extremely powerful and often evil, rather than in reality itself' (Press 1991, p. 209). This ideological, 'unreal', and culturally-reproduced dichotomy serves an attempt to divide and conquer a 'real', unified femininity, specifically and exclusively in re-lation to the concerns of patriarchal masculinity. There is, significantly, no masculine equivalent to the madonna–whore divide. The cultural oppo-sition between patriarchs and prodigals, while stereotypical, is by no means archetypally so. Moreover, it is not predicated exclusively on issues of sexuality, let alone issues of female sexuality, but is defined by the wield-ing of hierarchical power over others in terms of wealth, social status and knowledge.

The age differential inherent in the patriarch versus prodigal opposition does, of course, have strong ideological connotations of sexual impotence, which is feared as a consequence of ageing and of particular concern in a patrilineal context when a male heir has not yet been produced. However, in reality impotence is not necessarily related only to old age; it can strike at any time and for a variety of reasons. Nevertheless, in Pirandello's plays, as in western culture generally, it is exclusively associated with male senility. Female infertility, on the other hand, while inevitable with advancing age, features in the plays of Pirandello, as in those of D'Annunzio, as a possible problem for the pre-menopausal woman too (*La ragione degli altri*, and *Il beretto a sonagli*). Linked to this is the crucial dramatic consideration that while both older and younger male characters are major protagonists in the plays, not only is the status of the female protagonist *per se* debatable, that of the older/post-menopausal female character is one of existing very much on the margins.

PATRIARCHS AND PRODIGALS

Pirandello's plays deal with age and ageing as a male issue through a variety of relationships between older and younger male characters. Such pairings involve, first of all, non-related older and younger male characters, such as Ciampa and Fioríca in *Il beretto a sonagli*, and Zio Simone and Liolà in *Liolà*. It is the irony of the age-specific triangle in the latter play that this pair of male characters will become related as the drama unfolds, in that the younger Liolà cuckolds the older, impotent, Simone, thereby providing the wealthy and unsuspecting patriarch with a much-needed heir whom he will bring up as his own son. A second kind of pairing involves father–son dyads of different types: biological father–son pairs (Father and Son in *Sei personaggi in cerca d'autore*), social father–son pairs (Lello and the adopted Aldo, in *La Signora Morli, una e due*), or father and son-in-law pairs (Guglielmo and Leonardo in *La ragione degli altri*). The issue of male age also appears in a third variant that can be categorized as the older vs the younger self (Enrico's exploration, and attempted halting, of his own ageing process in *Enrico IV*, and Giuncano's similar preoccupation in *Diana e la Tuda*).

In all these pairings, the terms 'older' and 'younger' are used in preference to 'old' and 'young' in order to underline the relative, and relational, dimension of age. Rather than work with the dichotomous, fixed opposites of 'old' and 'young', the comparative terms 'older' and 'younger' allow more flexibility. As a general rule, the focus of this study is on generational, rather than simply numerical difference in age, with particular attention given to the presence of three generations and a correspondingly postfigurative culture as outlined above. The variants of the older–younger dynamic between male characters play themselves out in the areas of work, access to economic resources, possession of knowledge and exercise of reason (that archetypal and much privileged Pirandellian activity), the family (marriage, new family formation and issues of paternity) and female sexuality (competition for women, adultery and issues of virility). The male generation gap that works itself out in these various social spheres operates in the context of the particular class-belonging of the characters involved and in relation to their urban or rural setting.

Material wealth and sexuality are major issues defining the relationship between Zio Simone and Liolà in *Liolà*, one of the plays featuring an unrelated male pair, the first type of older–younger male relationship listed above. While the older Zio Simone is concerned with his material wealth and what he sees as his wife Mita's inability to produce heirs to inherit it, the younger Liolà busies himself in putting the latter situation to rights. The age difference between Zio Simone and Liolà, and their stereotypical association with impotence and super-potency, respectively, leads directly to the dramatization of one of patriarchy's nightmares. As Zia Croce says of Zio Simone: 'He's crying about his things; so many beautiful things that, at his death, would end up in other people's hands' (I). Linked to this is the unwitting bringing up by a man of means of 'the sons of other men' who will inherit his wealth (a phrase from Ariosto's *Orlando furioso*, which also deals with this dilemma).

Older masculinity is intrinsically linked to the possession of wealth and property in *Liolà*. Age alone is clearly not sufficient to empower Simone, who would be powerless without his farm. Pilcher's outline of the political economy perspective and exchange theory is relevant here. The political economy perspective argues that during later life and old age, as at any stage of the life course, access to societal resources, especially income from employment, is crucial in avoiding a position of structured dependency (Pilcher 1995, p. 104). Such a position is usually occupied by those at either end of the life course spectrum and often by women throughout their lives. This is at its most notable in a 'work society' where participation in the work force has great importance as an index of social worth. In terms of social relations based on exchange (a notion examined in chapter one), old age becomes impotent in direct relation to the decreasing ability to reciprocate or exchange (Pilcher 1995, p. 105). This inability stems not just from the limited physical resources which may bedevil old age and hinder the rendering of services, such as childcare, but, again, is contingent on restricted access to economic resources and the power deriving from such access. This contemporary position contrasts un-favourably with pre-industrial Europe, when 'participation in productive work roles, which, in modern societies, are largely associated with adult-hood, stretched over an entire lifetime' (Pilcher 1995, p. 83). As a result, old people were less likely to have experienced economic and social seg-regation (Pilcher 1995, p. 107).

It is this type of pre-industrial context which determines the power position of Simone in the rural *Liolà*, a position he maintains despite his advancing years. He does so in a setting that also allows for greater inte-gration of family life and work life than the urban contexts of many of Pirandello's other plays which focus, in the main, on families in crisis. In *Liolà*, families, albeit illegitimate, thrive. Moreover, Mead points out that while in the cofigurative culture typical of industrialized countries, society is based on a two-generational structure, a pre-industrial, post-figurative culture (such as that epitomized by *Liolà*) depends on the old retaining control of property, and therewith the power to sanction the behaviour of the young. While Simone has not lost control of his property, this potential situation is prefigured by his inability to father an heir. Producing (male) heirs is a sign of continued control over property, an intergenerational form of male control that is facilitated and serviced by a reproductive femininity.

Concern on the part of an older man for the production of an heir linked to real or feared impotence is of course not new to the twentieth century, with the situation of the wealthy but impotent older man marry-ing a younger wife who then takes a lover of her own age present in Boccaccio's *Decameron*, for example, in the story of Mona Sismonda (Day VII, Story 8). In the more distant past, in the Roman comedies as well as in those of the Renaissance, sons become prodigal with their fathers' wealth in their pursuit of young women, while on occasion fathers and sons com-pete for the same young woman (Machiavelli's *Clizia*). The older man, far from being venerated for his accumulated weath or wisdom, becomes a figure of ridicule in the sexual sphere as a result of what is seen as indeco-rous behaviour.

In *Liolà* Zio Simone is certainly the butt of ridicule. Yet he is also a dark, threatening figure. There are indications in the play that in his desper-ation to have an heir he has subjected Mita to domestic violence. Aunt Gesa's comment that this would not have happened if Mita had brothers to protect her illustrates only too well the all-male dynamic dominating relations (a dynamic similarly at work in D'Annunzio's *Più che l'amore*). The main players in *Liolà* are the older and younger male pair, playing ultimately for the stake of Simone's wealth by means of female bodies who are cajoled or beaten when they do not comply. This country comedy actually ends with an attempted knifing on the part of Tuzza, an impotent gesture of female frustration that is contemptuously dealt with by the hero, the play's young stud. While the play revolves around issues of virility and impotence, it also concerns itself very much with the lapse of control by third-age masculinity in favour of the younger Liolà, whose fathering of Simone's heir can be interpreted as a marker of his own rite of passage from youth to the prime stage of adulthood.

Liolà is the rustic version of a male generation gap between unrelated characters in a country setting where the patrimony lies in the land and its produce (in this case, grapes and almonds), a gap that is played out in urban surroundings in *Pensaci, Giacomino*. In this play the older man of seventy years, Professor Toti, takes in Lillina, a girl of sixteen who worked as a cleaner at his school, became pregnant by one of his young pupils, Giacomino, and was rejected by her family. Toti's marriage to Lillina is presented as a Pirandellian jibe by the individual against social convention. Toti aims to squeeze more money out of the State in the form of a longstanding pension for his young widow when he dies, as well as taking a poke at bourgeois convention by allowing Giacomino to visit Lillina in his home. However, a closer look at the relationship between the older Toti and the younger Giacomino reveals another strategy informing Toti's actions.

Toti's unexpected inheritance from his dead brother leads to an improvement in social status. Giacomino, on the other hand, is poor and unemployed, unless he agrees to accept help from the older, wealthier man. A conflict develops between them as Giacomino resists his positioning by Toti in this dependent and subordinate role. The cultural associations of the generation gap are visible here. The older man is wealthier but sexually inactive. The younger man, while in his sexual prime, has no money, job or family. Toti tries to lock Giacomino into the older man–younger man dynamic whereby he can dominate as the older of the two. 'Pensaci, Giacomino', he says towards the end. The title encapsulates much of the generation gap and its implications. The suffix -ino indicates Giacomino's youth, and he is told by the older man to think it over. In view of the fact that thinking is the prime activity of the Pirandellian hero, it becomes clear that this play is very much on the side of the older man.

By making Professor Toti the play's voice, *Pensaci, Giacomino* appears to argue implicitly against the decrease in social status resulting from the exclusion of the older, retired state employee from economic resources through employment. At the same time, the older man's actions ultimately act against the interests of the younger male character, who is also denied such access, but for different reasons that relate in part to his position in the age hierarchy. Giacomino is younger, at the other end of the age hierarchy, unemployed and, as an orphan, has no senior male relations to promote his interests. With Toti's paternalistic actions (making choices for the younger man without any real consultation), the two extremes of the age hierarchy compete, while at the same time occupying similar positions in relation to economic resources. Nonetheless, Toti has at least had employment, while Giacomino left Toti's school only to find himself unemployed. Pilcher's emphasis on the centrality of employment to the transition from one stage of the life course to another is relevant to the case of this young male character. She stresses the 'impact of unemployment on the two components of the transition to adulthood (transition from education to the labour market and the transition from family of origin to family of destination, or to some other form of independent household) and the consequences for the attainment of adult status and adult identities' (Pilcher 1995, p. 73).

Toti's rise in financial and social standing means that the older man is now in a position to 'help' the younger gain employment, while his own marriage to Lillina pre-empts any possibility of Giacomino, the biological father of her child, making the transition from family of origin to family of destination. This is portrayed in the play as a highly sensitive issue, with Giacomino's pride and honour in question, in an underlining of the male generation gap and its social and economic associations. As Toti informs Lillina: 'Giacomino will be there, I'm not saying he won't! But a position, in the eyes of the law, that he won't be able to give you, I'll have to be the one to do that' (I).

As far as Lillina herself is concerned, her point of view is never clarified. Weeping much, but saying little, she is portrayed as inarticulate, taciturn, emotional and ineffectual – in short, a victim. She, the actual mother, is not asked to think anything over, and appears as yet another Pirandellian *mater dolorosa*, the instinctual complement to masculinity's reason. Yet in terms of life course stages (rather than mere numerical age), Lillina has in fact reached adult status through her participation in the labour market as school cleaner. What is more, she has also reached adulthood in patriarchal terms by becoming a mother. Despite this, it is the dynamic of the male generation gap that structures the play, as indicated by the title's singling out of the central imperative spoken by the older to the younger man. On the surface, the play presents a subversive male protagonist who appears to go beyond society's regulations in his fight to retain a dominant power position, despite his advanced stage in the life course and its traditional implications of dependency and low status. At the same time, the play reinforces the predominance of relations between men over those between men and women, as well as over those between mother and child.

The outcome of another urban play portraying a relationship between unrelated older and younger male characters, *O di uno o di nessuno*, can also be interpreted in this way. This play depicts what seems at first sight to be an unusual set of events that are resolved in an unorthodox manner. Seen in the light of the male generation gap, however, the same stereotypical associations can be found. The female character, the unmarried mother Melina, is terminated in order to facilitate the organization of this ending, which concerns the fate of her newly-born son, by an all-male team. Tito and Carlino, one of whom is the father of Melina's child, are poorly-paid state-employed clerks who cannot afford to marry, while their involvement with each other also appears to preclude a transition from youth to adulthood through the formation of a new family. Their relationship illustrates, once again, the patriarchal prioritizing of relations between men over relations between men and women.

Two older male characters interact with the younger Tito and Carlino, namely Merletti and Signor Franzoni, with Franzoni, the *deus ex machina* privileged in terms of both class and age, appearing at the end of the play to become the social father of the child. Merletti, the lawyer who lodges in the same boarding house as Tito and Carlino, acts as their mentor throughout. In terms of career, Merletti is superior to Tito and Carlino, their position being conditioned by youth and lack of highly paid employment. While he also has the wisdom of age, the two young men appear foolish, a foolishness that fits the stereotype of the younger man in contrast with the older one, but that proves fatal for Melina. She is the mistress whom they share and all is well until she becomes pregnant but cannot tell them which of the two is the father. Tito and Carlino fall out, to be reunited only at Melina's death (caused not only by a weak heart but by *their* arguments over what should happen to the child).

Paternity, not maternity, is at the centre of this play, the title of which refers to the child, which must belong either to one man or to no one – least of all the mother. To smooth out the plot resolution, she is disposed of. The older, wealthier Signor Franzoni happens to have just lost his child in childbirth, and the logic of the play dictates that he and his wife should take in Tito/Carlino's baby. This is, of course, the logic of the all-male dynamic played out by the generation gap in all its implications. The older, wealthier man wins a *male* child and heir, a prize which neither Tito nor Carlino, despite the fact that one of them is the biological father, is entitled to according to the rules – they are young, poor and foolish. At the same time, this intergenerational, all-male dynamic excludes any female participation. Melina, the baby's biological mother, disappears from the plot on 'medical' grounds, while her baby's new social mother, Signora Franzoni, is similarly excluded from the action. She is portrayed as being in the process of recovering from the loss of her child at birth in a neighbouring villa offstage, and so outside the main action of the play.

In *Il berretto a sonagli*, another urban play dealing with an unrelated older–younger male pair, it is the older man, for a change, who loses out to the younger man in terms not just of sexual potency, but also of wealth. The older man is Ciampa, a clerk working for the younger and wealthier banker, Signor Fiorìca. This play focusses on the issues of age and career, and particularly on the effects of a reversal of traditional role and status on male sexuality. According to the stage directions, Ciampa is around forty-five years old, an age which he is portrayed as considering old. He blames his age, poverty and lack of good looks for the fact that his wife, who is younger than him, is having an affair with the young, wealthy and handsome Fiorìca. The generation gap creates a situation of conflict between the two men, complicated by the fact that the older man is the younger man's employee. Ciampa himself outlines all the implications of the particular type of generation gap in which he is involved, and the love triangle that results from it:

And how can you know, Madam, why someone . . . so often – let's say, *ugly, old, poor* – for the love of a woman who holds his heart tightly, as if in a vice, but who meanwhile doesn't make him say: – ouch! – who immediately prevents him from saying it with a kiss, so that this poor old man melts and becomes inebriated – how can you know, Madam, with what physical pain, with what suffering this old man is able to put himself down to the point of sharing the love of that woman with another man – *rich, young, handsome* – especially when this woman gives him the satisfaction of knowing that he's the boss and that things are done so that no-one notices? (III, 5, italics added)

Ciampa is clearly suffering as the loser in this particular generation game with his young boss. He also lives in a fool's paradise in that he gains satisfaction from the discretion with which his unfaithful wife pursues her affair – the empty, superficial blessing that she is abiding by the rules of social convention. This convention was of crucial importance in provincial Sicily of 1917. When Beatrice, Fioríca's wife, attempts to change the rules by making the affair public, Ciampa makes sure that it is she who ends up with the fool's cap, the *berretto a sonagli* destined for mad people. The absent young Fioríca, whose privileged position allows him to travel to the extent that he never puts in an appearance on stage, is thereby let off the hook in a plot that sees both conflict and cooperation between the two differently aged men. The accent is very much on sympathy for the predicament of the older man, a predicament solved through the use of reason (one bonus of older Pirandellian masculinity), and at the expense of femininity. Beatrice is enclosed in a mental asylum at the end of the play so that the all-male dynamic of generational conflict and cooperation, in which she has attempted to intervene, can resume its course.

In *Ma non è una cosa seria* there is a similar opposition between two unrelated male characters of different generations. The older, poorer Barranco concedes Gasparina to the younger, wealthier Speranza. Gasparina's attractions become irresistible when it transpires she is still a virgin, and the rivalry between Barranco and Speranza intensifies when Speranza decides to make his marriage to her 'serious' (in other words, he now wishes to consummate it). Interestingly, the delaying of marriage by Memmo (at thirty he is by no means in the first flush of youth) appears typical of the nineteenth- and early twentieth-century tendency to allow 'a wide spacing between the various elements of the transition to adulthood'. Jones and Wallace point to the mid-twentieth century as a time when spacing, particularly between leaving the parental home, marriage and birth of the first child, would narrow down (Pilcher 1995, p. 79). Memmo, like Cecé in *Cecé*, is not eager to marry, preferring to leave home and live alone. In the final stages of *Ma non è una cosa seria*, the two men argue it out while Gasparina stands by in a state of confusion, convulsion and on the verge of tears, with Memmo taking hold of her and shaking her in an act of possession. Once again, it seems that the generation gap, with its associations of material wealth and sexuality, plays itself out in the arena of female sexuality in its specific relevance to patriarchal concerns, while at the same time rendering mute the female point of view.

Unlike *Il berretto a sonagli* and *Pensaci, Giacomino*, both *Ma non è una cosa seria* and *Cecé* favour the 'handsome young man' over the 'old gentleman'. Both older male characters in the latter plays (Barranco and Squatriglia, respectively) are portrayed not only as less wealthy than their unrelated younger counterparts, but also as physically disadvantaged in some way. Barranco has a stammer, while Squatriglia has only one eye. Even taking this into account, there is no way in which the negative physical portrayal of older male characters matches that of older female characters in Pirandello's plays, a portrayal which, as will be seen later, is particularly virulent regarding the sexuality of these older women. The fact that Squatriglia shares his eye deformity with the hero of Pirandello's novel, *Il fu Mattia Pascal*, even points to a certain empathy on the part of the playwright with this character. The thirty-three year old Cecé, like Memmo, is delaying marriage and spends his time womanizing, using the older, less attractive Squatriglia as a pander in a trick played on a young prostitute, Nada (and recalling male trickery at female expense in the Renaissance comedies).

In *Il giuoco delle parti*, the respective ages of Leone, the estranged husband of Silia, and of her lover, are not made explicit. A recent production of the play interestingly assumed the husband to be older than the lover, with the former outwitting the latter in an exercise in reasoning and social role-playing (the game of roles of the title).[6] Reasoning powers, associated by Pirandello exclusively with male characters, also become a feature of older masculinity that dominates not just femininity, but also younger versions of masculinity. The younger Guido in this play is not simply outwitted, but meets his death as a result of being out-reasoned by Leone, thereby sharing his position of ingenuousness with Silia, his mistress.

The second type of pairing between older and younger male characters concerns, in the first instance, the biological father–son dyad. Remarkably few plays contain this particular type of older–younger man pairing; that is, pairs in which the son is at the youth or adult stage of his life course and thus old enough to form one half of the older–younger male pair. On the other hand, there are many instances of such pairs in which there is no familial relationship of any kind, whether biological or social. This tendency might appear surprising given the emphasis on the family in Sicily in particular, and within patriarchy generally. It may well be, of course, that while femininity is defined solely in relation to the family, this institution does not provide an exclusive context for the workings of masculinity, with its public rather than private face. In this case, the concerns of the male characters that predominate in Pirandello's plays, are more likely to be located outside, rather than exclusively within, a family scenario in general, and considerations of fatherhood in particular. It may also be the case that autobiographical considerations are at work here. Pirandello's relationship with his own father appears to have been problematic and unsatisfying (Giudice, 1963, p. 19). Another possibility is that Pirandello was simply not concerned with depicting successful father–son relationships, choosing instead to focus on problematic family situations which provided more complex, and so more dramatic, plot material.

This would not, however, explain why, on the other hand, there is no shortage of young male children in the plays. Children often exist as part of the plot even if they never appear on stage (Carluccio and Ninetto in *La morsa*, Didi and Federico in *Il dovere del medico*). It is remarkable, considering the fact that many of these young characters would be capable of at least some speech, that any stage appearance on their part is usually marked by silence (unless this can be attributed to theatrical caution in relation to child actors).[7] The end result is that they appear to act more as symbolic markers of their parents' reproductiveness than as characters in their own right. More precisely, the child characters in Pirandello's plays function to epitomize the primary creative power of paternity, while maternity plays only a secondary, nurturing role in reproduction.[8] Fanning's underlining of the primacy of paternity over maternity in Pirandello's plays would seem to offer another reason for the curious emphasis on male children, but not on older sons who are able to engage with their fathers on a more equal footing.[9] Paternity, as well as predominating over maternity in the plays, also appears to take precedence over actual fatherhood in the sense of a prolonged and more egalitarian relationship between father and son-as-youth/adult. It is noteworthy that the plays do not often focus on sons once they are reared beyond the dependent stage of childhood.

When a father–older son dyad does feature in a play, the relationship is often conflictual. This is the case in *Sei personaggi in cerca d'autore*. While the Father is verbose, the Son is taciturn and unresponsive, a tense dynamic that culminates in a physical fight on stage. Conflict between father and son is traditionally accepted as the norm and regarded as typifying intergenerational relations (a commonplace reiterated by Mead in her work on the generation gap), while a psychoanalytical subtext, in the form of the Oedipus complex, has long held sway as the psychic explanation for this and other familial dynamics. Despite poor relations between Father and Son, the play ends with both older and younger male characters remaining on stage together. Along with the Mother, they constitute the legitimate, nuclear family now purged of its illegitimate members, namely the Mother's three children by another man (the Little Girl and the Young Boy have died, and the Stepdaughter has run offstage). Father and Son remain bonded, however uncomfortably for each of them, by the family unit with which the play ends.

Self-interest and rancour characterize the attitude of the son towards the father in *Quando si è qualcuno*. While the nameless but famous Qualcuno (Somebody) enjoys the company of his new mistress and nephew, his own family, son Tito included, are portrayed as stifling his identity with their dependency on his fame and fortune. In the eyes of Qualcuno, his family prevents him from realizing his true self and recapturing his lost youthfulness (a process for which his mistress, Verrochia, is portrayed as indispensable). Tito is introduced unsympathetically by the stage directions as irritable and morose, and sets about orchestrating the ceremony that will endow him, as Qualcuno's heir, with the title of Count. Few words pass between father and son, with Tito bent on feathering his own nest through his father's success. At the end of the play, the father reluctantly relinquishes the new family he has recently acquired. In *Lazzaro*, Diego and his son Lucio do not speak to each other until Act III, after the father's miraculous recovery from an accident precipitated by his angry reaction at hearing that his son has given up his religious vocation. After a period of conflict, however, father and son are reunited by their faith.

A positive father–son relationship is, unusually, portrayed in *La Signora Morli, una e due*. Having abandoned his wife and young son, and emigrated to America on account of his debts, Ferrante's unexpected return years later marks the beginning of a strong bond with his son, Aldo, now eighteen years of age. Meanwhile it is made clear that the relationship between Aldo and Lello, his adoptive father, has not worked well. This latter relationship, one of the few examples of the social father–son pair in Pirandello's plays, is represented as unsuccessful precisely because Aldo is not Lello's biological son. As a result, Lello is reluctant for Aldo to be his heir. Biological fatherhood is idealized at the expense of social fatherhood in *La Signora Morli, una e due*. While this fits in with the stress on paternity in Pirandello's plays, it is nonetheless unusual to see a positive father–son relationship in which the son is no longer a child.

The emphasis in the plays remains predominantly on paternity and the early, dependent stage of male childhood. This tendency is reinforced by the centrality given to the related issue of potency, with impotence as the sign of declining manhood that accompanies the later life stage. The emphasis on paternity at the expense of maternity within patriarchal culture generally may represent the playing out of anxieties concerning the problematic nature of paternity. In this regard, Robbins identifies the 'inevitable failure of patriarchy – the Law binding the female Other – to live up to the impossible task for which it was instituted: maintaining the illusion of fixed paternity'. In a striking reversal of the classic ideological supremacy of (masculine) culture and the symbolic, over (feminine) nature and the material, Robbins pinpoints 'unsatisfiable paternal yearnings – unsatisfiable because of paternity's *merely* symbolic authenticity' (Robbins 1993, p. 138, italics added). Her observation that 'phallic, discursive potency is revealed as an inadequate substitute for the female reproductive power it must attempt to master', may help to explain the persistence with which patriarchal discourse attempts to colonize and appropriate this power of the Other that is so crucial to its concerns (Robbins 1993, p. 139).

Unrelated to issues of paternity, but linked to male competition for women, three plays in particular focus on the third and last variant of the depiction of age as a male issue, namely the older versus the younger self. Both *Diana e la Tuda* and *Enrico IV* feature a fatal rivalry between older and younger male characters. In addition, the plays also portray male fears of ageing, and feature the use of female characters who act as reflections of the desired younger male self. *Enrico IV* contains a particularly dramatic method of attempting to halt the ageing process. Not only does Enrico dye his hair (a practice condemned by Pirandello in the case of older women); he also chooses to remain locked in a fantasy world entered as the result of an accident in his youth (a fantasy that his class and wealth enable him to play out unhampered by any financial considerations). During the course of the play Enrico is confronted with Matilde, the object of his fantasies many years ago, and now also further along her own life course. She appears with her daughter Frida, the image of her mother in her youth and marking, for Enrico, the progression of the years. For the older Giuncano in *Diana e la Tuda*, the similarly aged Rosa, with whom he had an affair many years previously, also epitomizes his own advancing years.

In *Quando si è qualcuno*, one of Pirandello's last plays, written when he was sixty-six, the fifty-year-old Qualcuno, also a successful writer, is seen bemoaning the passing of his youth. He creates a young alter ego, Delago, as a pseudonym under which to continue writing, and much of the play revolves around the dilemma of characters who have mistaken Delago for a different, much younger, writer. The opening scene of the play shows two pictures of Qualcuno and Delago placed back to back on stage, with the latter picture depicting Qualcuno in his youth, in a dramatic visual depiction of two contrasting life-course stages. Female sexuality again serves to 'mirror' both older and younger male selves, as Qualcuno acquires a young mistress, Verrochia, who 'recognizes' the younger man still within him. Qualcuno's (older) wife and their children, on the other hand, are portrayed as tying him down to his numerical age. The sympathetic portrayal of the preoccupation of Qualcuno, Enrico, and Giuncano, with their advancing years, is not, however, reflected in Pirandello's treatment of older female characters.

THREE-GENERATIONAL PLAYS

This section concentrates on plays with three generations present in the plot (if not always on stage), corresponding to Mead's postfigurative culture discussed earlier. The term *third generation* is used throughout to refer to the oldest characters (grandfathers and grandmothers), with *second generation* referring to their sons and daughters, and *first generation* referring to their grandchildren. Both biological and social relationships between the generations are considered, as in the case of the previous section. In *La ragione degli altri*, for instance, the first generation is not biologically related to the third (Dina is the illegitimate child of Guglielmo's son-in-law, Leonardo). The play itself revolves around the distinction between biological and social motherhood, as Leonardo's wife, Elena, works towards the adoption of his daughter in order to reclaim Leonardo from his mistress, Dina's biological mother.

Pirandello's various dramatic portrayals of third-generation masculinity show both powerful, high-status male characters, and those who are not so powerful, in relation to younger male characters. However, it is the former type that can be seen to predominate. For example, Guglielmo Groa is a powerful third-age male character who dominates over his son-in-law, Leonardo, in *La ragione degli altri*. Guglielmo knows the newly-elected government minister personally, a fact that elicits respect and admiration in the newspaper office where Leonardo works. While the younger Leonardo is represented sympathetically, it is clear that his father-in-law is dominant, and not merely in terms of social status. It was Guglielmo who, in the antefact to the play, helped Leonardo out of financial trouble when the younger man's family hit on hard times, thereby also raising the older male character's status through economic channels. There is notably no third-generation female character, Guglielmo's wife having died in the antefact to the play.

In *Pensaci, Giacomino*, third-generation masculinity is seen to eclipse a much younger version of masculinity, particularly by forbidding the passage of the latter from one stage of the life course (youth) to the next (adulthood). While Toti becomes a social father to Nini through marriage, as far as life course progression is concerned, his position is, more accurately, that of social grandfatherhood. Like *La ragione degli altri*, this play offers a portrayal of a powerful third-generation male character. Interestingly, Toti is powerful despite the traditional withdrawal of access to the labour market which he experiences by forced retirement from the workplace (he is reluctant to end his career as a schoolteacher). This drop in status is deliberately obviated in plot terms by the sudden financial windfall that he receives in the form of an unexpected inheritance and as a result of which he becomes the most powerful shareholder in a bank. As in the case of Guglielmo in *La ragione degli altri*, Toti's economic situation is crucial in determining the degree of power and social status attributed to third-generation masculinity.

This becomes particularly clear when Toti's high status is compared with that of another third-generation male character in the play, namely Cinquemani, the old caretaker at Toti's school. Cinquemani's lower, working-class status is apparent in his obsequious behaviour, particularly towards the school director. He attempts to compensate for his lack of status by trying to maintain a position of power over his wife and daughter, who work as cleaners at the school. To Lillina he says: 'Order and obedience, by God! Back at home your mother's in charge; here at school I'm in charge' (I). However, he is thwarted in his attempt by both wife and daughter, his failure to assert any authority over them in the workplace providing a source of comedy. When Lillina's pregnancy is revealed, the Cinquemani grandparents-to-be erupt into a frenzy of physical violence towards their daughter and Giacomino. This scene, described in the stage directions as 'very violent', ends with Toti coming to Lillina's aid, a heroic rescue which he consolidates by removing her from her working-class context and promoting her to his own middle-class position by marriage.

The Cinquemani family becomes three-generational with the birth of Lillina's child, a biological three-generational family unit with an illegitimate new first generation. This is in contrast to the social, essentially three-generational family that Toti unconventionally creates by marrying the much younger Lillina in order to thwart the state's pension system, thereby also improving her social standing and legitimating her child. By not only allowing Giacomino to visit Lillina, but also using his new-found influence to find Giacomino employment, Toti offends the social conventions upheld by the working-class Cinquemani grandparents. In more ways than one, then, the unconventional, but middle-class, Toti, is the hero of *Pensaci, Giacomino*. The third-generation Cinque-mani, on the other hand, prove completely impotent in their attempts to influence events regarding their daughter, lacking both the economic and social status that enables their middle-class, third-generation son-in-law to dictate proceedings.

The picture is somewhat different in *Liolà*, as shown earlier. This rural play shows an older male character who, despite owning a farm and employing many of the other characters in the play, is not portrayed in quite so powerful a way as Toti and Groa. Zio Simone becomes a social father-to-be, or rather, as in the case of Toti, grandfather-to-be, to his young wife Mita's as yet unborn child by Liolà (the term *zio*, meaning 'uncle', is Sicilian usage for the third generation). The issue of patrilineality is fore-grounded in this rustic play, with its overt references to the ownership of land and the necessity for a male heir to continue the patriarchal line of property possession across the generations. Liolà epitomizes masculinity at its most 'virile', a position from which he can, moreover, infiltrate the patrilineal continuity of the older Simone's line with his own. Urban equivalents, like *La ragione degli altri* and *Pensaci, Giacomino*, show no such focus on patrilineality and the patrimony, nor do they revolve particularly around issues of virility and impotence.

Despite Simone's low-status role of cuckold in *Liolà*, he nevertheless retains a degree of dominance in the play, due to his ownership of land. The same cannot be said of Pirandello's third-generation female charac-ters, who are systematically represented as less powerful than their male counterparts. The topographical distinction between urban and rural contexts is once again of relevance here. Also significant is class differ-entiation within both urban and rural spheres, namely between urban working-class and middle-class characters (as in *Pensaci, Giacomino*), and between rural peasant and middle-class characters (examples of the rural middle class are Donna Fiorina Segni, a 'country lady' in *La vita che ti diedi*, and Sara in *Lazzaro*). Within the range of three-generational plays in which the third generation is represented by female characters, the status of older women, while almost invariably lower than that of older men, varies to some degree according to whether the setting is rural or urban. The rural, peasant context of *Liolà*, for example, while not affording the older female characters the same powerful position as that enjoyed by Zio Simone, at least allows them a respected and authoritative role in the community (as the term *zia*, or 'aunt', implies). Zia Ninfa, grandmother to Liolà's three young boys, speaks to Zio Simone as an equal, on one

important occasion confronting him and successfully preventing him
from taking Mita by force from her aunt's house, where she has taken
refuge. Zia Croce, the reluctant grandmother-to-be of her daughter's
future illegitimate child, is just as well respected, if not, in patriarchal
terms, as fortunate as Ninfa, whose son, by fathering three illegitimate
sons, is the hero of the community and of the play. Nonetheless, Zia
Croce, who is Simone's cousin, is seen in charge of the young peasant girls
shelling almonds in the first scene of the play, and again during the harvesting of the grapes towards the play's end. Moreover, these two older
female characters are not subjected to the combination of ageism and
sexism that repeatedly characterizes the portrayal of Pirandello's urban,
middle-class, third-generation *signore*.

In contrast to the two peasant grandmothers in *Liolà*, the portrayal of
the grandmother in *Il dovere del medico*, set in a southern town, is not particularly positive. With the description of Signora Meis as physically dis-
figured by her woes: 'her face . . . sharp, drawn and distorted by anguish
and pain . . . poor Signora, she's unrecognizable', life has taken its toll on
the body of this grandmother in a way that it is never seen to do in the case
of the male body in Pirandello's plays. This would seem to illustrate
Sontag's point that:

women do not simply have faces, as men do, they are identified with their faces
. . . A man lives through his face; it records the progressive stages of his life. In a
man's face lines are taken to be signs of character . . . A woman's character is
thought to be innate, static – not the product of her experience, her years, her
actions. A woman's face is prized in so far as it remains unchanged by (or conceals the traces of) her emotions, her physical risk-taking. (Sontag 1978, p. 78)

Not only has Signora Meis been recently widowed, but during the course
of the play she also tries unsuccessfully to persuade her daughter to leave
her husband, who has betrayed her with another woman and now lies
wounded after a suicide attempt. Signora Meis exits angrily from the play
before its climax, having failed to dissuade her daughter from resuming
relations with Tommaso.

In terms of the postfigurative culture of the play, she has been unable to
wield the authority associated with the third generation over the second
generation, despite her financially secure position. She leaves the stage to
resume her secondary, supportive role of childcare, returning home to
look after her daughter's two children, Didi and Federico, who have been
left in her charge. In dramatic terms, then, she has been unable to assert
any influence over the development of the plot, with her stage presence
diminishing in potency as the play proceeds. Female third-generational

authority over relatives of both second and first generations takes a different form in *Liolà*, where all three generations cohabit (Zia Ninfa, for instance, brings up her son's illegitimate children, and Zia Croce will doubtless help her daughter, with whom she lives, take care of her child when it is born). As a result of the cohabitation and working together of different generations in this rural play, intergenerational relations, while not always running smoothly, can at least be said to exist, with all three generations involved in each other's lives. Like Signora Meis in *Il dovere del medico*, Andrea's mother in *La morsa* also occupies the secondary dramatic role of taking care of her grandchildren in her own household while their father is away at work. She is not named and, unlike Signora Meis, never appears on stage (although the fact that relations with Giulia are poor would help to account for her non-appearance in her daughter-in-law's home, where the play is set). This third-generation female character occupies a very peripheral role, even in relation to the already subsidiary function of her counterpart in *Il dovere del medico*, with both urban grandmothers living in households separate from their children and grandchildren.

Despite the fact that there is no intergenerational cohabitation, *L'innesto* appears to depict more positive relations between the urban, middle-class Francesca Betti and her daughter, Laura, who is pregnant as the result of rape. This grandmother-to-be enjoys frequent stage presence during the first act, set in her daughter's marital home in Rome, where she supports her daughter in the face of her not very understanding son-in-law, Giorgio. Francesca is also on stage periodically during acts two and three, which are set in Giorgio's villa. However, the plot does not centre on the grandmother, but on the interaction between Laura and Giorgio. While Francesca's dramatic involvement is considerable initially, towards the end of the play Giorgio asks her to leave when she tries to intervene. Francesca waits in the wings for her daughter, who in the penultimate scene of the play decides to leave her husband and return to her mother. By contrast, relations with the second daughter, Giulietta, show evidence of the traditional generation gap, with Giulietta embarrassed by her mother's attitude towards her, which is summed up by the comment: 'I can't bear them, my dear Signora, girls these days, with all those airs and graces' (I, 1).

A similar embarrassment characterizes the interaction between third- and second-generation middle-class female characters near the beginning of *Questa sera si recita a soggetto*, as Signora Ignazia La Croce's four daughters, Mommina, Totina, Nenè and Dorina, in turn reprimand their mother for extolling their domestic virtues. Ignazia becomes a grandmother during the course of the play, as Mommina marries Verri in order to save the La Croce family from destitution after the death of its only male member, the father. Mommina gives birth to two girls who at a young age witness their father's acts of violence towards their mother. Ignazia continues to live in close contact with her three other daughters, having been unable to prevent Mommina's marriage to a man renowned for his violent jealousy. She cannot in the end protect Mommina from her son-in-law, who keeps her locked up and is responsible for her death. Ignazia's own financial position has been improved by Mommina's marriage, as well as by the successful singing career of Totina. The third-generation female character in this play returns to a position of economic security at the cost, first of all, of her daughter Mommina's life, and, secondly, at the expense of the family honour in terms of conventional views of the time which equated a singing career on the stage with prostitution.

The third-generation middle-class female character in *Il piacere dell'onestà* is also depicted as struggling against the sexual morality of the time with regard to the pregnancy of her daughter, Agata, as the result of an affair with a man separated from his wife. Signora Maddelena has considerable stage presence in terms of amount of actual appearance on stage. However, like Ignazia in *Questa sera si recita a soggetto* and Signora Meis in *La morsa*, her role is not a powerful one in terms of affecting plot movement. Neither she nor her daughter is involved in the negotiations that take place to salvage the family honour through marriage to a well-born stranger. As the male characters wheel and deal with Agata's future, mother and daughter take refuge in another room. Maddelena's middle-class role is one of economic stability; however, in dramatic terms her low status is linked to the status of women in society at the time, with the emphasis on her vulnerability and ultimate inability to save her daughter's 'honour' without the help of a team of male characters. Lastly, while two rural plays allow extensive stage presence to third-generation female characters (*La vita che ti diedi* and *L'altro figlio*), with the plot revolving around the figure of the grandmother in both plays, the focus, as will be seen shortly, is a negative one.

Within the urban setting characterizing many of Pirandello's plays, a class distinction must be made if the dramatic status of third-generation female characters is to be assessed correctly. Middle-class grandmothers, along with older female characters generally, are often negatively portrayed in terms of social, if not economic, status. The portrayal of a working-class grandmother like Marianna in *Pensaci, Giacomino*, on the other hand, has more in common with that of her rural, peasant counterpart in

Liolà, than with older, urban, middle-class *signore*. A crucial factor is that both rural peasant and urban working-class grandmothers in *Liolà* and *Pensaci, Giacomino*, respectively, are working. While this does not give them more economic power than the *signore* (who are better off financially even though they have probably never worked), they nonetheless acquire a more significant social identity. The identities of Marianna, Zia Croce and Zia Ninfa are consequently constructed, for the most part, around their working lives (and what they *do*), whilst those of the leisured *signore* remain fixed exclusively in their sexuality, and consequently in the body (and how they *look*). In relation to the former, it is, notably, in scenes related to their work that they achieve powerful dramatic status.

WOMEN AND AGE

Pirandello's portrayal of the generation gap involving older and younger versions of masculinity centres primarily on the relative capacities of these different generations for wielding power through access to material wealth and high social status. It also concerns itself with issues of male sexuality (most notably, impotence and 'virility'). By contrast, his treatment of female age and ageing plays itself out exclusively in relation to issues of female sexuality and the female body, and in concerns relating to the patriarchal emphasis placed on female reproductive power. In this context, the particular focal points are the onset of reproductive capacity with nubility, and the cessation of this capacity at some point during the menopause in later life. It is, notably, in the reproductive stage that the female body is considered to reach adulthood within patriarchy.[10]

Of strategic importance, but suppressed by the ideological and cultural focus on female sexuality and reproductivity, and to the exclusion of any other aspect of femininity, is the systematic denial of access to education, to the economic resources necessary for autonomy and to high social status in terms of empowerment. Instead, patriarchal culture foregrounds essentially disempowering idealizations that inform 'positive' images of femininity (the Virgin, the Madonna), while at the same time reinforcing condemnatory images of the other side of the man-made madonna–whore split, in other words, female sexuality and desire. In dramatic terms, in marked contrast to the older–younger male pairings, and indeed male relationships generally, dynamics between older and younger female characters remain peripheral, as do female relationships on the whole. Even a play such as *L'amica delle mogli*, whose title appears to promise a portrayal of the friendship between Marta and her married female friends, in the end centres on her romantic liaisons with male characters. Similarly, in *Così è (se vi pare)*, while the primary discursive power of the older male character, Laudisi, is placed in the limelight, older female characters merely play a supporting role. They fulfil the secondary supportive, nurturing function traditionally assigned to women, while their discourse is categorized as gossip. In this context, older female characters do not differ radically from their younger counterparts, whose discursive and reasoning faculties are often patronizingly underestimated (as in *Cecè*).

Theorizing about intergenerational relations is helpful in analysing the role of female sexuality within patriarchy. The survival of patriarchy through patrilineality, for instance, depends on the passing on of property and power from one male generation to the next, a process mediated by female reproductive power. This interlocks with the various stages of the life course within patriarchy, which involves progression from childhood through youth to the prime stage of adulthood and thence to old age. Of particular interest is the patriarchal strategy of blocking women's access to the economic resources necessary for autonomy and adulthood in such a way as to tie in with the similar subordination of children and the elderly. Adulthood is regarded as the prime stage in the life course, with higher social status than either preceding or subsequent life course stages. Old age, like childhood, does not carry prime, adult status, unless accompanied by some form of economic autonomy.

Sociological discussions of age and generation lead to the conclusion that women, like children and the elderly, are, through their exclusion from the workforce, similarly deprived of 'personhood, independence, and autonomy', in other words, the defining qualities of adulthood (Pilcher 1995, p. 84). 'Personhood in Western society', Hockey and James argue, 'is symbolized through ideas of autonomy, self-determination and choice' (Hockey and James 1993, p. 3). Age and generational difference link up with gender difference as far as the achieving of adulthood, or independent personhood through work, is concerned. As Pilcher comments, 'Children, young people, and the elderly emerged as dependent categories of persons (as did women), and so labour force participation became central to the attribution and withholding of personhood' (Pilcher 1995, p. 84). This is illustrated in *L'altro figlio*, a rural play dealing with disruptive emigration patterns that result in non-working, dependent and, by implication, low-status 'old people, *women*, and children' (p. 105, italics added) being left behind.

While Pirandello appears not to object to peasant and working-class women working, and accepts female domestic labour in the form of housekeepers and maids, his opposition to women occupying middle-class professions such as teaching, for example, is clear, and has been dealt with elsewhere.[11] In his article 'Feminismo' (1909), Pirandello rationalized his opposition to middle-class women working by idealizing domestic femininity and de-femininizing those women who choose to work. Pirandello's idealization typifies a cultural process that reinforces the institutional denial of entry by women into the public sphere of work and the consequent autonomy and social status available to working male adults. The survival of patriarchy, then, depends not only on patrilineality in terms of material property and institutionalized power, but also on the passing on of cultural property in the form of stereotyped precepts that help to maintain traditional power relations.

Another form taken by this type of ideological reinforcement is the process of infantilization of women and the elderly, a process that extends the asymmetrical power relation favouring adults over children to these other social categories.[12] Infantilization works by distancing non-adult life-course groups, or groups (like women) perceived as non-adult, from the adult stage by demoting them to the first and least powerful stage, that of childhood. Pilcher's following summary of Hockey and James on the infantilization of the elderly can also be applied to women:

Hockey and James argue that the ideological dominance of adulthood, its exclusive profile as the embodiment of concepts of independence and autonomy, is sustained through practices or strategies which operate to *distance* other groupings from it and its desirable qualities. One such practice identified by Hockey and James is the 'infantilization' of old and disabled people, where they are treated *as if they were children.* (Pilcher 1995, p. 87)

Infantilization finds expression in cultural production as well as in other types of social practice. The infantilization of women in particular at these levels allows, first, for the type of age control and surveillance in terms of space and time that characterize the treatment of children in the modern period, and, second, helps to ensure the restriction of femininity to patriarchally allotted spheres (such as reproduction) in domestic, private space.[13] Any notion of entry into adulthood for women is on the condition of motherhood. As Pilcher says, 'it has been suggested (Willis 1984) that whilst employment and a wage are important criteria of adulthood for men, motherhood is an important criterion of adulthood for women' (Pilcher 1995, p. 86).

Infantilization of female characters can be seen at work in the middle-class play *Il giuoco delle parti*. In this play, the married but childless Silia is referred to in childlike terms. Leone, her estranged husband, recalls how much he liked her singing voice, which he describes as that of a child: 'A dear little trilling voice, almost like a little girl's' (I, 3). It is not just her childlike voice that he finds congenial, but also the childlike nature which, unbeknown to Silia herself, provides a preferable alternative identity to that of the adult woman: 'Quite another, and she doesn't realize. A little girl who exists for a minute and sings, when she's absent from herself' (I, 3). Leone would have preferred Silia to remain at this infantilized stage, which he idealizes as: 'a dear, gracious way of being, that she could have, and doesn't' (I, 3). Silia's lover, Guido, copies Leone in the following scene: 'Ah, my dear!' he says to her, 'You seem like a little girl to me . . . can't you see that there's a crazy little girl inside you?' (I, 4). This amuses Silia, who has overheard Leone's words, and she playfully prolongs the metaphor of her infantilization until the end of the scene. However, a few scenes later she actually colludes with the process by reflecting Guido's words back to him in order to seduce him: 'I want to be your crazy little girl' (I, 6).

The adult male patronizing of Silia continues as Leone expresses his astonishment at her powers of comprehension, and is particularly evident in his use of the diminutive 'little head', in the first instance, and in his expression 'even she' in the second: 'Here's the miracle: in this *little head* that has been able to understand' (II, 3, italics added) and 'This is the game. *Even she* has understood that!' (II, 3, italics added). Stage directions further reinforce the infantilization of this female character. At one point she is described as speaking 'in an almost infantile way' (II, 3) and as clapping her hands in triumph when she thinks she has won a point in an argument. While Silia complains in the first scene about feeling imprisoned, and wanting financial and social autonomy ('rich . . . my own boss . . . free' (I, 1)), the rest of the play works against this possibility. One area in which it does so most effectively is precisely that of her infantilization.

As a married woman who is childless, she is already denied the adult status that motherhood ostensibly brings to womanhood within patriarchy. However, the idealization of motherhood does not bring with it the empowerment of women with true adult status. This is particularly evident as regards the mother's right of access to her own children in plays like *La morsa* and *O di uno o di nessuno*. In the former play, the husband's unilateral decision forbidding his wife ever to see their two young children again is made possible by the complete lack of power on the part of both mother and children. In this unequal power relationship dominated by the father, the mother is reduced to the same level of helplessness as her children. The play *O di uno o di nessuno* also marginalizes maternal rights, this time those of an unmarried mother over her child, in favour of (adult) male characters. In both plays the female characters are further written out by death (Anna in *La morsa* shoots herself, and Melina in *O di uno o di nessuno* dies of heart failure). The type of overt infantilization of childless female characters at work in *Il giuoco delle parti* also surfaces, if to a lesser degree, in *Ma non è una cosa seria* and *Diana e la Tuda*. *Ma non è una cosa seria* reiterates male approval of childlike femininity, with Memmo, like Leone in *Il giuoco delle parti*, fixated on the 'childlike mouth' of an ex-mistress (II, 3). In *Diana e la Tuda*, stage directions describe Tuda as having 'an almost infantile smile' (I, 1). As in the case of Silia in *Il giuoco delle parti*, this child-like quality is meant to enhance Tuda's sexual attractiveness, an enhancement that throws into sharp relief Sirio's rejection of Tuda as life incarnate, in favour of the artistic form that he seeks to derive from her.

Infantilized femininity is regarded as particularly attractive sexually, with the potency of this attraction lying in the increase in power differential that infantilization brings. The infantilization of femininity in these plays by Pirandello can be regarded as continuing the workings of patriarchy along its traditional trajectory of distancing femininity from the prime status of adulthood in the specific context of age as a social category. Infantilization provides one dimension to the denial of the rights of adulthood and personhood to childless female characters, while the prioritizing of paternity and fatherhood over maternity and motherhood in the plays serves the same function in the case of female characters who have borne children.

Emphasis on and attempted control of female reproductive power is part of patriarchal ideology of the woman-as-body. This follows the epistemological tradition traced throughout this work of binary opposites aligning the feminine with the body, matter, instinct, stasis and passivity, while the masculine is associated with the mind, form, reason, action and activity. The prime stage in a woman's life course is closely linked to her body, which must be young and fertile. As a result, the female body diminishes in cultural value with age, unlike the male body. Later on in the life course, ageing women are placed in a double-bind situation. While, on the one hand, only the young-looking female body is culturally acceptable, it is not permissible, on the other hand, for older women to attempt to maintain their position of acceptability by taking measures to retain their youthful looks. For Pirandello, such efforts provide the focus for particularly misogynist dramatization, a specific form of misogyny that combines sexism with ageism. The objects of Pirandello's most vehement outrage are the middle-class *signore*, into which category fall those female characters who try hardest to slow down their progression through the life course. His fascination with the ageing female body in decay also extends to the peasant class, despite the fact that no female peasant character in his plays shows concern about ageing. Sontag's comments on class difference in relation to ageing are of relevance here:

Aging also varies according to social class. Poor people look old much earlier in their lives than do rich people. But anxiety about aging is certainly more common, and more acute, among middle-class and rich women than among working-class women. Economically disadvantaged women in this society are more fatalistic about aging; they can't afford to fight the cosmetic battle as long or as tenaciously. Indeed, nothing so clearly indicates the fictional nature of this crisis than the fact that women who keep their youthful appearance the longest – women who lead unstrenuous, physically sheltered lives, who eat balanced meals, who can afford good medical care, who have few or no children – are those who feel the defeat of age most keenly. Aging is much more a social judgment than a biological eventuality. (Sontag 1978, p. 76)

Pirandello's interest in the ageing female body can be traced most productively by considering female characters in terms of class and work, as well as taking account of the way their attitude to the ageing process is portrayed. In his essay 'L'umorismo' (1908), Pirandello uses the example of his reaction to the sight of 'an old lady, her dyed hair oily with who knows what horrible pomade, ridiculously made-up and decked out in youthful clothes', to illustrate the difference between comedy and 'humourism'. His use of words like 'horrible', 'ridiculously' and 'decked out', coupled with the account of his reaction of laughter, are indicative of his attitude to attempts by older women to disguise the signs of ageing.

His analysis of the comic impression which the old lady has on him is that, instead of looking *like* an old lady (in other words, looking her age), she is '*contrary to* what a respectable old lady should be like' (Pirandello 1965, p. 127, italics added). Progression from the comic to the humouristic takes place when the perception of the contrary deepens into a feeling, and occurs as the result of an understanding of the old lady's motives. According to Pirandello, her motive is to retain the love of her younger husband. Underpinning this motive, however, is the fact that her denial of the ageing process is perfectly in accordance with the cultural convention that only the young female body is acceptable. Her behaviour, which is neither comic nor humouristic, is represented as such by means of this entrapment in the patriarchal double bind. This position results from the cultural encoding of ageing based on a double standard favouring the male gender, and combining sexism with ageism.

Ageing and the later stages of the life course have of course always been the butt of humour, not least as a result of the western perception of old age as a return to childhood. Ageist humour works in conjunction with the culturally-embedded process of infantilization of the aged, an insidious dynamic that is not present in Pirandello's plays.[14] Ageism and sexism can, however, be seen to combine in his plays to produce older female characters who are intended not only as sources of theatrical comedy, but who are also often virulently misogynist creations. In terms of class and working status, it is the leisured *signore* from both the urban and rural middle (and, in the case of *Enrico IV*, upper) class, together with a couple of *signore* working as landladies, who are represented as paying most attention to rejuvenating their appearance. These attempts are portrayed in a superficial manner, with varying degrees of derision that is at its most intense in relation to the leisured, *nouveau riche*, provincial middle class, and showing little 'humouristic' understanding of motive. There is no attempt to penetrate beneath the surface of this feminine behaviour, and Pirandello's portraits remain sketchy and repetitive.

The key word which recurs in stage directions regarding older female characters is the comic adjective *goffo*, or derivatives thereof, meaning 'odd', or 'awkward'. This word signals the comic intent of Pirandello in relation to the female ageing process and recurs particularly, but not exclusively, in the case of female characters from the provincial middle class. This trend continues into his last play, *I giganti della montagna*, begun in 1931 and left unfinished, in which La Sgricia is described as: 'a little old woman wearing a small bonnet, knotted *awkwardly* under her chin' (I, italics added). A progression can be traced in Pirandello's urban, middle-class plays, from the non-appearance on stage of the grandmother in *La morsa* (1898), to the patronizing but relatively benign description of Marta Marnis as 'poor old woman' in *Lumie di Sicilia* (1911), and the beginnings of a focus on the 'altered' female body, in the form of facial disfigurement through worry and age, of the grandmother, Signora Meis, in *Il dovere del medico* (1912), to the more overtly antipathetic portrayal of 'odd' older female characters in *Cosí è (se vi pare)* (1918). In this play, set among the provincial middle class, Signora Cini is described unsympathetically as: 'an *odd* old woman, full of greedy malice masked by an air of ingenuity' (I, 2, italics added). In the following act, she introduces her friend, Signora Nenni, whom the stage directions indicate as: 'an even *odder* old woman, and grimacing more than her' (II, 4, italics added).

Comedy is also the prime function of Zia Ernestina in *Come prima, meglio di prima* of 1920. This 'embittered, skinny old woman', her 'hair dyed with a horrible red pomade' (II), recalls the old lady in 'L'umorismo'. She has a fairly prominent stage presence, appearing for one half of the second act and most of act three (although taking a backseat during the final *dénouement* between Fulvia and Lidia). The type of comic relief which Zia Ernestina provides from the unfolding of serious events is always, however, at her own expense. Frequent stage directions ensure that she is constantly the butt of humour, rather than its deliberate initiator (as in the case of a Laudisi, for instance, or even Fulvia, whose foil she is in act two). While comical descriptions of Ernestina abate in act three, her function has by then already been established and a picture drawn, so that the audience laughs at, rather than with, this older female character.

Provincial-style age dissimulation, via cosmetics and clothing, is added to the comic awkwardness of the older woman with Signora Barbetti in *Tutto per bene* (1920), an urban play set in Rome: 'Mrs. Barbetti is sixty-three years old, but is all dyed and *oddly* decked out, like a rich provincial woman' (I, I, italics added). Two more older female characters from the provinces who are negatively portrayed in terms of both age and class, are the two sisters in *L'innesto* (1921), set both in Rome and the provinces. Signora Francesca is described in the stage directions as: 'a provincial old woman come into money, squeezed too tightly into an overly elegant dress that contrasts with her somewhat *awkward* air and way of speaking' (I, I, italics added). In view of Pirandello's ideas on comedy in his essay 'L'umorismo', his use of the concept of contrast is of particular interest here. Signora Francesca should stimulate laughter in the audience because she appears '*contrary to* what a respectable old lady should be like' (Pirandello 1965, p. 127, italics added). In other words, while her clothes are elegant, her manner is awkward (*goffa*, Pirandello's key comic word).

The fact that her clothes are also too tight signals that she is no longer as slim as she would like to believe (and as her culture requires her to be). Another recurring feature of Pirandello's older female characters is the fact that their figures have lost their shape. Signora Francesca's sister, Signora Nella, while elegantly dressed, also possesses a figure that is 'already ruined' by age. She forges on nevertheless (and mistakenly, in her creator's eyes), fancying herself to be still in good enough shape for a world that is no longer for her (I, I). The attempt to disguise the ageing, shapeless female body in fashionable clothes on the part of Donna Fiorina Segni, this time in the leisured rural middle-class setting of *La vita che ti diedi* (1924), is depicted with the usual comic idea of clumsiness, now combined with unreserved distaste for the degenerating body itself: 'a modest country Signora of around fifty years, she sports the latest fashions, which sit somewhat *oddly* on her old body shapeless with age' (I, italics added).

In comparison with the older female characters from the leisured urban and rural middle class, the efforts of the upper-class Marchioness Matilde to delay the ravages of time in *Enrico IV* are described less negatively, albeit still critically, in the stage directions. This may be because, at forty-five years of age, Matilde has only just, according to Pirandello, entered the age range at which the female body begins to degenerate: 'she's around forty-five years old, still beautiful and shapely, even though she repairs the inevitable ravages of age rather too obviously, with the use of violent, if wisely chosen, make-up, which gives her the proud head of a valkyrie' (I). Around seven years older than Matilde, at the age of fifty-two years, is Signora Maddalena in *Il piacere dell'onestà* (1918). This older female character from the leisured urban middle class is described approvingly in the notes preceding the play. She makes no attempt to appear younger and does not aspire to be sexual, which, Pirandello implies, would be inappropriate. No longer entitled to her own sexual passion, she 'passes it on' to her daughter, 'through whose eyes alone she sees'. In other words, she is the perfect older woman and asexual mother: 'fifty-two years; elegant, still beautiful, but resigned to her age; filled with passion for her daughter, through whose eyes only she sees'.

Maddalena is portrayed in positive terms because, unlike many other female characters of her age, she has relinquished her sexuality. Or rather, she has transferred it to her daughter, through whom she continues to live vicariously. The mother does not compete with the daughter in sexual terms in this play; indeed, Maddalena even encourages her daughter's affair with an unhappily married man, in her concern that, at twenty-seven years of age and still unmarried, Agata may never experience sexual passion. It is perhaps because of the mother's decision to nurture her daughter's desire, rather than her own, that the mother–daughter relationship in this play is portrayed as mutually sustaining. In *Enrico IV*, on the other hand, Matilde makes sure that her nineteen-year-old daughter, Frida, remains in her shadow. The mother's competitive sexual attitude to her daughter results in Frida being: 'saddened in the shadow in which her imperious and showy mother keeps her' (I). Matilde's behaviour elicits social disapproval, so that her daughter 'is also offended, in this shadow, by the idle gossip provoked by her mother, but not so much on her own account, as on her mother's' (I). The selfless attitude of the daughter, who is more concerned for her mother's reputation than for her own, indicates that Pirandello's sympathies lie with Frida, rather than with her mother.

Attempts by older female characters who are also mothers to retain their sexuality and remain physically attractive, are thus represented not only as undignified, but also as reprehensively damaging to the daughter. It is the younger daughter who should be allowed to enjoy the limelight, rather than being kept in the shadows by an 'inappropriately' sexual mother. *Come prima, meglio di prima* contains a particularly negative mother–daughter relationship that breaks down completely at the end of the play, when Livia realizes that Fulvia, the 'whore' with dyed hair who has moved in with her father and borne him a child, is her own long-lost mother. The play culminates with Livia fainting into her father's arms, while Fulvia makes a dramatic final exit with her new baby and an ex-lover. At the younger end of Pirandello's range of problematic older mothers (she is presumably in her mid to late thirties, as she met Silvio when she was eighteen, and Livia is now sixteen), it is, again, her overt sexuality that is made responsible for her daughter's unhappiness. Had Fulvia reappeared in Livia's life in the guise of the matronly Maddalena in *Il piacere dell'onestà*, for instance, then the mother–daughter dynamic would almost certainly been more positive.

Preceding the first appearance together of Fulvia and Livia in act two, and functioning almost as a portent of their catastrophic encounters, is a rather extreme, almost caricatural example of the bad, sexual mother and her victimized daughter in the first act. The widow Naccheri who, at fifty years of age, has a bony face with sunken eyes, tries various ways of appearing young, each more bizarre than the last. These include an elaborate wig, make-up that makes her face look like a painted death's head, and a youthful style of dress that makes her look absurdly slim:

Widow Naccheri, around fifty years, has a curious thick, wavy little wig, full of tiny curls on the forehead and tied up in a small net. Her thin, angular face with pale, lashless, sunken eyes, gives the impression of a mask, all white as it is with powder and *oddly* painted; but with the horrible effect of a death's head with make-up. She dresses youthfully, forcing her old body to look ridiculously slim and laughably shapely. (I, italics added)

That this grotesque and condemning portrait of a fifty-year-old female character, whose face is already like a fleshless skull, is meant to be a comic portrait, is indicated by the usual word 'oddly', as well as 'funny' and 'ridiculous'. Moreover, Naccheri is jealous of her twenty-eight-year-old daughter Giuditta, whom she treats badly and who is completely cowed by her.

Naccheri is not one of the leisured middle-class *signore*, but works as a landlady in a boarding-house. *Vestire gli ignudi* (1923) contains another 'painted' landlady, Signora Onoria, whose age and efforts to disguise it are negatively portrayed (she is 'squat, *odd*, painted and a gossip' (I, italics added)). Madama Pace in *Sei personaggi in cerca d'autore* (1921) is an example of an older female character whose work involves running a brothel. A more exotic character than the norm in Pirandello's plays (she is Spanish), Madama Pace nonetheless shares many negative features with other older female characters in that she has a painted face and dresses with an 'awkward' elegance. In the description of this character, comedy intertwines with ageism and sexism: 'an enormously fat witch, with a pompous woollen wig, coloured orange and flaming rose on one side, in the Spanish style; all painted, dressed with an *odd* elegance in gaudy red silk' (II, italics added).

The two landladies of *Come prima, meglio di prima* and *Vestire gli ignudi*, and the procuress in *Sei personaggi in cerca d'autore*, albeit all working women, can be said to operate in the domestic sphere, and are linked more with the private than with the public sector. Rosa's job in the newspaper office in *L'imbecille*, however, is a rare Pirandellian acknowledgment of the increasing presence of female labour in the part of the tertiary sector relating to office work.[15] While the description of her in the stage directions contains no reference to her covering up her age, the portrayal of the working, bespectacled Rosa links her masculinization and her unmarried state (*signorina*) with her advancing age, the latter reinforced by the choice of surname, Lavecchia (*la vecchia* means 'old woman'): 'Miss Rosa Lavecchia, around fifty years, red-haired, thin, bespectacled, dressed in an almost masculine manner' (p. 130). Zia Lena, an older female character in *Come tu mi vuoi*, does not attempt to disguise her age, but is portrayed as disguising her gender, with her 'strange' hair, horn-rimmed glasses, and dark clothes, all signalling the masculine. Masculinization of female characters in Pirandello's plays, as in his article 'Feminismo', is intended as a negative trait.

While both the working Rosa and the leisured Zia Lena are unusual older middle-class female characters in relation to many of the others in the plays, they are also hallmarked in terms of age. Relatively unmarked by comparison is the description, in *Come tu mi vuoi*, of Zio Salesio as 'a little old man' (already a more endearing term because it is in the diminutive form) who has dyed his hair and moustache. As in *Enrico IV*, *Il berretto a sonagli, Diana e la Tuda* and *Qualcuno si è qualcuno*, male anxiety about ageing is dealt with sympathetically. In the statement: 'Elegance is the first duty, and perhaps even martyrdom, of Uncle Salesio' (II), the 'task' of appearing elegant is a euphemism for the fear of ageing, and compassion for the 'little old man's' discomfort underlies the comic intent.

Portraits of older female characters, on the other hand, are frequently barbed with misogyny. The ageing female body, far from being considered 'inelegant', is treated with nothing short of loathing, whether or not its unfortunate owner is preoccupied with attempting to halt or disguise the process. This is the case in the often detailed descriptions in the stage directions (possibly in part as a throwback to the earlier, narrative matrix from which many of the plays are taken). It also surfaces verbally on stage in what male characters say about older women. The description in *L'uomo dal fiore in bocca* by the husband of his thirty-five-year-old wife reveals male disgust at the female body already in degeneration, even though this is attributed to her grief at her husband's cancer: 'she doesn't seem like a woman any more, more like a duster. Even her hair has turned permanently white, here on the temples; and she's barely thirty-five years old' (p. 133).

Another male character to express a combination of ageist and sexist sentiments is Virgodamo in *Ma non è una cosa seria*, with his comment: 'woman is terrible; especially at a certain age' (I, 1). In this play, work and female ageing are linked as the miraculous rejuvenation of a female character, Gasparina, takes place when she ceases to work as the landlady of a boarding house and becomes a lady of leisure after marrying Memmo Speranza. A similar process can be observed to take place in the rural play, *Lazzaro*, in this case as the result of a change in class status. Sara loses years in appearance when she abandons her position as leisured rural *signora* to take on that of a working peasant. The theme of rejuvenation, which dates from classical and mediaeval times, reinforces the patriarchal perception that young female bodies are highly prized, with the ageing female body as a particular focus of contempt and disgust. No equivalent exists in relation to the male body.[16]

While ageing middle- and upper-class female characters are often portrayed negatively in the plays, especially when they try to disguise their age, ageing peasant women, none of whom exhibit concern about ageing, also become the focus of scrutiny. The description of Maragrazia, a peasant woman of over seventy years of age in *L'altro figlio*, goes to great lengths to outline her wrinkled face, her sparse hair, and her appearance that resembles a pile of greasy rags (p. 101). The old male peasant, Jaco

Spina, on the other hand, is merely referred to as 'an old peasant'. Even younger peasant women in this play do not escape the playwright's concern with female ageing. La Gialluzza, who is only around thirty years old, is already experiencing a change in hair colour ('with hair, once blonde, now straw-like' (p. 101)).

Instances in which older female characters are not described at length, and whose age thus remains relatively unmarked, are often those characters belonging to the retinue of servants working in middle-class households. Like Jaco Spina, the 'old peasant', and Cinquemani, the 'old caretaker' in *Pensaci, Giacomino*, these female characters are to be found named in relation to the work they do; for example, the older Elisabetta in *La vita che ti diedi* is called 'the old nurse' (I), just as the older Giovanni in the same play is called 'the old gardener' (I). Fana in *Il berretto a sonagli* is similarly described in the list of characters simply as 'old servant'. It is also the case that neither of the two peasant grandmothers in *Liolà*, Zia Croce and Zia Ninfa, is described at all in terms of the body; and that the urban, working-class Marianna Cinquemani, who becomes a grandmother during the course of *Pensaci, Giacomino*, remains unmarked dramatically in terms of age.

Pirandello's plays show a markedly positive interest in older masculinity and its socioeconomic power, with many older male characters as major protagonists who influence plot development and enjoy a dominant stage presence. Many plots also hinge on the bonding yet competitive relationships between older and younger male protagonists, with some culminating in victory for the older side of the male generation gap. As regards older femininity, the plays reveal a negative fascination with the female ageing process, with particular focus brought to bear on the degenerating female body. Especially vilifying portraits characterize those women in the plays who attempt to halt or disguise the ageing process and who continue to consider themselves as sexual beings. Such vain presumption is sometimes linked to bad motherhood, as the older female character tries to eclipse her daughter, the younger and culturally more admissible version of herself, to the detriment of the daughter's personal development.

In terms of class, Pirandello's depiction of female ageing appears to embody the western situation in which middle-class women tend to be both more concerned about the ageing process and more able financially to try to compensate for it, than their poorer lower-class equivalents. The plays show a range of rejuvenating methods used by middle-class (and in the case of Matilde in *Enrico IV*, upper-class) female characters, none of which appear to have any effect other than actually drawing attention to the ageing process: wigs, make-up, tight clothes following the latest fashions for younger women. While peasant and working-class women are not depicted in the plays as trying to compensate for the ageing process, and so do not incur the most vicious portrayals of which Pirandello is capable, the plays nonetheless focus at times in microscopic detail on parts of the body ravaged by time. Defined exclusively in relation to their bodies, female characters in general, and older women in particular, are fixed by the plays in a patriarchal double-bind. While, as Sontag says, 'one of the norms of "femininity" in this society is being preoccupied with one's physical appearance', older female characters who exhibit such a preoccupation in the plays are regularly depicted by comedy laced with a combination of ageism and sexism (Sontag 1978, p. 79). This type of portrayal is entirely lacking in the case of older male characters. Any male ageing crisis is represented by comedy informed by understanding and sympathy.

Given the fact that men as well as women age, such unequal portrayal of the male and female ageing process is clearly the sign of an evaluation of ageing as a 'social judgment' rather than simply a 'biological eventuality' (Sontag 1978, p. 76). This is coupled with Pirandello's preference for the dynamics of the male, rather than the female, generation gap, as the foundation for dramatic action. By contrast, the female generation gap mostly takes to the stage in terms of dramatic appearance, rather than action; in other words, the focus is on how female characters *look*, rather than on what they *do*. We are back in the realms of the traditional perception of the actress always invariably playing herself *as a woman*. Yet at the same time, true to the circular reasoning informing patriarchal ideology, the woman-as-body is already always an actress: 'To be a woman is to be an actress. Being feminine is a kind of theater, with its appropriate costumes, decor, lighting, and stylized gestures' (Sontag 1978, pp. 76–7).

CHAPTER SIX

Centre stage: Franca Rame's female parts

In contrast to the marginalized position of female characters waiting in the wings in Renaissance comedy, female parts in the plays of Franca Rame are placed firmly centre stage. Nowhere is the feminine point of view more clearly expressed than in the one-woman satires, both those written by Rame herself and those written in collaboration with Dario Fo. Foregrounding the feminine perspective in these plays is achieved partly, on the formal level, by the fact that the female character is not, as is usually the case, competing for audience attention with other characters, who, in mainstream theatre, are predominantly male. Of course, sole occupation of the stage by a female character would not, in itself, be enough to privilege a genuinely feminine viewpoint. The norm, as the previous chapters have shown, is for the female character to be constructed in such a way as to merely reiterate and reproduce Other subjectivities. To place her alone on stage could quite possibly even augment the recuperative effectiveness of her reiteration. As it happens, female monologues and soliloquies, along with active female protagonism, have tended to be outweighed by those of male characters, as has also been observed.

What differentiates the female characterizations of Franca Rame is their overt critique of femininity as defined and circumscribed within patriarchy. This is in marked contrast to the predominantly *covert* means used by patriarchal ideology to contain femininity in plays such as those examined in the previous chapters. The aim of Rame's plays is to unmask traditional assumptions concerning gender relations in a fundamental set of mostly everyday social spheres (sexuality, work and the family), spheres whose interaction is inflected by historical, political and socioeconomic issues. Rame's critique is frequently made pleasurable, and so more penetrating, by the comic genre which expresses it; and it is on her comic, rather than her 'obscenely tragic', female parts that this chapter concentrates.[1]

Plate 6. In control of her image: contemporary femininity and modern technology in
Una giornata qualunque, 1986, with Franca Rame as Giulia.

The key questions to be asked are, how effective a critique is achieved
in Rame's plays, and how much of patriarchy still remains inscribed
within the dramatic fabric? In addressing these questions, a number of
issues need to be explored, such as who, or what, exactly is now centre
stage, given the current debate not just about female subjectivity, but
also postmodernism's fragmentation, and even denial, of the 'subject'
itself. In what ways do Rame's plays reflect the contemporary context
within which gender relations work today? How are gender relations
portrayed differently from the ways they were in the preceding eras and
dramatists examined, in terms of both thematic and formal dramatic
areas? Can a progression be traced that situates Rame's plays as the culmination of an evolution of female characterization from stage absence,
marginalization, problematization, antagonism and reactivism, to a
position of dramatic centrality as protagonist with a proactive role corresponding to that of central male characters? Or would it in fact be
unrealistic to expect a complete revolutionizing of earlier dramatic representations of femininity, given that patriarchy still holds sway, albeit
in a more complex, technological world (such as that portrayed in *Una
giornata qualunque* and *La donna grassa*)? In any case, how could one expect
this different portrayal of femininity, which would also have to be a
portrayal of a different femininity, to function on stage?

The first step towards the creation of genuine dramatic female protagonism might be to deconstruct traditional female characterization
in order to reconstruct a more authentic feminine version (a process
rather akin to that of *autocoscienza*, the equivalent in the Italian women's
movement of American 'consciousness raising', but with the additional
element of 'self reconstruction'). The stereotypical female character
would then be displaced by an alternative, more proactive version that
would function differently in both formal and thematic aspects to its
patriarchally constructed, and constricted, counterpart. The dramatic
criteria set up in the first chapter on Renaissance comedy can be enlist-
ed here as a yardstick for female characterization. It will be remembered that the first requirement for dramatic female protagonism is
freedom of stage movement, without being hampered, marginalized or
even completely excluded, because of the sociodramatic constraints of
time and place based on age, class and marital status (of female, but not
male, characters).

Secondly, in the realm of dramatic action, direct involvement and
agency in plot development are crucial, while the plot should be of relevance to the lives of women themselves, rather than women exclusively in
relation to male interests. Most importantly, the unfolding of the plot and
the development of its issues should be seen from an authentic feminine
viewpoint, rather than from that of the idealized or demonized female
character of patriarchal fantasy. Of course, 'authentic' feminine subjectivity, as will shortly be seen, is not so easy to delineate as might at first
sight appear. Nonetheless, making female protagonists representative of
women of all ages, for example, in place of patriarchy's dramatic focus on
the reproductive phase of the female life cycle, would certainly be a step
in the direction of broadening the spectrum of femininity portrayed. In
conjunction with this notion of a female voice, the third dramatic component, that of speech, should allow female characters to speak for themselves, rather than have their thoughts ventriloquized by male characters
(let alone be replaced and caricatured by vestiges and fetishes of femininity in the form of male cross-dressing). As regards speech vehicles, the
female protagonist should be allocated across the full range of the dramatic speech hierarchy (prologue, monologue, soliloquy, aside, dialogue,
polylogue), irrespective, once again, of her age, class and marital status.[2]

Franca Rame's female parts appear in many ways to work in diametric opposition to traditional female characters. Her female parts have
freedom of stage movement, are involved in plots based on issues relevant to women's lives, and speak for themselves. Indeed, her at times
complex performance technique means that her female characters on

occasion even 'speak for' male characters (as well as other female characters). It remains to be seen whether her female parts nevertheless
still function along patriarchal guidelines, particularly in the type of
women's lives they represent. Bearing in mind the three basic dramatic
criteria, this chapter attempts to pinpoint areas of adherence to patriarchal dramatization of femininity, and areas in which the stereotype is
subverted.

The term *female parts* is used to indicate not merely the female characters created by Rame, or co-written with Fo (and as they appear in
the dramatic text), but refers also to the fact that these parts have often
been played by Rame herself (in the ever-changing recreation of the
role in performance). This exceptional combination results in the inte-
gration of writer/actress/character to produce a complex blend of the
diegetic and extra-diegetic, especially in view of Rame's star status. In
other words, Rame's own personality and life experiences enter the
equation in her approach to the issues she dramatizes, as well as in-
fluencing the way the audience perceives her characters. Rame's
writing/acting/directing activities are most strongly in evidence in the
dramatic form of the monologue, such as the one-woman satires
grouped together as *Tutta casa, letto e chiesa*, which brought her various
dramatic talents into a wider public arena in 1977. Later plays, such as
La donna grassa of 1991, also include polylogues, containing several
speaking parts, both female and male.

While plays such as *Lo stupro*, *La donna grassa* and *L'eroina* were written
by Rame, and in the latter two cases, produced by Fo, it is not always so
easy to distinguish the dramatic contributions of Rame and Fo. The
form of their collaboration, particularly pre-1977, the year when Rame
began to work independently of Fo, is complex and varying in combination.[3] Fo's introduction to *Venticinque monologhi per una donna di Dario Fo e
Franca Rame* is devoted almost exclusively to an elaboration of the initial
statement that almost all the twenty-five monologues were written, as
he puts it, by two pairs of hands ('a quattro mani da me e Franca'). He
breaks down the collaborative writing stage as follows:

It often happened that Franca would suggest an idea to me, I would set out its
'treatment', we'd discuss it either more or less vivaciously and then I got the
job of dramatizing it in its entirety. On other occasions it was Franca who
would hand me a plot outline to read, I'd give her my opinion, and she'd con-
clude the writing out. (Fo 1989, intro.)

Rame–Fo theatre, however, does not mean the simple transference
of the written text from page to stage, as in the case of the dramatists

examined in the previous chapters. The plays of Rame and Fo, even as regards the actual words spoken by the characters, take shape on stage, in that performance considerations, and particularly audience response, determine the final performance product (final, that is, for the duration of that performance). In this sense their plays cannot be considered to be in the tradition of those dealt with in the rest of this work, in that they trace their lineage back along a different route, to the mediaeval *giullari*, or jesters, and to the Renaissance *commedia dell'arte*. Unlike the scripted erudite Renaissance comedies explored in the first two chapters, *commedia dell'arte* plays began with a *canovaccio*, or plot outline, which was then elaborated on stage, a tradition that Goldoni worked against by providing his actors with a complete written script, and which Rame–Fo theatre takes up again.[4]

The important implication here is that Rame the actress, rather than just Rame the writer and producer, has an input into her collaboration with Fo that is significant for the purpose of this chapter. Her playing of female parts involves re-creating the role during performance, a recreation that feeds into the next version of the written text, and consequently into the version on which this study is based. In other words, the female *characters* in the Rame and Rame–Fo plays examined in this chapter as they appear in the written text, are very often the descendants of a line of female *parts* (based on characters) that have been shaped and reshaped by Rame.[5] Fo explains the process of this shaping in the following terms:

Most of the working out of the text took place directly on stage. Night after night Franca, using the input of the audience, which is always our greatest collaborator, would vary the rhythm and structure of sentences, speed up passages, put in or leave out remarks, etc. In that way, after a couple of months, the text seemed to us to be completely transformed, almost unrecognizable compared to the original text. (Fo 1989, intro.)

It is to Franca Rame's female parts, then, rather than simply to her female characters, that this chapter devotes its attention.

FEMALE SUBJECTS

Subjectivity

The dramatic status of the female character in Renaissance comedy was assessed in the opening chapter on the basis of visibility and audibility, twin aspects of stage performance that are central in determining audience perception of femininity. With female parts centre stage in the plays of Rame, the mere matter of being both seen and heard now gives way to considerations such as protagonist action or antagonist reaction as features of her characterization of femininity. Rame herself actually denied the role of protagonist to the central female characters in *Tutta casa, letto e chiesa* of 1977, despite the fact that this collection of plays is all about women: 'The out and out protagonist of this show about women is the man. Or rather, his sex! He isn't present "in flesh and blood", but he's always here among us, big, enormous, getting in our way . . . and he squashes us!' (Fo 1989, p. 5).[6] To this male protagonist (*protagonista maschile*) she then counterposes female characters (*personaggi femminili*) (Fo 1989, p. 7). One could accept Rame's assessment of her characters (and that of some of her feminist critics) at face value, and go on to explore whether a female protagonist, or subject, does evolve over the following fifteen years (with, for instance, *L'eroina* and *La donna grassa* of 1991), or whether her female characters continue to be typified by antagonist reaction, and relegation to the object position.[7] Alternatively, and this is the approach taken by this study, one can focus on the plays themselves in order to trace the precise nature of the female parts which they foreground so emphatically.

The centrality and complexity of Rame's portrayal of femininity allow for, and indeed necessitate, a more sophisticated discussion than earlier representations. The spotlight on her female parts straightaway reveals a set of issues around the female subject, notably those of subjectivity and femininity, particularly in the face of patriarchy's presumption of the male, but denial of the female, subject. There is then the further question of defining feminine subjectivity not only in itself, but for the purposes of its study in a dramatic context. Leading on from the arguments surrounding subjectivity and femininity are the debates in feminist identity politics and, especially given the politicized nature of Rame's gender critique, the various discussions on the workings, and particularly the effects, of power. A brief overview of the relevant issues in these areas can lead the way to a working definition of dramatic feminine subjectivity.

In the first place, the question arises of how, if at all, the subject is to be pinned down; and, even if its existence can be established and delineated, is it possible for the writing/acting 'I' ever to be a 'she', or is it always inevitably a 'he' in the patriarchal symbolic order? Or is the notion of the subject, in all its determinist fixity, to be replaced by that of subjectivity as a process and a practice? As for femininity, is it to be thought of in terms of femininities, as in the case of feminism (radical feminism, essentialist feminism, materialist feminism)? Linking the vexed definitions of subjectivity and femininity is the fact that the notion of a single feminine viewpoint, or identity, so long assumed necessary for political cohesion and effectiveness, has been thrown into question by the postmodernist fracturing of the essentialist 'I', whatever its gender.

Writing on subjectivity and femininity, Vintges considers the contemporary European penchant for decentring and deconstruction of the subject, with a view to theorizing a feminism not tied to an essentialist feminine subject. The mid-seventies, the era of Rame's *Tutta casa, letto e chiesa*, saw a particular assault on the coherent, unified subject, the seamless, pre-discursive Descartian 'I' that indisputably pre-existed thought, being and action. Instead, ideological and psychoanalytical theories decentring the subject reduced its social role from causal agent to interpellated effect (Althusserians) and undercut its sentient dominance in the symbolic by reinstating the unconscious and partially relocating the subject within the imaginary (Lacanians) (Vintges 1991, p. 230). Even more radically, deconstruction of the subject denied its existence altogether, replacing it with variegated subject forms and subject positions (Foucault, Deleuze, Guattari) (Vintges 1991, p. 230). Vintges concludes the following implications for femininity:

If we assume that a unified subject does not exist, then we can no longer speak in terms of a feminine subject. There are only feminine positions, roles and places in practices and discourses, which offer and structure being a woman . . . Instead of assuming that there are women who are subsequently confronted by all manner of practices and approaches, the relationship is reversed: which woman-positions do we find in our society? (Vintges 1991, p. 231)

However, as noted by Foucault, two major problems arise in relation to subject positions, illustrating the cardinal workings of power not simply as that exerted by state institutions (juridico-political, educational, scientific, medical, religious), but as manifested in its effects. The first problem is that these subject positions are in themselves liable to become fixed and normalized, rather than remaining flexible and, as Deleuze and Guattari argue, true to the actual multiplicities of existence:

Standardized subject forms are imposed on us in all kinds of ways, and . . . herein lies the greatest power effect in our culture: countless technologies, techniques and practices – interwoven with the humanities – produce subject positions which we have to assume on pain of exclusion and/or sanctions . . .

what are in fact multiplicities become caught in subject forms, and thus subjected to the existing order. (Vintges 1991, p. 232)

The second problem is that the mere fact of occupying subject positions can give the illusion of existing as a subject: 'The fact that we live in these subject positions and experience ourselves as subjects, forms the mechanism of *the* dominant power type in our society, characterized by Foucault as normalization and disciplinary power.' This illusory subject, however, is not an agent, but, rather, an 'effect of disciplinary power' (Vintges 1991, p. 232). It is only when a subject position, and the contingent, temporary identity it confers, is recognized *in the moment of its taking up*, in other words, as a process and a practice of signification, rather than a pre-established place to be filled, that control over it as an effect, and thence agency, can be achieved.

This line of thinking has moved feminist identity politics on from the essentialist, unified Woman-position to a multiple identity politics, where identity is understood as a process featuring diversification and change. Noting the roots of identity politics in the resistance to dominant culture and politics, Wright defines identity as a matter of one's 'sense of history, understanding of social relations and personal possibilities, modes of reasoning, values and expressive styles' (Wright 1993, p. 1). The sense of agency implicit in this definition underlies theories of identity politics that 'build on the development and/or reconstruction of a strong, resilient "self"', able to survive with dignity in societies which deny or degrade it' (Wright 1993, p. 1), a tenet encapsulated by Italian feminism's *autocoscienza* and its emphasis on self reconstruction. The 'self' in this case is not to be understood as a reversion to the pre-discursive subject with a fixed identity; there is no such thing, Wright argues, as 'a single and exclusive identity affiliation' (Wright 1993, p. 3). On the contrary, the multiple identity model means the interaction of identities that are permeable as well as flexible.

In this context Wright emphasizes the importance of recognizing that the multiple identity model of being is made up of identities that are not only 'oppressed', but also 'privileged', in relation to the dominant ideology. This complex model of identities, or subject positions, that not only intertwine and interact, but also contradict each other, may appear paradoxical when measured against the simplistic, unified pre-discursive subject of dominant ideology. As a more nuanced and variegated model, however, its contrapuntal processes are more reflective of the multiplicities of everyday existence, as well as offering genuine, rather than merely illusory, possibilities for agency.

Franca Rame's one-act monologues allow for a variety of subject positions to be observed in the process of being taken up. Alone on stage, the actress enacts significant life choices and subsequent changes in her character over a period of time (as in *Abbiamo tutte la stessa storia*). As another variant, the actress may also play, by implying their presence onstage, other characters in addition to, and alternating with, her central female role (*Abbiamo tutte la stessa storia* and *Michele lu Lanzone*). Alternatively, she may dialogue with implied offstage characters, whose parts she also speaks, by repeating what she has 'heard' them say (*Una donna sola*). At issue here is the foregrounding, at the formal level, of the taking up of subject positions *as a process*, with the important implication of intervention and agency. This is at its most pointed when the central, onstage female character changes and develops in response to the viewpoints of other, implied female characters. These 'characters' thereby take on the guise of 'personified', alternative subject positions available to her. The performative nature of these subject positions is made particularly overt by the fact that one actress plays them all *by implication*, rather than as separate female characters in individual stage appearances (as in the case, for example, of Silvia and Gioconda, personifying asexual domesticity and sexual artistic creativity respectively, in D'Annunzio's *La Gioconda*).

Neither decadent nor realist theatre allows for the same degree of complexity in playing with subject positions, their characters remaining relatively fixed throughout the play. One partial exception is the device of cross-dressing, such as that found in Renaissance comedy, both at the first, formal level (boy actors in female parts) and at the second, plot level (character–character) (see chapter two). In the context of the process of taking up subject positions, a character cross-dressing to take on the identity of another character of a different gender (such as Lidio pretending to be Santilla in *La Calandria*), can be seen as playing with gender identity as contingent and as a process. However, this type of cross-dressing could also be considered as the mere exchange of one traditional, unified subject for another. Alternatively, a character can cross-dress as a newly-created character (as Lelia does when she calls herself Fabio in *Gli ingannati*), in which case Lelia (in reality a boy actor), fashions Fabio according to 'her' own style. In the case of Franca Rame's one-act monologues for women, on the other hand, the fact of an actress (rather than a boy actor) playing, or rather implying, one or more characters, and enacting a series of life stages and changing feminine subject positions, ensures that the focus remains exclusively on the practice of a self-reconstructing femininity, in line with the practice of *autocoscienza*.

Self-styling (Wright's 'expressive styles') is one particular development of the key promise of agency in theories positing multiple identity, subject positions and effects of power as processes. Building on Foucault's later work on Greek and Roman discourses of sexual behaviour, which he characterizes as arts of existence that lie outside state-institutionalized discourses, Vintges argues for a feminism that takes up 'the possibility of constructions of self-identity which escape subject being as a result of normalization' (Vintges 1991, p. 236).[8] Two crucial Foucauldian points are taken up by Vintges here. The first is the de-naturalizing or deconstruction of the seamless slippage in dominant ideology from *normativity* ('the construction and application of norms and values, and of giving meaning in general') to *normalization* and discipline ('the power of the Norm, which determines what is normal, what is deviant') (Vintges 1991, pp. 232, 233). The splitting of normativity, with its particularity and free-wheeling difference, away from normalization, generality and discipline is made possible by Foucault's separation of self-styling, or personal ethics, from hegemonic forces:

For centuries we have been convinced that between our ethics, our personal ethics, our everyday life and the great political and social and economic structures there were analytical relations . . . I think we have to get rid of this idea of an analytical or necessary link between ethics and other social or economic or political structures. (Foucault 1983, p. 230, quoted in Vintges 1991, p. 236)

It could of course be argued that this mode of reasoning comes full circle back to an essentialist viewpoint that denies the relevance of historical, social, economic and political context in the formation of identities and subject positions, resulting in a dangerous de-politicizing of the issues of identity and reinstating the seamlessness with which dominant ideology covers its processes. However, while there is no doubt that social, economic and political change is vital for the freeing up of subject positions, the drive towards such change has come from somewhere, namely from outside the dominant ideology, and in reaction to it. It is in the interstices of hegemonic structures, or, more specifically, in Foucault's terms, at the effects end of the workings of power in everyday life, that a space resides for agency in the form of self-styling.

Self-styling offers feminism a mode of agency that is freed from the constraints of patriarchal truth and morality about femininity, and so from the essentialist, unified female subject. Femininity, or rather, femininities, can now be construed in terms of the *process of taking up* multiple 'styles of living' (the effects, subject positions and identities that are self-created through specific practices and discourses), rather than in terms of pre-discursive subjects *allocated*, under the guise of individual choice, to a limited, and limiting, set of pre-existing, patriarchally-defined feminine roles. The female subject as fixity can now be replaced by female subjectivity as process, 'perpetually construed and constructable' (Vintges 1991, p. 237). In the context of identity as a process, Butler argues that: 'Paradoxically, the reconceptualization of identity as an *effect*, that is, as *produced* or *generated*, opens up possibilities of "agency" that are insidiously foreclosed by positions that take identity categories as foundational and fixed' (Butler 1990, p. 147). It is in the production or generation of identity as a process, that Butler locates the functions of the repetitive, the performative and the public, functions which are all recognizably theatrical.

Taking signification as the first locus of agency and identity, Butler notes that, just as 'signification is *not a founding act, but rather a regulated process of repetition* that both conceals itself and enforces its rules precisely through the production of substantializing effects', so too 'the rules that govern intelligible identity ... operate through *repetition*' (Butler 1990, p. 145). It is in repetition as a practice, in other words, as ongoing, that possibilities reside for intervention and subversion. Repetition as constitutive of identity is linked by Butler to the performativity of gender, with the term 'performative' echoing its use in speech act theory, where it denotes the 'executive' force of all utterances (Elam 1980, p. 158):

There is no gender identity behind the expressions of gender; that identity is performatively constituted by the very 'expressions' that are said to be its results ... In what senses, then, is gender an act? As in other ritual social dramas, the action of gender requires a performance that is *repeated* ... Gender ought not to be construed as a stable identity or locus of agency from which various acts follow; rather, gender is an identity tenuously constituted in time, instituted in a exterior space through a *stylized repetition* of acts. (Butler 1990, pp. 25, 140)

Gender performativity as repetitive self-styling transports the whole issue of identity as a practice into the theatrical arena: 'Consider gender, for instance, as a *corporeal style*, an "act", as it were, which is both intentional and performative, where "*performative*" suggests a dramatic and contingent construction of meaning' (Butler 1990, p. 139). It is in the inherently fabricated nature of self-styling that the essence of performativity, and so of theatre, lies, as a set of acts and gestures characterized by 'made-upness' and contingency, and as a preoccupation with 'surface' (with the focus on 'surface' reiterating the issues of fetishism explored in chapter two):

Acts, gestures, and desire produce the effect of an internal core or substance, but produce this *on the surface of the body* . . . Such acts, gestures, enactments, generally construed, are *performative* in the sense that the essence or identity that they otherwise purport to express are fabrications manufactured and sustained through corporeal signs and other discursive means. (Butler 1990, p. 136)

This performative theory of gender, in which gender is not a pre-existing identity, but is constituted by specific actions, is particularly reminiscent of Renaissance perceptions of sexuality not as a once-and-for-all defining factor of identity, but simply as an act that might or might not be repeated (see chapter two).

Another feature of the enactment of self-styling as identity is the necessity for this process to be collective, rather than isolated and private: 'Although there are individual bodies that enact these significations by becoming stylized into gendered modes, this "action" is a public action. There are temporal and collective dimensions to these actions, and their public character is not inconsequential' (Butler 1990, p. 140). Theatre is once again invoked here, in its definition as a public event: without an audience, there can be no theatre. The repetitive, the performative and the public elements that constitute the process and practice of taking up subject positions and identities may account for the irresistible appeal of theatre and other visual performance arts that are also defined by these elements. In watching and listening to actresses and actors enact the taking up of particular subject positions, 'repeating' their parts, often performance after performance (one form of repetition particularly foregrounded by the Characters in Pirandello's *Sei personaggi in cerca d'autore*), the audience are able to rehearse and reevaluate their own subject positionings.

In that her monologues particularly emphasize the practice of taking up multiple subject positions and underline identity as a performative process, Franca Rame's work can be described as quintessentially theatrical. Her focus on the process and contingency of identity formation treats identity, in Foucauldian terms, as an effect that is on-going, rather than pre-discursively ordained. In this sense, her plays deal with power in the area of its effects, namely power brought into effect by virtue of being repeatedly brought to surface, or enacted, in everyday life, and therefore open to subversion at this point through self-styling. However, her plays also deal with those purportedly exclusive sites of power, namely state institutions (the law, police, religion) and their underpinning by patriarchal ideology. These regulatory systems conceal the fact that they are in fact practices and discourses, and in order to perpetuate this concealment, require and produce fixed, unified, *pre-discursive subjects* with an illusion of agency in their adherence to the norm. At the same time, these systems also work to exclude the mobility and plurality of *discursive subjectivity* and difference in disciplinary repression and denial of the effects end of the dynamics of power. Through the viewpoint of their female parts, Rame's plays often explore the interaction between these two cardinal sites of power, albeit rarely with a positive outcome.

In the light of the preceding discussion, what definitions of the dramatic feminine subject or dramatic feminine subjectivity are now available for an exploration of the female parts that Franca Rame places centre stage? It seems that identity can no longer be perceived as monolithic, or pre-ordained, and that the unified subject has been replaced by multiple subject positions and identities. It may, then, be impossible to talk of, or from, one fixed subject position, let alone a fixed female subject position. As a consequence, there may well *be* no female subject to be dramatically reproduced and represented. Any attempt, whether in political or cultural representation, to produce and reproduce a single stable female subject position or identity, must, in that case, be regarded as ideology breeding false consciousness. Vintges' answer to this question in her essay 'The vanished woman and styles of feminine subjectivity', is that 'the subject woman does not exist, long live feminine subjectivity!', a solution that can be appropriated for the purposes of this chapter in the form of dramatic feminine subjectivity (Vintges 1991, p. 236).

The modernist dramatic feminine subject of the previous chapters can now be defined as the representation of a fixed, unified identity, more often than not idealized or demonized according to the patriarchal fantasy of a femininity circumscribed by compulsory reproductive heterosexuality. Postmodernist dramatic feminine subjectivity, on the other hand, can portray the taking up of multiple subject positions and identities through enacted discourses, and dramatize the possibility of holding a variety of even contradictory ideological and political standpoints (Wright's combination of oppressed and privileged identities), depending on repeated patterns of self-styling (Vintges' Foucauldian lifestyle ethics). Dramatic feminine subjectivity, as a portrayal of a process and a practice, can illustrate the occupation, simultaneously or at different times, of varying feminine standpoints (for example, those defined within essentialist feminism, radical feminism or materialist feminism). Importantly, dramatic feminine subjectivity can also represent the possibility of participating in practices other than those related to reproduction and sexuality, such as, for instance, those associated with work or leisure.

In Rame's plays, dramatic feminine subjectivity appears in line with feminine subjectivity as a process by the way in which her female parts play out the search for subject positions in various areas of their lives. This search is often informed by three salient characteristics in Italian feminism, namely the practice of *autocoscienza*, the prioritizing of relations between women, and an active awareness of the political and economic context.[9] The drive towards *autocoscienza*, the process of an emergent awareness of the self and the consequent move towards its reconstruction, provides the impetus guiding plot development in many of Rame's plays, such as *Una donna sola, La mamma fricchettona*, and *La Medea*, as well as the more recent *Una giornata qualunque*. As *Una donna sola* progresses, for example, Maria develops an awareness of the exploitative nature of her domestic situation, which sees her locked indoors by her husband and the object of sexual harassment on the part of her live-in brother-in-law, a neighbour with binoculars, an obscene phone caller and an ex-lover. The play takes the form of a self-revealing, confessional-style monologue that provides the therapeutic vehicle enabling Maria to simultaneously externalize and recognize her anger at her situation, thereby giving her a new sense of self (the first stage of *autocoscienza*). Until now she has been used to speaking and doing everything internally, rather than speaking out and risking a beating by her husband (Fo 1989, pp. 16, 17). She is helped in this process of externalization by a female neighbour to whom she addresses her thoughts, and whose encouraging comments and questions, which are either 'repeated' or implied in Maria's monologue, perform the function of a therapist's prompts. Interestingly, this 'therapy' is not conducted with Maria lying down, or even sitting, but takes place while she is carrying out a host of domestic duties that are executed with comic frenzy. The implication here is that of the insidiously disciplinary motto 'busy hands are happy hands'; her lifestyle allows her little space for herself, let alone for the important process of reflection on her condition (a negative feature of the female experience of traditional family life that the Donna in *La mamma fricchettona* particularly resents (Fo 1989, p.46)).

By focussing on the growing self-awareness of one female character in response to the interventions of another, implied, female character who is clearly more aware, *Una donna sola* highlights the emphasis in Italian feminism on individual feminine subjectivity very much in the context of a collective feminine identity. In a manner akin to Sibilla Aleramo's 'I'-narrated novel *Una donna*, Rame's dramatic monologue *Una donna sola* is the story of one individual woman, and at the same time that of many women (also a particular feature of *Abbiamo tutte la stessa storia*, which literally means 'We all have the same story'). Apart from the fact that Aleramo's novel is autobiographical, while *Una donna sola* is not, there is another notable difference between the two works. Written at different moments in the history of the Italian women's movement (1906 and 1977 respectively), the former speaks from the viewpoint of an isolated female 'I' that is separate from other women in its struggle for autonomy (most notably from the mother, whom the narrator only truly comprehends in later life on discovering her mother's own writings left behind after her suicide). Rame's play, on the other hand, shows the beginnings of a sense of female community, a feature of Italian feminism that is also present in *Una giornata qualunque* of 1986, and that was to develop into the bond of *affidamento*, or entrustment, between women. The interplay between individual and collective femininity is particularly dramatized on the formal level in *Una donna sola* by the use of the monologue form which at the same time implies a dialogue.

Friendships between women and recourse to women rather than to men as the primary reference point, are an important part of Italian feminist political practice that finds expression in some of Rame's female parts. Rame herself, however, has said that 'after the great battles, campaigning for divorce, abortion, or the law against sexual violence, women in everyday life are the worst enemy of women' (Rame, *L'Unità*, 14 December 1991, in Rame 1992, p. 114). This is certainly true of the many 'other', and usually also younger, women, in her plays, who act against the interests of wives in their liaisons with husbands (but who are, curiously, never really held to account). Competition between women for men, the result of internalization of patriarchal misogyny, can be countered within feminism by strengthening the bonds between women. Making choices in 'everyday life', such as steering clear of other women's husbands, as well as restructuring female identity around something other than sexuality, are particularly contemporary possibilities of self-styling and *autocoscienza* that do not appear available to Rame's female parts.

Nonetheless, affirming relationships between women play an important role in many of her plays. These appear, interestingly, to be restricted predominantly to non-related women (*Una donna sola, Una giornata qualunque, Ho fatto la plastica*), while in some plays, non-related female voices dialogue with each other on feminine issues in a professional capacity (*Monologo di una puttana in manicomio, Voce amica, La donna grassa*). Mother–daughter dyads, on the other hand, do not always function amicably (*La donna grassa, L'eroina, Una donna sola*). In *Una donna sola*, Maria finds she can confide not in her daughter, from whom she appears estranged, but in her new female neighbour, who, during the course of the play, is upgraded from 'una signora' to 'una cara amica'. *Una giornata qualunque* shows Giulia turning her attention away from her ex-husband, for whom she can be seen making a video-recorded suicide note at the beginning of the play, to Carla, whom she gets to know only as a voice on the telephone. Carla's methods of dealing with her problems closely mirror those of Giulia, even down to the specific details of the eating habits/disorders that they have in common. As a result, Giulia is forced into the realization that her problems are not particular to her, but are also shared by other women. This has the positive effect of deflecting her from her original plan to commit suicide and redirecting her anger outwards, rather than turning it on herself. As she explains through the intercom to the policeman standing ominously outside her front door:

No, I've already saved myself . . . when this dear friend of mine, Carla, telephoned me, it acted like a mirror for me . . . enormous . . . grotesquely deforming . . . and I understood! She spoke with my very own words . . . An absurd photocopy! See, like a flash of lightning! I appeared so funny to myself . . . unreal. Those are the words for it: funny and unreal. I realized my madness, do you understand? As if at last projected in perspective. I said to myself: OK, Giulia, you're a bit down, but do you really want to kill yourself? You must react! (Fo and Rame 1991, p. 70)

As a result of her interaction with Carla, Giulia's attention switches from unhealthy introspection as an isolated individual marooned indoors, to a place in the collective: 'Enough navel-gazing (. . .) You must leave this house that's driving you mad (. . .) . . . I want to go out . . . talk to people . . . tell about my experiences' (Fo and Rame 1991, p. 71).

However, Giulia's new self-awareness and her subsequent resolve to take up a different, active subject position in relation to the patriarchal order (in other words, the process of *autocoscienza*, or self-styling, that she has set in motion as a direct result of her growing awareness of other women), are cancelled out by the direct intervention of state systems of power. On the one hand, this intervention illustrates the politicized nature of Italian feminism, with its perception of the state as patriarchal and inimical to women (the third characteristic of Italian feminism, it will be recalled). On the other hand, it is a critique that looms large over the end of the play to deny any positive *dénouement* for the female part, in that it problematizes Giulia's blossoming *autocoscienza* by misappropriating it for patriarchal medical discourse: at the very moment of Giulia's dramatic self-realization, the forces of law, order and medical science, in the form of a policeman and a doctor, force their way into her home to take her away to a mental asylum. There is also the implication that Giulia's new-found voice cannot, and must not, be heard, as her entry into the symbolic is firstly interrupted by the criminal patriarchal under-world (in the form of two male burglars who break into her home), and then silenced by the law enforcers, who are more concerned with what she is *saying*, than with what the burglars have *done*.

Carla's reaching out to Giulia is also ineffectual. Giulia is unable to dissuade her from suicide (unlike the neighbour in *Una donna sola*, who successfully prevents Maria from shooting herself). Moreover, Carla's attempt to get the police to stop the burglary taking place in her new friend's home ironically puts into motion the disciplinary and punitive forces that culminate in Giulia's enclosure (in an ending reminiscent of Pirandello's *Il berretto a sonagli*, which sees Beatrice taken away to an asylum after she has tried to 'interfere' with male codes of honour). *Una donna sola* ends similarly. Maria's response to her oppression takes the form of an extreme final solution: on the advice of her female neigh-bour, she decides not to kill herself, but to eliminate her oppressors instead (she pushes her wheelchair-bound brother-in-law out of the fourth-floor window of her flat, shoots the voyeur with the binoculars, and awaits her husband's return, gun in hand). Chillingly comic, these actions crown her growing self-awareness in such as way as to prob-lematize it. Her *autocoscienza* may not become medicalized, but her actions will doubtless summon the forces of law and order, and so ensure a punitive postfact to the play.

Both *Una donna sola* and *Una giornata qualunque* end with failure on the part of the female character to implement effectively what has been gained in terms of *autocoscienza* and female community during the course of the action. These two positive developments are in line with Italian feminism, but appear negated by the third, political, element in a closure marked by pessimistic determinism. In the following section, an exploration of issues related to femininity in Rame's plays will attempt to distinguish the ways in which her female parts remain inscribed by patriarchal definitions of femininity policed by internalized strategies of self-victimization and powerlessness, leading to continued entrapment in circumscribed roles; and the ways in which dramatic treatment of these issues attempts to empower their female parts.

Subject matter

Ostensibly as a result of the type of subject matter commonly associated with writings by women, an entire area labelled 'women's writing' has been separated off and accorded either low status by patriarchal ideology, or high status by essentialist feminism. These assessments derive directly from conflicting views of the 'female subject' behind the writing. Essentialist feminism both extols the female subject as Woman, and argues for 'writing-the-body' from a pre-Oedipal, pre-discursive position lying outside the patriarchal symbolic order. For patriarchy, the 'female subject' is a contradiction in terms, and by extension the 'female writing subject' an impossibility, in that the universal subject of the symbolic order is presumed to be an 'I' that is only ever a 'he'.[10]

Replacing the notion of the subject with that of subjectivity, however, means that both feminine and masculine subjectivity are seen as constituted through discourse in ways that not only free up the regulatory female/feminine and male/masculine pairings, but also allow for new and changing gender identities. One implication for the subject matter usually linked with women's lives and with their writing is that, far from being 'naturally' and predeterministically 'feminine', and so low-status, issues regarding the personal and the private (the emotional and instinctual, the domestic, the familial), are in fact neither gender-specific nor inconsequential. The corollary is that so-called masculine issues of the political and the public (the rational and intellectual, work, war) also concern women, rather than being the exclusive province of high-status masculinity.[11]

Gender mobility across these two sets of issues, encapsulated in the concept 'the personal is political', is a feature that sets 'subjectivity' apart from the 'subject'. In what sense, then, is it still a valid project to speak in terms of 'feminine' subjectivity, and in terms of the performative practice of dramatic feminine subjectivity and identities ? Butler points towards an answer in her comment: 'If one "is" a woman, that is surely not all one is' (Butler 1990, p. 3). While not automatically jettisoning all stereotypically feminine issues in favour of those that are categorized as masculine (and thereby acceding by default to patriarchal divisions), dramatic feminine subjectivity should play out the taking up of *non-patriarchal* subject positions across a range of different discourses. At stake, then, are the subversive feminine subject positions in, and radical comprehensivity of, the discourses engaged with by Rame's female parts, or their conservative perpetuation of a patriarchally-circumscribed set of roles.

There is no doubt that Rame's female parts are constructed through a wide range of discourses traditionally associated with both femininity and masculinity. In keeping with contemporary socioeconomic developments, they are not always exclusively associated with the personal, private, domestic sphere (as in *Una donna sola*), but are also wives and mothers who additionally participate in the labour force at various levels, although never in top-ranking professional positions. They are to be found as workers (*Il risveglio, La casellante*), as office and other salaried staff (*Rientro a casa, La mamma fricchettona*), and in middle-class careers (*Coppia aperta, quasi spalancata, Una giornata qualunque, La nonna incinta*). Occasionally they are, or have been, workers whose marital status is unspecified (*La maestra di ballo, Il pupazzo giapponese, Monologo di una puttana in manicomio*). They are not only politically aware (*Il risveglio*), but also politically active (*La mamma fricchettona*).

However, the particular subject positions that they take up in some of these different discourses appear to fluctuate in the degree of their subversiveness, with the result that traditional images of femininity are at times reinforced. This is particularly clear in the way many of the plays end. A final denial of multiple possibilities for feminine identity and subjectivity clouds many of Rame's plays, despite the fact that the motor force of *autocoscienza* actually drives them. At the last moment, fate and determinism seem to cut short what the female parts have been working to achieve, as any agency is ultimately ruled out by state forces. Now allocated exclusive possession of power in terms of both its source and its effects, the state effectively dominates the final scenario in a reinforcement of the 'analytical or necessary link' between personal ethics of existence and 'other social or economic or political structures', an illusory link according to Foucault, and, by implication, existing only as part of dominant ideology (Foucault 1983, p. 230).

A crucial factor here is the Italian historical and political context for a perception of the state marked by suspicion of centralized state powers. Still the subject of debate, the 'distrusted state' is seen variously as the result of strong regional roots, the failure of the *Risorgimento* as a class revolution, the unresolved north–south divide centring on the misalliance between northern capital and southern land ownership, and the overall failure of the state to function in the interests of civil society. The unrest that peaked in 1968 in Italy, as elsewhere, was to continue over the decade that saw both Rame's own political activism and the flowering of her theatrical career (while other countries returned to stability relatively quickly) (Lumley 1990, pp. 11–18). This context, in conjunction with continuing patriarchal hegemony, informs the way in which Rame's female parts explore a range of discursive spheres. They proceed with this exploration from the initial viewpoint of the particular juncture of class, age, familial and marital status that, were they to be regarded in terms of representing fixed, unified subjects, defines and preconditions their actions. In terms of representing subjectivity, on the other hand, this juncture signals an essentially arbitrary point of entry into a set of interactive discourses, and thus into a performative scenario where multiple identity (including both 'oppressed' and 'privileged' identities) can be enacted and re-enacted.

In the personal sphere of sexuality and body-imaging, the female parts enact a complex blend of subversion (rebellion on the part of the oppressed identity) and reiteration of the status quo (failure of the oppressed identity to rebel, or complicity on the part of the privileged identity). The plays deal with both recreative and procreative feminine sexuality. In terms of recreative, as opposed to procreative, female sexuality, Rame's plays take up the forbidden position not only of female sexual desire, but of desire unrelated to reproduction, a position relegated by patriarchy to the negatively-valued side of the madonna–whore division. In marked contrast to the fantastic demonization of female desire in the decadent plays of D'Annunzio examined in chapter four, Rame's female parts give matter-of-fact expression to their sexual expectations when their erotic needs are ignored. Maria in *Una donna sola* (1977) and Caterina in *Rientro a casa* (1983) both resent the selfishness with which their husbands treat them sexually. Maria's husband uses her rather like one of the household appliances ('Yes, used, like an electric shaver, a hair-dryer'), and always expects her to be instantly available ('always ready instantly! Like Nescafé!' (Fo 1989, pp. 18, 17)). For Caterina, sex with her husband ('My 21-second dear') makes her feel like a video-game being played at speed. Like Maria, Alice in *Alice nel paese senza meraviglie* (1977) experiences sexual exploitation from all directions, this time from fairy-tale creatures and even trees. In a dream-like fantasy setting, this play satirizes the sexual liberation of the late 1960s and 70s which, in the guise of 'allowing' female sexual desire, merely ratified the continuing use of female bodies for male pleasure. The plays abound in expositions on female desire. Images recur of the female body likened to a butcher's chart or map of Italy, with differently coloured areas sometimes denoting regions of varying erogenous intensity (*Una donna sola*, *Monologo di una puttana in manicomio* (1977), *Ho fatto la plastica* (1988)).

Rame's female parts do more than merely lament their lot. The Donna in *Contrasto per una sola voce* (1977), for instance, actively pursues sexual satisfaction. In this Boccaccesque play, set in the fourteenth century, the female character uses her parents' absence to dictate when her lover may visit her and, by convincing him that they are still in the house, regulates both his speaking part and his sexual behaviour. With the *orgasmo adulto* in *Una donna sola*, female recreational sexuality has come of age (Fo 1989, p. 16). The fact that Maria is both sexual *and* a mother is particularly effective in countering the patriarchal madonna– whore divide. In Rame's plays, mothers, and grandmothers (*Ho fatto la plastica*) are portrayed as possessing sexual desire as a matter of course, rather than being vilified for it in terms of patriarchal morality that desexualizes motherhood and ageing female bodies (as in the plays of D'Annunzio and Pirandello).

Yet alongside the affirmation and assertion of female desire, its fulfilment is nonetheless still represented as illicit and of carnivalesque temporariness, taking the form of adultery (*Una donna sola* (1977), *Rientro a casa* (1983), *Coppia aperta, quasi spalancata* (1983)), and parental deception (*Contrasto per una sola voce* (1977)). In a more recent play, the satisfaction of female desire through solitary fantasizing is portrayed as alienating and pathetic (*La donna grassa* (1992)), while in *Voce amica* (1988), the caricatural Donna Disperata is confused by her sexual relations with countless men, whom she can only identify by numbers corresponding to their ages. There is no *autocoscienza* at work in this play, with the Donna Disperata sleep-walking into a variety of beds, a metaphor for lack of self-awareness in a character far more naïve and ignorant than Maria a decade previously in *Una donna sola*.

This later female part is used to poke fun at female desire not only as excessive, but also as automatically leading to pregnancy. While the *voce amica*, the friendly voice of a female psychologist at the end of a telephone, listens sympathetically to the Donna Disperata's worries about the paternity of her baby, the only outcome is her frantic decision to transform her lovers into numbers to be played in the lottery. This resolution, while comic, masks a darker complicity with patriarchal misappropriation of female sexuality, which removes it from female control, seen here to be faltering. Moreover, unlike Maria and her implied female neighbour in the earlier monologue, the Voce Amica and the Donna Disperata are written as speaking parts to be played, more conventionally, by two different actresses (with the former as an offstage voice). In terms of performance politics too, mobile feminine subjectivity has been implicitly sacrificed here in favour of fixed feminine subjects.

One striking common denominator of many early female parts, such as those in five out of six of the monologues in the play cycle *Tutta casa, letto e chiesa* of 1977 and the more recent Carla in *L'eroina* and Mattea in *La donna grassa* of 1992, is that they are all mothers. As in the case of recreative female sexuality, exploration of the procreative dimension is double-edged, in that it both posits a critique, and harbours reinforcement, of the patriarchal status quo. Alignment with traditional values is particularly evident in the assumption, pre-shaping many of the female parts and reaffirming the specifically Catholic patriarchal tenet of compulsory reproductive heterosexuality, that all women are, or will at some point become, mothers; moreover, they will do so within marriage. Only rarely, as in the interactive prologue to *Una madre* (1980), is there a nod in the direction of women who are not mothers, the result here of an audience reaction that surprised Rame and indicates the assumption of motherhood to be unrealistic. Rame asks seemingly unconvinced female members of the audience to imagine that they are the mother of a terrorist shown on the television news: 'It's your son! I'm talking to you . . . "your" son . . . It's absurd? It's not possible? Why? Don't you have children? A brother then . . . a sister . . . Just pretend' (Fo 1989, p. 260).

Motherhood is omnipresent in the plays, in contrast to the marked absence of mothers in the Renaissance comedies and their marginalization in the plays of Pirandello. In Rame's plays it is more a case of absent fathers, and husbands, unless they are to be considered as 'not present in flesh and blood', but nonetheless 'oppressively here among us' (Fo 1989, p. 5). In *Il risveglio*, for instance, the father/husband is 'present' but asleep. The stage directions indicate that he can be replaced with a mannequin, since he has no lines (as in the case of Maria's brother-in-law in *Una donna sola*). Although deprived of a voice, his pseudo-presence is, however, loaded with significance. He is enjoying sleep, while the mother/wife frantically prepares their child for school and herself for work. The unequal sharing of domestic responsibilities in a household where both parents work allows him a lie-in (while the last straw for this working mother is the realization that she does not have to go to work after all as it is Sunday). Motherhood is comically omnipresent in *L'uomo incinto* (1977), with all three family members (mother, daughter *and* father) realizing they are pregnant. Informing the comedy in this play, as in many others, is a critique of procreative female sexuality as problematic. The unexpected pregnancy of the father, who has inadvertently taken his wife's contraceptive pills, shifts the problem into the male court to expose double standards in patriarchal values idealizing motherhood. While self-sacrifice and suffering is the lot of the ideal woman-as-mother, it will not do for men. Other plays point out the valorization of femininity exclusively in terms of reproduction ('as if we were thoroughbred cows meant for reproduction', Lisistrata says to other mothers in *Lisistrata romana* (Fo 1989, p. 151)), while for Medea, children are the means whereby men subjugate women (Fo 1989, p. 74).

In other female parts, critique of motherhood comes close to reinforcing the ideal patriarchal stereotype of the *mater dolorosa*, the particularly Catholic image of motherhood-as-suffering that pervades Pirandello's plays. The prologue to *Passione arcaica dei Lombardi: Maria alla croce* defines the play as 'the anti-passion, the drama of non-acceptance of sacrifice' on the part of Maria, mother of Christ. However, despite her imprecations at her role as suffering mother *par excellence*, the only solution offered by the closure of the play is an expression of her desire to die, followed by some comically irreligious berating of the Angel Gabriel. Other similar maternal female parts suffer in the fate of their children: the mother of an imprisoned terrorist and drug addict in *Una madre*, the mother of a peasant-hero murdered by landowners in *Michele lu Lanzone*, mothers of murdered children in *La strage degli innocenti*, and the mother of a young man murdered by Fascists in *Mamma Togni*. In *Mamma Togni*, the son's death deprives his mother of motherhood itself, a role that she is bereft without, and that subsumes her entire identity: 'Boys, my son is dead, now I've no-one to call me mummy anymore . . . and I . . . need . . .'. This identity is returned to her as the other injured young partisans, after a long silence, cry out 'Mamma, mamma', after which 'I was always Mamma Togni to everyone' (Fo 1989, p. 215, first performed 1971).

Unhappy relationships between mothers and older children appear to haunt motherhood (*Una donna sola*, *La mamma fricchettona*, *La donna grassa*), including domestic violence inflicted by a drug-addicted son in *L'eroina*. Any positive images of motherhood in the plays mostly revolve around younger children. For Maria in *Una donna sola*, her baby is the only member of the family whom she cares about, while in *Il risveglio* and *Abbiamo tutte la stessa storia*, young children become the addressees of monologues spoken by the female parts. While some plays toy with the possibility of abortion (*Abbiamo tutte la stessa storia*, *L'uomo incinto*), one play stands out in its exploration of a female subject position that takes exception to motherhood as the norm. *La Medea*, a monologue reworking a Euripidean theme, is introduced in the prologue as being the most politically feminist play in *Tutta casa, letto e chiesa*. Medea's response to Jason's infidelity and marriage with a younger woman is to kill both their children (as well as her rival and the latter's father). By killing her children, she intends to break out of the cage of motherhood in which patriarchy ('the society of men') has imprisoned her, and to recreate her identity anew ('to be reborn a new woman' (Fo 1989, pp. 74, 75)). A different female subject position echoes the traditional womanhood-as-motherhood tenet: 'You should think like a worthy mother, not like a haughty woman', advise other female voices from outside Medea's house (Fo 1989, p. 71) (a position that reiterates the Father's view of the Mother: 'She's not a woman, she's a mother', in Pirandello's *Sei personaggi in cerca d'autore*, Act I).

Although infanticide in *La Medea*, 'the most politically feminist piece in the whole show' (Fo 1989, p. 67), is intended as a purely allegorical act of self-awareness or *presa di coscienza* (p. 69), its association with feminism is unfortunate. Not only does it lend credence to extremist anti-feminist discourses, among them that of feminists as bad mothers and second-rate women generally, but it fails to locate the true source of Medea's problems by simply reiterating, rather than deconstructing, the patriarchal ideology underpinning the original play. The site of Medea's problems is, importantly, her internalizing of motherhood defined in patriarchal terms as the bearing children *for a man* – the children are, after all, hers as well as Jason's. Her problems of course also relate to the entire complex of femininity as understood within patriarchy. It is not in fact until Jason leaves her for a younger woman that Medea finds fault with motherhood. While recognizing the internalization by other women of patriarchal values regarding the female body and double standards regarding ageing, she paradoxically fails to recognize her own acquiescence with patriarchal motherhood. As a result, she falls into the erroneous belief that the complete destruction of motherhood, rather than its reinterpretation and reappropriation into her control, will lead to the demise of 'male law' and allow her to redefine herself anew. However, she not only fails to reclaim motherhood by rejecting her role as 'envelope enclosing the stakes of social circulation . . . the place, the sign, of relations between men' (Irigaray 1977, p. 181). By acting the archetypally 'bad mother', she also plays into the hands of a patriarchal society that can simply classify her as 'mad'. Ultimately, her action is one of unproductive false consciousness, rather than a true *presa di coscienza* leading to successful self-reconstruction (*autocoscienza*).

Another feature of this play is that the female part continues to situate motherhood within marriage and the patriarchal family unit, with the *pater familias* at its head. This traditional definition of the family unit prevails in Rame's plays, reinforcing heterosexual parenting as the norm and heterosexual, reproductive femininity as compulsory. At the same time, the patriarchal family appears as the prime locus of oppression for many of the female parts, with its many inherent double standards the object of critique: in terms of the work/unpaid housework debate (*Il risveglio*, *La mamma fricchettona*, *I piatti*), and exploitation that is both sexual (*Una donna sola*, *Rientro a casa*) and emotional. In *Una giornata qualunque*, Giulia thinks back on thirty-five years of family life with a husband as the exclusive centre of attention:

waking up every morning and thinking about you . . . not you as you . . . but you as husband . . . you were the centre of the family . . . I'm not being ironic . . . what with thinking about food . . . the ironing, the washing . . . about your work . . . your career . . . About your problems . . . that were always also my problems . . . then about my problems too, that somehow always remained just my problems. (Fo and Rame 1991, pp. 40–1)

An even darker side of family life is exposed in the domestic violence which female parts have experienced at the hands of husbands (*Una donna sola*, *Coppia aperta*, *quasi spalancata*) or sons (*L'eroina*), leading, in turn, to a desperately violent reaction on the part of the abused wife (*Una donna sola*).[12]

Some female parts openly reject family life. Caterina in *Rientro a casa* regularly leaves her husband and two children because of his sexual behaviour, an oppressive family situation that she realizes is common-place. On returning in a drunken haze to the wrong home one foggy evening, she spends the night in a block of flats and in a family set-up identical to her own, including the statutory mother-in-law with her crochet, who, barely turning round, comments: 'Is that you, are you back already?' (Fo 1989, p. 119). The Donna in *La mamma fricchettona* has left her husband and adult son, and an existence that never allowed her 'a moment for myself', and opted for a part-time job and a life 'among people, among women', only to be denounced to the authori-ties by her husband and son for abandoning the conjugal home and forcibly taken back by the police at the end of the play. Despite the critique of traditional family life in these plays, no viable alternative is posited. There are no representations, even in more recent plays, of, for instance, single working women living alone quite happily. With the notable exception of *La mamma fricchettona*, women on their own are mostly portrayed as not coping, and as desperate for another marital set up (*Una giornata qualunque, Coppia aperta, quasi spalancata, La donna grassa*).

In the personal sphere of the female body and self-imaging, Rame's female parts similarly occupy multiple positions of critique and rein-forcement in relation to dominant discourses on ideal femininity. These particularly concern body size and shape, as well as the associat-ed area of ageing explored in the previous chapter. Orbach noted in 1978 that concern with body size as a focal point for the definition of feminine self-image became part of the consciousness-raising process of the 1970s. In particular, she situated thinness as a recent and specifi-cally western ideal in countries where food is plentiful, and its produc-tion monopolized by multinational corporations that target women catering for families as primary purchasers (Orbach 1988, preface to 1978 edition, p. 17). A decade later, she records ever-increasing prob-lems of compulsive eating, and the related conditions of bulimia and anorexia as a direct result of internalization of body size as definitive of individual worth (Orbach 1988, p. 19). By the time of the written ver-sions of Rame's *Coppia aperta, quasi spalancata* (1983), *Rientro a casa* (1983), *Una giornata qualunque* (1988), *Ho fatto la plastica* (1988) and *La donna grassa*, or *The fat woman* (1991), all plays featuring body size and shape as a concern for their female parts, it was still the case that 'obsession and preoccupation with the body had increased, rather than abated' (Orbach 1988, p. 20).

Mattea, the 'fat woman' of the play's title, is obsessed with her weight, and experiences an ambivalent attitude towards food that appears to bear out the fact that, as a result of the 'thin aesthetic which has dominated over the last twenty years . . . women absorb a powerfully contradictory message *vis-à-vis* food and eating. It is good for others, but bad for the woman herself; healthy for others, harmful to the woman herself; full of love and nurturance for others, full of self-indulgence to herself' (Orbach 1988, pp. 20–1). She appears also to be caught in another double bind, on the one hand subscribing to the magazine *Grasso è bello* (*Fat is beautiful*), and on the other, desperate to lose weight. Orbach expresses a similar paradox. Despite her understanding of the perception of body size as conditioned by cultural and historical context, she still assumes thinness as the ideal, and her work is geared to the goal of losing weight. While Mattea's deliberations about fatness and food are comical, she remains trapped in the position of victim to poor self-image. This is emphasized by the closure of the play, which sees her deflated at the news that her ex-husband has fathered a child and is about to remarry. The play ends with her returning to her electronic lover (a tape-recorded male voice) for comfort. She is ultimately problematized in her body not only in terms of size and its assumed negative implications for sexual attractiveness, but also in her reproductive power, in which she has also been supplanted by another woman.

Other, earlier plays also engage with dominant discourses of the female body by similarly restricting their female parts to positions that, however comically, manage to illustrate and perpetuate, as well as critique, the status quo. In *Coppia aperta, quasi spalancata*, a satire on open relationships ending unexpectedly with the husband's, rather than the wife's, suicide, Antonia's own son orchestrates her transformation in terms of body image, so that she can successfully find another man to replace her unfaithful husband. Satisfied with her new wardrobe and hairstyle, he turns his attentions to her weight: 'Well done, Mum, it's going well . . . you've changed your wardrobe, your hairstyle . . . but you're fat, Mum, you'll have to slim, Mum' (Fo and Rame 1991, p. 12). His next comment, 'you've got to make yourself appetizing', recalls the metaphors of consumption frequently associated with the female body in Renaissance comedy. Despite her witty retort ('What am I, a guinea fowl?'), she follows the exercise routine and diet he sets for her, and loses weight, reshaped by male hands, a man-made woman made ready for other men, in a process she refers to uncritically as adaptation ('I adapted to look for another man') (Fo and Rame 1991, p. 29).

In *Rientro a casa*, the feeling of well-being after an unexpected afternoon in bed with Oreste, a colleague at work, is automatically translated into weight loss by the unhappily married Caterina ('I've certainly lost at least three kilos') (Fo 1989, p. 118), in a direct equation of positive self-imaging and thinness, and bearing out the view that fatness and thinness 'are not so much descriptions of body size as they are emotional categories: emotional categories that carry the weight of cultural dictates we have all internalized' (Orbach 1988, p. 22). Stage props like the exercise bicycle in *La donna grassa*, and Giulia's diet book in *Una giornata qualunque*, signal the body-styling industry that has grown up alongside the food industry to encourage and capitalize on current concern with body size, shape and fitness. They also serve to illustrate the 'technologies, techniques and practices' that 'produce subject positions which we have to assume on pain of exclusion and/or sanctions' (Vintges 1991, p. 232).

Mattea's response to the possibility of a television appearance in *La donna grassa* is a feeling of inadequacy leading to a comically grotesque fantasy of drastic body-reduction (and revealing a passing awareness of body-styling as a western luxury): 'I'll have seven liftings done . . . I'll have five kilos taken off each breast . . . twelve from my stomach . . . eighteen from my behind . . . and what's left over I'll donate to the Third World' (Rame 1992, p. 79). Body-styling is taken a step further in the form of ludicrously extensive cosmetic surgery and 'lifting' in the satirical *Ho fatto la plastica*, with stitches unravelling at crucial social moments and resulting in total paralysis at the moment of the grandmother's first sexual triumph in her new, Frankensteinian body. The final comment by the female part that she might as well be a motionless mannequin in a shop window forces home the point that, far from signalling the beginning of a new lease of life, eight hours-worth of cosmetic surgery have only created a facsimile of woman.

In this play, as in *La Medea* and many others, deterioration of body shape is associated exclusively with the ageing of the female body (while concern with body-styling is of course expected in women of all ages). There appears to be no escape in any of the plays from the patriarchal double bind that valorizes femininity in terms of youth and ideal body size, and at the same time problematizes women who attempt to counter the effects of ageing. On the positive side, many of Rame's female parts represent later, rather than earlier, stages in the female life course, in itself a broadening of the spectrum of dramatized femininity. They are placed centre stage to grapple comically with the patriarchal double bind, with the audience exposed to a feminine viewpoint (unlike Pirandello's older female characters, who rarely step beyond their pejorative descriptions in the stage directions). However, it is a feminine viewpoint still entrammelled and confined by patriarchal definitions and parameters, with a preponderance of negative dramatic closures sealing the inability of the female parts to find fulfilment in what they *do*, rather than how they *appear*, and particularly, how they appear in the eyes of men.

It appears that the body, sexual relationships, marriage and the family remain the spheres within which they continue to construct their identity, with a notable recurrence of the age-old commonplace of the *malmaritata*, or unhappily married woman, dating back to beyond the Renaissance. While working female parts are by no means absent, the working-class workplace is more often than not considered in its burdensome interaction with housework and childcare (*Il risveglio*), or in the light of the dangers it presents to women's health (*La maestra di ballo: catena di montaggio*). Antonia in *Coppia aperta, quasi spalancata*, is a rare and relatively recent example of a middle-class female part who places importance on the new job she has found since leaving her husband, and on her voluntary evening work at a local centre for drug dependency: 'It's very important to work . . . you're among people, you don't brood . . . you're independent' (Fo and Rame 1991, p. 18). In most plays, however, work is defined in terms of a breadwinning activity rather than a fulfilling career that might afford a sense of identity beyond being a woman. There is, moreover, a complete absence of any leisure activities that, particularly in contemporary society, provide another means of self-development. The question to be asked of Rame's female parts is, if they are women, and taking up positions in discourses of femininity, ideal or otherwise, is that all that they are?

PERFORMANCE POLITICS

Complementing the previous discussion on *what* Rame's female parts portray, attention to *how* they function on stage reveals that they often differ formally from traditional female characters, such as those examined in the previous chapters, in ways that draw on popular mediaeval performance practice. Specific performance strategies are particularly crucial in facilitating and enhancing the dramatization of the *performativity* of a feminine subjectivity aware of itself as a process and a practice.

This is achieved in the context of an often intimate and humorous stage–audience dynamic established in the prologue and/or during the course of the play, and geared to provoke critical reflection rather than the complacent catharsis of a fourth-wall response. Her use of comedy is particularly important in that it counteracts one of the dominant stereotypes of feminism as unattractively bitter and humourless. More significantly, the fact that her critique takes place within the context of heterosexuality and marriage also disavows one popular misconception of feminism as a position definable as radical lesbian separatism, rather than a plurality of positions, as is in fact the case. Dominant ideological forces propagate this misrepresentation in order to mask the existence of other feminist positions, notably the particularly threatening ones working within, rather than outside, heterosexuality and marriage. In her use of the comic genre as a vehicle for critique, Rame follows a long tradition. Explaining her use of comedy, she says:

When you go to the theatre and see a tragedy, you identify, get involved, cry your heart out, and then go home and say: 'What a good cry I've had tonight!', and you sleep relaxed. The political content has passed you by, like water off a duck's back. In order to laugh, on the other hand – and this is still Molière talking – you need intelligence, sharpness of mind. It's not only your mouth, but also your mind, that opens wide with laughing, and into your mind go the nails of reason. (Fo 1989, p. 9)

A grotesque vein often provides an edge in realist comedies that epitomize the everyday (*Una donna sola, Rientro a casa, Coppia aperta, quasi spalancata, La donna grassa* and most of her other plays), and in comic surrealist fantasy (*Alice nel paese senza meraviglie*), comic mythical allegory (*La Medea, Lisistrata romana*) and farce (*La maestra di ballo, Il pupazzo giapponese*).

The stage–audience relationship set up by Rame also works to reinforce the strengthening of bonds between women, visible in several of her plays, and recognized by Italian feminism as crucial to *autocoscienza* (and thence to the freeing-up of multiple feminine subject positions). Direct address and interaction with female members of the audience are features of her performances that find their way, in turn, into subsequent versions of the dramatic text. In evaluating the perception by female and male spectators of Rame's female parts in terms of the dramatic criteria of stage setting (time and place), action and speech vehicles, and comparing the subsequent stage–audience dynamics with those explored in earlier chapters, a scenario comes into focus, the complexity of which mirrors that of Rame's female subjects discussed in the previous section.

As one would expect in plays dealing with contemporary everyday life, many of Rame's female parts have freedom of movement. They appear unproblematically in the street (*Il problema dei vecchi*) or indoors (*Coppia aperta, quasi spalancata*), or move between both outdoor street and indoor domestic scenes, irrespective of the time of day (*Rientro a casa*). They are shown outside the home in the public sphere of work (*Il pupazzo giapponese, La maestra di ballo: catena di montaggio, La casellante, La nonna incinta*), or at the wheel of a car in a transcontinental rally (*Parigi-Dakar*). Of course many are older, married female parts who would also have been allowed to appear unchaperoned in street scenes in the comedies of the Renaissance and Goldoni. There they would have functioned, however, mostly as minor characters, with plot interest usually revolving around younger, nubile female bodies. A shift of interest towards older married and unmarried female characters, albeit mostly pejorative, is discernible in the plays of both D'Annunzio and Pirandello. Rame's older female parts, on the other hand, take centre stage to take issue with patriarchal stereotypes.

While they occupy a variety of stage settings, for a number of female parts, however, both outdoor and indoor scenarios have negative connotations. An outdoor job as street vendor in an insalubrious area, exposed to all weathers and to the violent criminal underworld, has become the lot of Carla, an ex-teacher of Latin and mother of heroin-addicted children who is accidentally shot dead at the end of the play (*L'eroina*). Other working female parts are also in danger. As factory workers in *Il pupazzo giapponese*, they are drugged to increase efficiency, and have also lost limbs because of poor safety standards. In *La maestra di ballo: catena di montaggio*, their ability to have children has been severely damaged through repetitive strain injury on the production line. Adverse conditions of work and housing for the female level crossing keeper in *La casellante* mean constant ill-health for her family. On the indoor front, Maria in *Una donna sola* is permanently locked indoors by her husband. Mattea in *La donna grassa*, Antonia in *Coppia aperta, quasi spalancata* and Giulia in *Una giornata qualunque* all experience isolation and alienation in their homes. For some female parts, 'inside' means being locked up in a mental asylum (*Monologo di una puttana in manicomio, Il pupazzo giapponese, Una giornata qualunque, Michele lu Lanzone*), while references to madness by the female parts themselves are not uncommon.

In assessing Rame's stage settings in terms of positive development

for the dramatic representation of femininity, these negative stage settings demand closer attention. The place where the female parts are
seen to carry out their self-exploration is particularly significant in
terms of the visual aspect of the stage–audience dynamic; the stage setting can therefore never be considered as mere background, but always
carries meaning (as discussed in chapter one). Moreover, in the case of
stage settings that are mimed, audience attention is specifically directed by the actress to her surroundings (*Abbiamo tutte la stessa storia*). In the
complex coexistence of critique with reinforcement of patriarchy in
Rame's plays, it is not always easy to unravel the status of the stage
settings. Sometimes the stage setting is openly criticized as part of the
particular aspect of contemporary society under scrutiny. This is the
case of many of the ubiquitous indoor, domestic settings in Rame's
plays, and ties in with her focus on unmasking traditional home and
family as idealized patriarchal institutions harbouring female oppression. At other times, however, the setting remains unmarked, receiving
no comment.

The domestic habitat confining and defining patriarchal femininity
is made the overt object of critique, in different degrees, by both
Antonia in *Coppia aperta, quasi spalancata* and Giulia in *Una giornata
qualunque*, so that the audience is forced into an awareness of the formal
dramatic element of place, and of its implications for feminine subjectivity. For Giulia, the urge to 'get out of this house that's driving you
mad . . . to go out . . . talk to people' (Fo and Rame 1991, p. 71) is an
important step as she proceeds towards *autocoscienza* during the course
of the play. In the case of Antonia, her move towards self-development
in finding work and taking part in activities outside the house and
among people in *Coppia aperta, quasi spalancata* has already taken place,
and is recounted as antefact. The play is set in the new home she has
established after leaving her husband, but with the emphasis remaining on her relationships with men (ex-husband, son, lover), the critique
of place remains passing and momentary, rather than forming part of
the *dénouement*, as in *Una giornata qualunque*.

On the other hand, no critique of the traditional alignment of femininity with the domestic scenario takes place in *L'uomo incinto* (first performed in 1977). During the course of this play the action moves from a
scene with the Mother (*Madre*) and the Daughter (*Figlia*), set in the
Mother's home, to a scene with the *Industriale* (the father and husband)
and the *Professore*, in the latter's medical study, with the naming of the
characters further reinforcing stereotypical gender roles. (There is also

a female nurse (*Infermiera*) whose menial role is established when she is summoned to take an order for refreshments.) While the play offers a critique of patriarchal double standards regarding reproductive roles, the audience is never distanced from, and therefore made aware of, the value-laden scenarios which the stage settings represent.

In *Una donna sola* critique of place is closed down by a no-exit ending, as in *Una giornata qualunque*. The fact that the apparently ordinary household setting in which Maria appears is actually one in which she is physically imprisoned is revealed during the course of the play in such a way as to surprise and shock her female neighbour, who points out that her husband is breaking the law in locking her indoors. Yet hand-in-hand with this critique of female enclosure is the implication that Maria is in effect powerless to prevent it. This is made evident by her reason for not reporting either her husband or the male voyeur to the authorities, namely that the law is patriarchal and would undoubtedly favour the two men. Her own illegal, and impotent, solution of violence at the end of the play reaffirms the hopelessness of her situation. While on the one hand, multiple feminine positions beckon as the play progresses, on the other, possibilities are shut down by the play's closure. Her enclosure in a private prison remains intact, with her imprisonment in a state prison an almost inevitable next step.

Prevalent in Renaissance Italy, and integrated into the stage practice of the classical comedies, the enclosure indoors of women continues to find stage space centuries later in the plays of Pirandello, together with forced confinement of women in mental asylums for patriarchal convenience (*Il beretto a sonagli*).[13] While Rame's *Una donna sola* at least offers a critique of female enclosure in the home, plays like *Monologo di una puttana in manicomio*, *Il pupazzo giapponese* and *Una giornata qualunque* appear not to explore enclosure in mental asylums as a form of medicalized discipline that has always been imposed on women in particular.[14] Even though *Michele lu Lanzone* contains criticism of the illegal but continuing practice of wrapping unruly inmates tightly in wet sheets until they faint (*la strozzina*), the fact that the Mother is there at all receives no attention.

Stage settings tend to portray stifling domestic surroundings and hazardous lower-class workplaces, in line with the aspects of contemporary industrialized patriarchy that Rame singles out for critique. Yet even in plays figuring middle-class female parts with occupations that are not problematic, the locus of action still remains exclusively in the domain of the domestic and the sexual. Any shift in focus away from patriarchal definitions of femininity, with its domestic, familial implications, to a femininity with other elements, such as a career or leisure pursuit also contributing to its identity, remains but a glimmer. Even *La nonna incinta*, set not in a factory, but in an artist's studio, and opening with Franca seen creatively at work restoring a statue, is concerned with her pregnancy. One could, of course, choose to read the nature of her pregnancy (her bearing of a child on her daughter's behalf, engineered by the son-in-law to safeguard his wife's lucrative career), as a violation of her own career. However, the play never explicitly acknowledges any pleasure or fulfilment that she might be experiencing in her work.

In conjunction with the type of action depicted in the plays, exploration of the precise form that this takes on stage raises the issue of how the female parts use their bodies in performance. In particular, do the dancing female bodies in *Una donna sola* and *La maestra di ballo: catena di montaggio* function exhibitionistically as spectacle, providing opportunities for audience voyeurism and interrupting narrative progression (like, for example, Basiliola's erotic dance in D'Annunzio's *La nave*, or the Stepdaughter's dance in Pirandello's *Sei personaggi in cerca d'autore*)?[15] Do enlarged female screen images (*Una giornata qualunque*) and outsized female silhouettes (*La donna grassa*) act as the monstrous feminine, an excessive, alarming, sharp-toothed femininity that threatens to disempower masculinity and that must be cut down to size (like Pirandello's Tuda, who appears on stage initially in the form of a giant silhouette, only to become anorexic during the course of *Diana e la Tuda*)?

Maria enters the stage in *Una donna sola* dancing frenetically to rock music, clad in a transparent, low-cut negligée that led to objections from feminists. While gratuitous, sensationalist exhibition of the female body reinforces patriarchal definition and objectification of femininity *as* body (in opposition to masculinity as subject and intellect), to deny the female body runs the danger of obliterating female eroticism altogether. *Una donna sola* can be read as an attempt to reappropriate female eroticism for a non-patriarchal femininity currently besieged by various forms of exploitation and harassment. In this context, Maria's revealing costume is not gratuitous, but, functioning as semi-nudity rather than semi-nakedness, forms an integral part of the satire on a femininity grotesquely abused from all angles.

In addition to her selfish and violent husband, her brother-in-law's gropings, a voyeur and a lover, all seeking gratification at her expense, she is also subjected to obscene phone calls. While swelling an already absurdly long list, the inclusion of a phone caller (who presumably does not know what she is wearing) also indicates that her sexual harassment is not 'caused' by her transparent attire, thereby undercutting the patriarchal assumption that women are to be held responsible for men's sexual reactions to them. At the same time, the sheer extent of male sexual response to this particular female part serves to ridicule the patriarchal fantasy/nightmare of an excessive female sexuality that cannot be contained, with Maria's 'sexual powers' emanating well beyond her domestic prison. Importantly, however, Maria is no *femme fatale* (a factor that helps to differentiate her from D'Annunzio's Basiliola, for instance). As the prologue makes clear, Maria is 'simple' and 'naïve', modelling herself on television images of femininity (Fo 1989, p. 7). Yet, unlike Flaubert's Emma Bovary, who remains attached to her romantic, literary blueprints and interested only in male characters, Maria makes significant progress towards *autocoscienza* through her new female friendship.

Together with her revealing stage costume, Maria's dance is also to be read in a satirical context. It is neither erotic, nor, coming as it does at the beginning of the play, interruptive of narrative progression, to which, on the contrary, it functions as a trigger. The frenetic speed at which the dance takes place, to the accompaniment of loud rock music, together with the basket of ironing that Maria holds, serve to deny interpretation as sultry, erotic spectacle catering for voyeurism. Dancing female bodies are particularly central to *La maestra di ballo: catena di montaggio* (*The dancing mistress: assembly-line style*). In this play, dance movements are foregrounded in a critique of exploitation of the female workforce in the context of contemporary industrialized Italy. Three aspiring female factory workers are trained by a dance mistress in the twenty-four different movements they will need to perform repeatedly at the machines. These numerous, repetitive movements are disguised as an enjoyable form of art, or a means of keeping fit, in order to fill the workers with enthusiasm and so maximize production on the assembly line. Coupled with this disguise is encouragement of the alienation of women from each other in the form of cross-class competitiveness: 'Have you seen how simple it is? Then there's the further advantage of firming-up the pectoral muscles and getting rid of cellulite. Who knows how many ladies would pay to be in your place!' (Fo 1989, pp. 80–1).

The dance mistress is the only speaking part, while the factory girls merely dance, with the occasional quizzical look at their teacher. Once

they have mastered the movements, they dance 'with a by now obses-
sive rhythm' (Fo 1989, p. 81). However, any notion of gratuitous spectacle is immediately undercut by the intervention of an offstage voice
from a loud-hailer that accompanies the dance, intoning the injurious
effects on women's gynaecological health of the repetitive strain of performing forty thousand five hundred awkward movements each day
(Fo 1989, pp. 81–2). As in the case of *Una donna sola*, the female bodies in
La maestra di ballo: catena di montaggio do not function to provide sensationalist sexual exhibitionism. In both plays, the female body is
incorporated into a critique of patriarchal exploitation in contemporary society, while the use of distancing effects (fast music, props,
voiceover) maintains audience awareness of the formal properties of
performance.

The female body also takes to the stage in Rame's plays in the form
of images projected on to a screen or backcloth. The role of the media
in producing and reproducing images of femininity in *Una donna sola*
raises issues of femininity *as* image. The inherent notion of surface and
the consequent implications of fetishism for femininity have been
explored in chapter two, while the screen imaging of femininity that
exploded with the advent of cinema has been a major focus of feminist
film studies.[16] Rame's middle-class female parts have access to the
technology allowing them to produce their own images of themselves.
Franca in *Ho fatto la plastica* makes a video of her new, surgically 'lifted'
and rebuilt self for a female friend in a play that opens with a denuncia-
tion, by a *male* television presenter, of the 'pervasiveness of stupid
moralisms' that make women undergo cosmetic surgery 'as if it were a
sin, a horrendously shameful act, to be confided only to a close female
friend' (Fo and Rame 1991, p. 167). During the course of making this
video, an image construction of yet another reconstructed surface (the
female body), the female part comes to finally reject the complete
subsumption into surface and image to which the media's mediation of
femininity has reduced her.

Enlarged screen images of femininity figure in *Una giornata qualunque*,
a play that makes extensive, and particularly farcical, use of television
and video, along with other, more mechanical devices. Like *Ho fatto la
plastica*, this play opens with the making of a video as a modern technological means of communication that can replace the written letter.
An enormous screen placed at the back of the stage is filled with an
image of Giulia, an image that she plays with, adjusting both her
clothes and, by means of signals to unseen stage hands, the lighting and

camera angles. In a passing comment, she reveals that she is familiar with camerawork ('I'm so nervous . . . I'm used to being behind the camera, not in front of it' (Fo and Rame 1991, p. 38)), while a complex system of warning gadgets that spring into action when she tries to drink and smoke illustrates that she is at home with modern technology.

As she creates her image on the screen, she plays with the enlarging effect of placing her hands close to the camera, while the slow music she has added as a sound-track suddenly erupts into blaring rock music, and the telephone keeps ringing. By showing the feminine image in the process of construction by the female part herself, and by breaking playfully into the process, the audience is distanced from the enormous image before it. Constantly reminded of the constructability of the image, and so of the performativity of a feminine subjectivity in control of its own constitution, the audience is not allowed to identify with the image, or to occupy a voyeuristic position in relation to it. Images from television replace Giulia's images as she postpones her suicide for a chicken dinner and one last episode of her favourite soap. Screen images and real life intermingle comically when she believes herself to be addressed by a policeman in a crime thriller on the screen (but presaging the real policeman who helps the doctor take her away at the end of the play). Comically immersed in images generated by the media and modern technology, it is in fact a combination of this technology, in the form of the telephone, with the written medium (a magazine) that brings her, however accidentally, into contact with Clara. This is not only an indication that technology can bring people together, rather than alienating them from each other, but also points to a future where the inside–outside dichotomy, as utilized by patriarchy, may no longer have meaning.

The enormous female image at the beginning of *Una giornata qualunque* recurs in *La donna grassa*, this time in the form of the outsize silhouette of Mattea. In this play devoted to the female body and the contemporary western patriarchal template for ideal female body size, Mattea's actual body is not always visible on stage, disappearing at regular intervals to leave behind only a voice. In the opening scene, a female and a male voice are heard emanating from a bed, but neither is seen in the flesh. Mattea then gets up, to vanish shortly afterwards into the bathroom, at which point the audience sees 'Mattea's rather abundant "silhouette"' (Rame 1992, p. 62). However, this is no erotic silhouette (like that of Tuda which opens Pirandello's play *Diana e la Tuda*), but one that is sitting on the toilet having a pee ('fa pipì'). Mattea disappears from view again later in the play, on the arrival of a stranger. She puts up a dividing screen and proceeds to converse with him from behind it. On her reappearance, and after a brief interchange, he exits, and the audience once again sees her silhouette, this time as she washes herself. She is joined in the bathroom by her daughter, Anna, who undresses and mimes having a shower. This time, both women are watched by a Young Man, Mattea's colleague, in an act of voyeurism discovered and cut short by Mattea, who sends him into the kitchen. Anna reappears, wrapped in a towel, finally going back into the bathroom, where she gets dressed.

While the play on Mattea's silhouette comically deflates any possibility for audience voyeurism, it is difficult to see why Anna should spend so much of her time undressed, particularly in the presence of someone she has never met before. A further area for debate in this play is the frequent use of Mattea's disembodied voice. While the voice of the Man in bed is of course even more disembodied, being in the form of a tape recording, the frequent disappearance of the female body raises the issues of invisibility and a voice for femininity explored earlier in relation to the Renaissance comedies. On the one hand, the omnipresence of Mattea's voice can be read as positive in terms of feminine subjectivity, and notably so when detached from the body, which is, after all, the defining factor of patriarchal femininity. There is also a reversal of the traditional dynamic of masculine voyeurism–feminine exhibitionism/spectacle (as exemplified by the Young Man watching the women's naked silhouettes) in the episode when Mattea can see the stranger who visits her, while he can only hear her. On the other hand, this reversal is only temporary, ending with the stranger's exit when, having at last presented herself to him, Mattea threatens to strip. Moreover, the reason for the reversal in the first place is a negative one, namely her poor self-image. As far as her voice is concerned, while it is always to be heard, a denial of the female body, as discussed earlier, is not to be advocated, given the relative invisibility of feminine subjectivity within patriarchy.

The notion of a feminine voice is central to the third and last dramatic criterion, that of speech vehicles. In the Renaissance comedies, the dramatic feminine voice was relegated to the wings not just on the basic level of the transvestism of boy actors as female characters, but also in terms of the female characters themselves. Enmeshed with the frequent ventriloquizing of their views by male characters went the standard dramatic practice, informed by the sociocultural context, of severely limiting their stage presence and curtailing their access to the full range of speech vehicles according to their age, class and marital status. In diametric opposition, Rame's female parts (most notably in the monologues and plays written for several parts but performed as monologues) speak for themselves and take over the speech of other parts, both male and female, in ways that have already been mentioned.

In the monologue *La mamma fricchettona*, for example, the priest's contributions to the dialogue with the Donna, and her arrest and handcuffing by policemen, are all inferred by the audience from the female part alone on stage, a dramatic practice recalling the mediaeval jester's performance 'in which the storyteller, in this case myself, a woman, acts all the parts through allusion' (Fo 1989, p. 159). While in this play the priest and policeman are not represented in any physical form, in *Il risveglio*, for instance, a mannequin is used to play the part of the slumbering husband, whose viewpoint in arguments belonging to the play's antefact is ventriloquized by the Donna in her monologue. The female part in the mediaeval *Contrasto per una sola voce* denies her male lover, who has a walk-on part only, any form of speech apart from the odd sneeze, using the pretext that her parents are sleeping nearby. Even in *La donna grassa*, a play including two speaking male parts, the main female part has constructed a third male voice according to her own desires. Moreover, Mattea in this play, like Carla in *L'eroina*, maintains a position of centrality in a polylogue context, by virtue of the fact that she is always the main addressee of all the other parts.

Organization of the speech vehicles around the female part is an important contribution to audience perception of a dramatic femininity that is centre stage. This is complemented by another performance strategy, namely that of direct address. Direct address to the auditorium constructs the audience *as* audience, formalizing the relationship between stage and auditorium by breaking down the fourth wall, and counteracting the dynamic of non-critical, escapist identification and voyeurism. In particular, direct address to female spectators means a strengthening of bonds between women (a necessary part of *autocoscienza* in a patriarchal context) across the stage–auditorium divide. Women are addressed in the prologue (*La Medea, Una madre*), as well as during the course of the play itself. Stage directions in *Abbiamo tutte la stessa storia*, for instance, state that the Ragazza 'directly addresses the women present at the front of the auditorium' (Fo 1989, p. 53), while in the prologue to *La Medea*, Rame dedicates each performance of this favourite play to 'all the young, and not so young, present in the theatre' (Fo 1989, p. 71).

Direct address is a prominent feature of *Coppia aperta, quasi spalancata*, a polylogue with three speaking parts. Significantly, Antonia addresses the audience much more frequently than her ex-husband (named generically as 'Man' in the stage directions). The thirty-nine stage directions instructing her to directly address the audience, or to turn towards them, in comparison with the Man's seven, ensure Antonia's greater rapport with the audience in a context where attention is divided between two characters on stage. Also included is a direct address by Antonia to the women in the audience, with whom she strikes up a special relationship through mock didacticism: 'The first rule . . . you women at the front, take notes from now on . . . you never know . . . my experiences might be useful . . . the first rule, as I was saying, is to leave home' (Fo and Rame 1991, p. 11).

The use of direct address and, in the monologues, the playing of multiple parts by one actress, are central to Rame's performance politics. Her adherence to a type of stage practice derived from pre-Renaissance times functions particularly well in ensuring the dominance of a dramatic feminine voice. Moreover, many of the plays dramatize the taking up of a variety of feminine subject positions, rather than adhering to the limited feminine stereotypes fantasized by mainstream dramatists. In a fertile blend of past dramatic methods with contemporary concerns relevant to women's lives, her female parts break the mould by offering a critique of patriarchal definitions of femininity. However, at times this critique appears to sit alongside the actual reinforcement of traditional values. It is tempting to see the problem of authorship resurfacing here, and to designate the patriarchal viewpoint as Fo's contribution. Alternatively, one could attribute the two contrasting standpoints to Rame's own multiple feminine identity, and read the combination as indicative of the specific historical and socioeconomic context of her personal, political and theatrical development. Beyond all doubt, however, is the fact that Rame has made an important contribution. This is to be found in the particular kind of link she forges between the dramatic and ideological spheres, in that her plays work to activate not simply feminine subjectivity itself, but feminine subjectivity as a performative process that is ongoing and so open to change.

Notes

1. See, for example, Hartsock 1983.
2. Critiques of western epistemology can be found in Alcoff and Potter 1993; Hekman 1990; Jay 1981; and Nicholson 1990.
3. This is one of the many issues concerning the reader and meaning-construction addressed in Mills 1994.
4. This distinction is explained in Elam 1980, p. 3.

I   WAITING IN THE WINGS: FEMALE CHARACTERS IN ITALIAN RENAISSANCE COMEDY

1. According to Pietropaolo, the comedies accounted for 90 per cent of all performances. This study is limited to the following: Ariosto, *La cassaria* (*The affair of the chest*), 1508, *I suppositi* (*The substitutes*), 1509, and *La Lena* (*Lena*), 1528, in Ariosto 1954; Machiavelli, *La mandragola* (*The mandragola*), 1518, and *Clizia* (*Clizia*), 1525, in Machiavelli 1964; Gli Intronati, *Gli ingannati* (*The deceived*), 1537 (first performed 1531), and Bibbiena, *La Calandria* (*Calandria*), 1513, in Borsellino 1962, 1967, vols I, II; Aretino, *La cortigiana* (*Court affairs*), 1525, in Aretino 1968. For plot summaries and discussion of the development of this genre in Renaissance Italy, see Andrews 1993, and Radcliff-Umstead 1969.
2. The plays belong mostly to what Andrews calls the 'pioneering period' in this tradition, a period that produced at most only fourteen plays; the pace of production accelerated thereafter, so that the years 1528 to 1555 saw over a hundred new erudite comedies, while by the end of the century the total was over 250 (Andrews 1993, p. 64).
3. On the *sacre rappresentazioni*, see D'Ancona 1966.
4. See Radcliff-Umstead 1969; Duckworth 1971; Beare 1968; Hunter 1985, on the Roman plays, and the first two authors on Roman influence on the Renaissance comedies.
5. Toffanin believes that 'Renaissance society, especially the family, had not altered so radically from ancient Rome that the influence of Plautus and Terence led dramatists to present a distorted portrayal of life in modern Italy' (Radcliff-Umstead 1969, p. 19). Herrick states: 'a surprising number

of learned comedies continued to keep respectable women off stage as did the ancient Romans' (Herrick 1960, p. 66).

6. Theoretical treatment of the unities became widespread in Italy only from 1536, the date of a new published edition of Aristotle's *Poetics*, and five years after the latest play under consideration here (Andrews 1993, pp. 204–8).

7. For the application to English Renaissance texts of this suggestive notion of the ventriloquizing of the female voice, see Harvey 1992.

8. Curfew did at times exist, but is not mentioned in these plays. Klapisch-Zuber notes fifteenth-century instances in some towns (Klapisch-Zuber 1985, p. 268). Brucker refers to curfew in Florence in 1453 (Brucker 1986, p. 20).

9. Writing on theatre in his *Second book of architecture*, 1545, Serlio says: 'In other scenes the sun rises, moves on its course, and at the end of the play is made to set with such skill that many spectators remain lost in wonder' (Hewitt 1958, p. 24). See also Molinari's reference to a 1539 production of *Commodo* using an imaginary but realistic sun which 'in the perspectival sky . . . progressing gently, made known step by step the supposed time of day' (Molinari 1964, p. 69, n. 22). He also notes that in a performance of *Alidoro* at Reggio in 1508 the same sky covered both stage and auditorium (p. 69, n. 22).

10. Sabbattini introduces Book 2 of his *Manual for constructing theatrical scenes and machines* as follows: 'In the first book we dealt with the method of making scenes and stage devices: now in the second we shall deal with the *intermezzi*, for today it seems that no good show can be presented without complete or partial change of scenery' (Hewitt 1958, p. 98).

11. On the playwright's obligation to work within the Serlian framework, Pietropaolo says: 'Once the Serlian scene became the orthodox setting, the playwright had little to say on the matter. The spatiality of his play was not something of his making, but rather an independently determined starting condition which imposed obvious restraints on his imagination. Of course, he could choose to locate the action in any city . . . three houses shown in perspective on the right, three on the left, and a church at the back of the stage defined the performance space of virtually every comedy' (Pietropaolo 1986, p. 38).

12. Pfister similarly notes the influence of stage setting on the content of a play. On the subject of a German play of 1890, he writes: 'Replacing the type of public locale that unity of place in classical and classicizing drama was based on by a private interior is therefore primarily of thematic importance' (Pfister 1991, p. 252).

13. In his account of the love affair between Giovanni and Lusanna in fifteenth-century Florence, Brucker writes: 'Lusanna was also a frequent visitor to the Servite Church of Santissima Annunziata, with its famed image of the Annunciation, a particular object of veneration of Florentine women hoping to become pregnant' (Brucker 1986, p. 9).

14. Pietropaolo points out the perspectival significance of the position of the church on stage: 'Being the meeting place accessible to all social groups, the church on whose door is significantly located the vanishing point of the parallel plane of the set, is another centripetal focus of demographic motion and may . . . be regarded as the enclosed counterpart of the public square that extends in front of it' (Pietropaolo 1986, p. 39).

15. The binary opposition is one of a set of epistemological structures that shape western thought and that are currently under critique within feminist postmodernism. See Introduction, note 2. For an account of the Renaissance inheritance of dualities from Greek thought, see Maclean 1985; for a discussion of the impact of binary oppositions and other epistemological structures on definitions of power in the context of Machiavelli's *Il principe*, see Günsberg 1995.

16. For an account of the importance within patriarchy of the various stages of female sexuality, see Hastrup 1978.

17. See Machiavelli, *Il principe*, chapter 17. On the status of women in Renaissance Tuscany, see Brown 1986.

18. With reference to the citizenship of women, Chamberlin notes that a woman was 'denied all political rights and was, according to both civil and canon law, reckoned as being subject to her husband' (Chamberlin 1969, p. 198). For the prevalence of the enclosure of women in the home, particularly in Florence, see Brown 1986.

19. Serlio goes on to argue against this practice as follows: 'I do not recommend this practice, however, because although the figures represent living creatures they show no movement.'

20. Trickery has a long tradition, particularly in the history of western comedy, and was already established in the *Atellanae*, the southern Italian rustic farce of the third century BC in which Plautus began his theatre career as an actor and upon which he was to base the characters of his comedies (Harwood 1984, pp. 69–70). Firth goes even further back to Epicharmus of Syracuse in the fifth century BC, 'writing on Italian soil the earliest recorded comic pieces'. She sees his work as expressing 'in a prophetic germ two themes . . . one, the preoccupation with the concept of identity; and two, the insistence upon wit or intellectual virtue as the ultimate human value' (Firth 1978, p. 63). See this study for an informative introduction to Italian comedy.

21. In their regard, Brucker notes that it was in fact common for the sons of wealthy men to delay marriage, and to have sexual liaisons and children with women from lower classes, then eventually marrying women from their own class for reasons of lineage and patrimony (Brucker 1986, p. 78).

22. A longer version of this section appeared as 'Commodification of the female body in Italian Renaissance comedy', *Romance studies*, 1994, 24, 41–57.

23. On realism, see Belsey 1985.

24. While following certain Roman practices, *La mandragola*, *La Lena* and *La*

cortigiana, unlike the other five plays, do not appear to be directly indebted to any of the Roman plays in particular. Information on sources is included in Andrews 1993; Duckworth 1971; Herrick 1950; Radcliff-Umstead 1969. The following Roman comedies will be examined as the most likely classical influences on our Renaissance plays: Terence, *Eunuchus, Andria, Heautontimorumenos, Phormio,* in Page 1912, vols. I, II; Plautus, *Captivi, Casina, Menaechmi, Mostellaria,* in Page 1956–7, vols. I–III.

25. Anderson cites the following reasons for the weak urban economy of the ancient world, with its manufactured goods restricted to textiles, pottery, furniture and glass-ware: the high cost of transport, simple techniques and limited demand (Anderson 1985, p. 19).

26. Anderson notes: 'Mercantile and banking capital, always lamed in the classical world by the absence of the necessary financial institutions to ensure its secure accumulation, now expanded vigorously and freely with the advent of the joint-stock company, bill of exchange and double-account book-keeping: the device of the public debt, unknown to ancient cities, increased both State revenues and investment outlets for urban rentiers' (Anderson 1984, p. 152).

27. Writing about *I suppositi,* Andrews notes that 'illicit seduction being regularized by marriage has something about it of the mediaeval *novella,* and thus represents a pattern of sexual intrigue far more familiar to a courtly audience' (Andrews 1993, p. 39).

28. The plot of Plautus' *Mercator* concerns a merchant family with landowning origins. Charinus states in Act I, scene I (which functions as prologue) that his father, Demepho, sold the farm he inherited 'and with the money bought a ship of fifteen tons burden and marketed his cargoes of merchandise everywhere'.

29. Radcliff-Umstead believes that *La Calandria* in fact owes more to the *Decameron* and to humanistic comedy than to *Menaechmi,* from which it borrows only the device of mistaken identity facilitated by using twins (Radcliff-Umstead 1969, pp. 146–52).

30. People spent their money on 'food and clothes, furniture and moveable decorations being considered relatively unimportant' (Chamberlin 1982, p. 201).

31. See Irigaray 1977.

32. See chapter 2 for a discussion of fetishism.

33. See Herlihy 1978, chapter 14. Whenever reference is made in these Roman plays to the financial settlement upon marriage, this is always in terms of a dowry, and never a counter-dowry (*Menaechmi,* Act V, scene 2; *Andria,* Act V).

34. See D'Ancona on the effect of warfare on theatre performances (D'Ancona 1966, vol. II). On Renaissance criminality, see Chamberlin 1982.

35. Klapisch-Zuber writes: 'kinship, friendship, and neighborliness are thus almost always evaluated in terms of their social utility' (Klapisch-Zuber 1985, p. 68).

36. Interestingly, a similar situation appears to have existed in English Renaissance drama. See Mack 1979.

37. Of the eight Roman comedies which are believed to have most influenced these plays, three contain mothers: Cleostrata in *Casina*, Nausistrata in *Phormio* and Sostrata in *Heautontimorumenos*.

38. Hewitt notes that 'since the performance on the floor of the hall of dances, combats, and tourneys was often as important as anything on the stage, the auditorium required brilliant lighting both for the performance and for the well-dressed audience', and that even when 'the performance came to be concentrated more and more behind the proscenium', and 'there was less necessity for brilliant light in the auditorium', nevertheless 'the audience would expect some light throughout the performance, for not until recent years would there be the means or the convention for the audience to see a performance from a dark auditorium' (Hewitt 1958, p. 15).

39. On dramatic terminology, and on the debate concerning the distinction between the soliloquy and the monologue, see Pfister 1991.

40. See Silverman 1983, for an introduction to this field.

2 GENDER DECEPTIONS: CROSS-DRESSING IN ITALIAN RENAISSANCE COMEDY

1. This chapter examines the same corpus of early sixteenth-century erudite comedies as the previous chapter. See chapter 1, note 1, for details.

2. Of particular note is Suor Annalena Odaldi, whose convent farce uses cross-dressing. See Bloomsbury 1992; Weaver 1986.

3. Duckworth notes that this method appears in half of Plautus' plays and also in those of Terence (Duckworth 1971, p. 169).

4. Disguise is used in Boccaccio's *Decameron*, while the epic poems of Ariosto and Tasso each contain female warriors fighting in male guise (Bradamante and Marfisa in the *Orlando furioso*, and Clorinda in the *Gerusalemme liberata*). For a discussion of these female warriors, see Günsberg 1991. For disguise in popular culture, see Burke 1978.

5. On gender inversion in the context of the world-upside-down, see Stallybrass 1991, and Babcock 1978. For the classical origins of the inversion motif, see Curtius 1973, pp. 94–8.

6. Signor Parabolano, at the end of *La cortigiana*, concludes that the play 'è di Carnovale'. See D'Ancona for details of performances of the comedies during Carnival in Rome in 1508 (when, in conjunction with celebrations of the wedding between a nephew of Pope Giulio II and one of the Colonnas, 'three meals and two plays were prepared' (D'Ancona 1966, II, p. 77)), 1510 (p. 78), 1513 (pp. 83–4), in Urbino in 1513, when the *Calandria* was performed at the court of Duke Guidobaldo (p. 102) and in 1542 in Mantua (p. 440). See also Bristol 1985.

7. Reference is also made in this study to an Italian woman who used male disguise to work as a sailor during the Battle of Lepanto, 1571, and to Catterina Vizzani, a Roman cross-dresser who was reported in an eighteenth-century text as having spent eight years working as a servant, and who was found to be female upon her death (p. 113).

8. See chapter 1, note 13. For an account of this system of attributes as portrayed in Italian Renaissance epic poetry, particularly as regards female cross-dressing, see Günsberg 1991, pp. 174–8.

9. Brown notes that the earliest known such legislation, in late thirteenth-century France, advocated death by fire for both men and women committing an act of sodomy with the same, or opposite sex, for the third time, a recommendation that was repeated by Bartholomaeus de Saliceto in the fifteenth century. She goes on to say that 'it was not until the sixteenth century, when the Catholic and Protestant reformations brought about a growing concern with legislating moral conduct and curbing heresy, an offense traditionally associated with homosexuality, that such harsh views became common in the few laws and juridical commentaries that discussed the subject. The two laws of the period that specifically mentioned women in connection with same-gender sex both provided the death sentence. Charles V's statute of 1532 stated: "If anyone commits impurity with a beast, or a man with a man, or a woman with a woman, they have forfeited their lives and shall, after the common custom, be sentenced to death by burning." Treviso's law similarly noted that: "If . . . a woman commits this vice or sin against nature, she shall be fastened naked to a stake in the Street of Locusts and shall remain there all day and night under a reliable guard, and the following day shall be burned outside the city"' (Brown 1989, p. 72).

10. Gamman and Makinen identify three types of fetishism in western culture: commodity fetishism, anthropological fetishism and 'psychiatric' or 'pathological' fetishism (with the latter referred to as 'sexual' fetishism) (Gamman and Makinen 1994, p. 15). For a discussion of these types of fetishism, see their first chapter.

11. I am indebted here to Stallybrass's focus on a crucial quotation from Freud's essay on 'Fetishism' (Stallybrass 1992, pp. 78–9).

12. Cecchini writes that in 1621 it was 'fifty years that women have been in the habit of appearing on stage'; Riccoboni writes that they were introduced around 1560 (D'Ancona 1966, II, p. 448, n.1).

13. See also his chapter 'Le donne nella Sacra Rappresentazione' (D'Ancona 1966, II, pp. 632–43).

14. See Duchartre 1966; Firth 1978, p. 64; Gilder 1960, p. 51.

15. In the prologue to *La Calandria* mention is made of the fact that the play 'is not in Latin: because, having to be performed before infinite numbers, who are not all learned, the author, who above all seeks to please you, wanted to write it in the vernacular; with the intention that, understood by all, it should delight each person equally'.

16. D'Ancona notes the celebratory reception for an actress such as Vincenza Armani on her entry to a new town: 'on her arrival in some towns, artillery was fired, and that's no fable' (D'Ancona 1966, I, p. 403 n.2).

17. See Case 1988, and Ferris 1990.

18. See also Duchartre 1966, p.28.

19. Isabella d'Este writes on 12 November 1503 concerning the performance by 'the pupils of master Francesco from the school' of a play by Apuleius; in November 1521, Equicola notes that a Latin comedy was performed in a private house 'by various young men' (D'Ancona 1966, II, pp. 388, 397).

20. See Metz 1977, and Mulvey 1989.

21. On the comedies as 'an integrated spectacle in which words, scenery, music, dance and performance were all equally important', see Andrews 1993, p. 96.

22. On *intermezzi* see also Jacquot 1964, and Nicoll 1938.

23. Isabella Gonzaga d'Este writes of her disappointment that there were only two *intermezzi* during what she describes as a long and tedious performance of *Bacchide* at Ferrara in 1501 (D'Ancona 1966, II, p. 385).

24. D'Ancona refers to the separation of women from men in the audience (D'Ancona 1966, II, p. 383). On the presence of the lower orders, Radcliff-Umstead, however, writes that 'the learned comedy never reached a wide audience in Italy, for it was confined to the larger towns and even within these larger towns to a limited audience of educated people who could relish a literary performance as well as slapstick. Outside of Italy the learned comedy was known only to the highly educated few or to the professional playwrights who could make use of it in their own work. Popular comedies before 1550 were religious plays or farces' (Radcliff-Umstead 1969, p. 210).

25. These theories of spectatorship, which originate in studies on film, can be fruitfully extended to the theatre, bearing in mind of course that film constructs the spectators' look in a highly complex and complete manner, while theatre allows the audience to focus anywhere on stage. Without the medium of the shot, a wide range of which is available to film (close-up, panning shot, reverse shot etc.), the theatre has taken recourse instead to other means for guiding audience attention, such as the use of speech vehicles like the soliloquy and monologue (see chapter 1 of this book). On female spectatorship, see also Pribram 1992.

26. See, for example, Stacey 1994.

27. Ariosto's epic poem *Orlando furioso*, 1532, contains such a boy–man pair, namely Medoro and Cloridan. Medoro, furthermore, is associated with femininity, so that Angelica's preference for him over and above the masculine warrior-heroes, whose pursuit of her is a major plot strand, is of great interest. See Günsberg 1991.

28. This summary is taken from the overview of current scholarship in Howard 1993, pp. 43–4, n. 3.

29. Radcliff-Umstead argues that almost all the comedies by this group are

addressed to the ladies in the audience (Radcliff-Umstead 1969, p. 197).

30. Garber 1992; Stallybrass 1992. The term *fetishism* was first used to denote a sexual (and criminal) form of obsession by Krafft Ebing in 1886, while Alfred Binet's sexual orientation of the term in 1888 also predates Freud (Gamman and Makinen 1994, p. 15).

31. For a summary of these arguments and objections to them, see Schor 1992, pp. 114–15. For an evaluation of feminist writing on fetishism, see Gamman and Makinen 1994, chapter 6. See also Grosz 1991.

32. A similar episode with lesbian undercurrents occurs in Ariosto's *Orlando furioso* (1532). In an episode narrated by Ricciardetto, Fiordispina falls in love with Bradamante, a female warrior who has had her hair cut short and who seems to Fiordispina to be male. Later, Bradamante is changed into what is described as 'the better sex' (*miglior sesso*) in that her twin brother, Ricciardetto, appears before Fiordispina to satisfy her desires.

33. The following contemporary Goliardic student song encapsulates the castration threat at the heart of fears about female sexuality:

> Hostelry number twenty!
> If vaginas had teeth,
> How many penises would be in hospital,
> How many vaginas in court!
> (Osteria numero venti!
> Se la fica avesse i denti,
> Quanti cazzi all'ospedale,
> Quante fighe al tribunale!)

I am grateful to Richard Andrews for bringing this song to my attention. On the *vagina dentata*, see Creed 1993; Theweleit 1990, p. 201.

34. Jardine argues that the association of cross-dressing with illicit desire is a trope informing textual instances of cross-dressing (Jardine 1992, chapter 3, especially p. 35, n. 5).

35. Jardine draws attention to 'the "moralizers" trope of the vulnerable boy captured in service by dominating female householders', giving as examples Plautus' *Menaechmi* and Secchi's *Gli ingannati* (Jardine 1992, p. 37, n. 24).

36. The oration can be found in Fratri 1928, pp. 251–62.

3   ARTFUL WOMEN: MORALITY AND MATERIALISM IN GOLDONI

1. See pp. 49–87 above.

2. While a play could of course be set entirely indoors, with no need for scene changes, an outdoor setting allowed for greater variation in the combinations of characters on stage. In *Il teatro comico* (1750), Goldoni's mouthpiece in this theatrical manifesto, Orazio, indicates the relevance of theatre technology to a play's content when he attributes the fact that the Ancients observed the unity of place to their inability to change scenes: 'The ancients did not have our facility for changing scenes, and that is why

they observed the unities' (II, 3) (Goldoni 1972). Quotations from the plays will be taken from this edition unless otherwise indicated.

3. Venice had grown to a city of over 100,000 by the end of the seventeenth century (Anderson and Zinsser 1988, II, p. 233). See this work also for a discussion of the implications for family life of expanding urban centres. On the rising population in the latter half of the eighteenth century in Europe, with Italy increasing from eleven to eighteen million, see Woloch 1982, pp. 107–9.

4. On the reception of actresses and on *La locandiera*, see Ferris 1990, chapter 4.

5. Andrieux states that seven permanent public theatres already existed to cater for a population of 130,000 when more were forbidden by a law of 10 November 1757 (Andrieux 1972, p. 182). Steele contrasts this situation with the predominance of temporary, private theatres elsewhere in Italy, and notes that Goldoni wrote for three of Venice's public theatres: the Teatro San Samuele (1734–40), the Teatro Sant'Angelo (1747–53), and the Teatro San Luca (1753–61) (Steele 1981, p. 15). Kennard accredits Venice with sixteen public theatres 'at a time when London had only six and Paris ten' (Kennard 1967, p. 164). It is possible that he includes temporary theatres in this number.

6. The western patriarchal splitting of femininity into angel and monster has a long history dating back to classical mythology. It is present in Dante's *Divina commedia*, for instance, in the form of the celestial Beatrice and the Siren. The notion of the angel in the house, with its particular connotation of domesticity, was crystallized by Coventry Patmore's poem *The angel in the house* in 1885. Ever since Virginia Woolf declared that, for women to write, the 'angel in the house' must be 'killed', the phrase has come to epitomize a stereotype of domesticated femininity limited exclusively to the private sphere (Gilbert and Gubar 1984, chapter 1).

7. See pp. 6–48 above.

8. For a discussion of chastity in terms of use and exchange value, see Günsberg 1994, pp. 7–8.

9. The genesis of Richardson's epistolary novel was a set of model letters for all social occasions, which he then imbued with a moralizing tone and enhanced with a plot. One of Pamela's main activities in the novel is in fact her letter-writing. See Woloch 1982, pp. 194–6.

10. On Venice as a pleasure centre, see Steele 1981, p. 20. On courtesans in Europe, and on Venice and Rome as European capitals of prostitution, see Anderson and Zinsser 1988, II, pp. 69–78.

11. This is the definition of prostitution given in Irigaray 1977, pp. 170, 181.

12. See Mangini 1974.

13. On gambling and the theatre, see Anglani 1983, pp. 140–3, and Cervato 1993, chapter 4.

14. Goldoni 1978.

15. The *Ménagier de Paris* instructed wives to restrain their husbands 'from follies and silly dealings' (Anderson and Zinsser 1988, I, p. 442).

16. Goldoni 1891, III.
17. See Sombart 1967.
18. See pp. 49–87 above.
19. See Howe 1992, pp. 37–65.

4   MASTERFUL MEN: DIFFERENCE AND FANTASY IN D'ANNUNZIO

1. Quotations from the plays are taken from this edition. For one-act plays, page references will be given; for plays divided into acts, but not scenes, the act reference will appear.
2. *Cavalleria rusticana* was intended as part of a dramatic trilogy that would exhibit the impersonal technique in three different class settings: the urban lower class in *In portineria*, and the upper class in *A villa d'Este*, or *Amori eleganti*. While *In portineria* was performed, albeit unsuccessfully, on 16 May 1885 at the Teatro Manzoni in Milan, no trace remains of the upper-class play of the trilogy (Barbini 1970, pp. 149, 151). Verga's unfinished narrative realist cycle, *I vinti*, shows a similar penchant towards lower- rather than upper-class ambiance, with only *I Malavoglia* and *Mastro-Don Gesualdo* being completed and *La Duchessa di Leyra* remaining half-written, while *L'onorevole Scipioni* and *L'uomo di lusso* never saw the light of day.
3. On alternative views of the concept of power, see Elshtain 1985 and Hartsock 1983.
4. This is also the opinion of Andrea Sperelli in D'Annunzio's novel *Il piacere* (1889).
5. The courage of Theseus, the hero of *Fedra*, in leading the siege against Thebes, is described by a messenger in terms of inhuman virtue (I). Marco Gratico in *La nave* is of leonine stock, while the heroes in *La gloria* are titanic and lion-hearted, and die on their feet (V). They have a wild energy and 'a will that can conquer even death' (II, 1).
6. This discussion of sadomasochism draws extensively on Benjamin's analysis of the master–slave relationship (Benjamin 1993, chapter 2).
7. Stoller writes on the male subject's attempt at differentiation as follows: 'he must separate himself from his mother's female body and in his inside world from his own already formed primary identification with femaleness and femininity. This great task is often not completed' (Benjamin 1993, p. 75).
8. For a discussion of the dynamic of fear and desire in the gothic novel, see Day 1985.
9. For an introduction to the concepts of ideology and false consciousness, see Bottomore 1985.
10. See Günsberg 1994, pp. 26–34.
11. For an analysis of Sade's Juliette and other female characters, see Carter 1979.
12. Female exhibitionism has been theorized in relation to male voyeurism in

film theory. See Silverman 1983; Mulvey 1989; Kuhn 1982. For a discussion of voyeurism and exhibitionism in relation to theatre, see Günsberg 1994, pp. 35–6.

13. The homoerotic and sadomasochistic dimensions of the relations of exhibitionism and voyeurism in *Le Martyre de Saint Sébastien* would have been altered, however, when the part of Sébastien was played by a woman in a 1911 performance. This performance would have returned the gendering of sadomasochistic relations to its traditional male/sadist, female/masochist format (Mutterle 1980, p. 6). Mutterle also notes that the performance, with the ballerina Ida Rubinstein in the title role, caused a scandal and was condemned by the religious authorities.

14. Long red hair also recurs as an indicator of female sexuality in Pirandello's *Come prima, meglio di prima*, *All'uscita* and *I giganti della montagna*. See Günsberg 1992, pp. 41–6.

15. See pp. 49–87 above for a discussion of fetishism.

16. Ovid, *Metamorphoses*, 10: 243–97; see also Hall 1974.

17. Mila in *La figlia di Iorio*, Basiliola in *La nave*, Pantea in *Sogno d'un tramonto d'autunno*, and Evadne in *Fedra*. Other female deaths take the form of drowning (Bianca Maria in *La città morta*), suffocation (Pisanelle in *La Pisanelle*), asps (Gigliola in *La fiaccola sotto il moggio*) and a pin (Ipponoe in *Fedra*). Both female and male characters die by poison (Fedra in *Fedra*, Cesare in *La gloria*, and Mortella's father in *Il ferro* (by overdose)), stabbing (Francesca and Paolo in *Francesca da Rimini*, Ruggero in *La gloria*, Gherardo in *Il ferro*, and Giuliano in *Sogno d'un mattino di primavera*), beheading (Parisina and Ugo in *La Parisina*) and torture (female and male religious martyrs in *Le Martyre de Saint Sébastien*). Only male characters are dispatched through arrows (Sébastien in *Le Martyre de Saint Sébastien*), strangling (the usurer in *Più che l'amore*) and an axe (Lazzaro in *La figlia di Iorio*).

5   PATRIARCHS AND PRODIGALS: THE GENERATION GAP IN
PIRANDELLO

1. Quotations from the plays are taken from the Einaudi, *Mondadori teatro e cinema* edition. For one-act plays, page references will be given; for plays divided into acts, but not scenes, the act reference will appear.

2. The most recent work on theories of age, Jane Pilcher's *Age and generation in modern Britain*, 1995, opens with a reference to Finch's 1986 description of this area as 'relatively uncharted territory'. This chapter draws extensively on Pilcher's theoretical contribution on age (which, rather than inter-age relations, is her main concern), while at the same time reorienting her ideas away from the context of modern Britain to suit the historical, social and cultural context of Pirandello's late nineteenth- and early twentieth-century Sicily.

3. 'Camaraderie in competition: male bonding and male rivalry', Günsberg 1994, chapter 3.

4. Mead's other two cultural types are the *cofigurative*, in which future genera-tions are guided by the present, and *prefigurative*, in which elders learn from children and the future is prefigured by the young.

5. Gender-differentiated portrayal of access to education in Pirandello's plays is dealt with in Günsberg 1994, chapter 4.

6. *The rules of the game* was produced by Jonathan Kent, translated by David Hare, and performed by the Almeida Theatre Company in London from 7 May – 27 June 1992. For a review of the production see Tandello 1992.

7. See Firth 1994 on children in Pirandello's short stories in this context.

8. See Delaney 1986.

9. See Fanning 1996.

10. For an account of the 'marked' stages of women's lives as opposed to the 'unmarked' progression of the lives of men, see Hastrup 1978.

11. See 'Danger: women at work', Günsberg 1994, chapter 4.

12. See Pilcher 1995, chapter 3, and Hockey and James 1993, chapter 1.

13. For a discussion of the actual enclosure of female characters in Pirandello's plays, see Günsberg 1994, pp. 96–100 *et passim*.

14. See Hockey and James 1993, pp. 11–12.

15. Istat figures for 1921, one year prior to the first performance of the play in Rome, show 5,841 women as opposed to 571 men working as typists, stenographers and copyists (Günsberg 1994, p. 110).

16. Curtius deals with the rejuvenation theme in his section 'Old woman and girl'. It is interesting that the equivalent male topos, the *puer senex*, dealt with in the preceding section entitled 'Boy and old man' (pp. 98–101), con-tains no element of rejuvenation, with both Boy and Old Man coexisting in the same body (Curtius 1973, pp. 101–5).

6 CENTRE STAGE: FRANCA RAME'S FEMALE PARTS

1. This phrase is used by Rame to describe the grim monologue *Io, Ulrike, grido . . .* (Fo 1989, p. 243).

2. For a definition of *polylogue* and other dramatic terms, see Pfister 1991.

3. One indication of the ambiguous nature of this area is the appearance of the volume entitled *Venticinque monologhi per una donna di Dario Fo e Franca Rame* as part of the collection *Le commedie di Dario Fo* (rather than perhaps independently). Yet some of the same plays are listed under *Il teatro di Franca Rame* at the end of Rame's *Parliamo di donne* (containing *L'eroina* and *La donna grassa*) of 1992 (a volume with only Rame's name on the cover, but describing *Parliamo di donne* on the flyleaf as 'two one-act plays by Franca Rame and Dario Fo'). On the intricacies of the Rame–Fo collaboration, see Rame 1992, pp. 116–17, Hood 1993, xiv, Mitchell 1986, pp. 79–80.

4. See Goldoni's *Il teatro comico* (1750).

5. The play collections referred to in this chapter are as follows: Dario Fo, *Venticinque monologhi per una donna di Dario Fo e Franca Rame*, 1989; Dario Fo and Franca Rame, *Coppia aperta, quasi spalancata, e altre quattordici commedie*,

1991; Franca Rame, *Parliamo di donne*, 1992. While many of the plays in the 1991 collection were originally written for television, they have been included in this study because they are considered by their authors as suitable for the stage, and have indeed been performed in a theatrical context (Fo/Rame 1991, p. vi).

6. The Italian for sex (*sesso*) also denotes the penis, leading to ambiguous word-play in the following sentence, in which the pronoun 'he' can also be understood as 'it'.

7. On the feminist reception of Rame's plays, see Hirst 1989 and Rame 1992.

8. Foucault 1985, 1985a, 1987.

9. See the introduction in Kemp and Bono 1993.

10. For further discussion of the status of 'women's writing', in particular women's autobiography, see Günsberg 1993.

11. See Hartsock 1983.

12. While sexual violence against women in a family context does not appear in any of the plays, its perpetration against women in the workplace (*Il pupazzo giapponese, Monologo di una puttana in manicomio*) and in the streets (*Lo stupro, Previsioni meteorologiche movimenti di stupro in Italia*) is brought out into the open and placed on the dramatic agenda.

13. On female enclosure in Renaissance Tuscany, see Brown 1986.

14. For a discussion of patriarchal methods of dealing with female 'madness', see Showalter 1987.

15. On female spectacle and narrative interruption, see Mulvey 1989.

16. See, for example, Bruno and Nadotti 1988, Kuhn 1982 and Penley 1988, to name but a few.

Bibliography

Alberti, L. B. (1969) *The family in Renaissance Florence (Libri della famiglia 1438–41)*, ed. R. Watkins (Columbia, SC, University of South Carolina Press)

Alcoff, L. and Potter, E. (eds.) (1993) *Feminist epistemologies* (London, Routledge)

Anderson, B. S. and Zinsser, J. P. (1988) *A history of their own: women in Europe from prehistory to the present* (London, Penguin, 2 vols.)

Anderson, P. (1984) *Lineages of the absolutist state* (London, Verso)
  (1985) *Passages from antiquity to feudalism* (London, Verso)

Andrews, R. (1993) *Scripts and scenarios: the performance of comedy in Renaissance Italy* (Cambridge University Press)

Andrieux, M. (1972) *Daily life in Venice in the time of Casanova* (London, Allen & Unwin)

Anglani, B. (1983) *Goldoni: il mercato, la scena, l'utopia* (Napoli, Liguori)

Ardener, S. (ed.) (1978) *Defining females: the nature of women in society* (London, Croom Helm)

Aretino (1968) *Tutte le commedie*, ed. G. B. De Sanctis (Milano, Mursia)

Ariosto (1954) *Ludovico Ariosto: opere minori*, ed. C. Segre (Milano, Riccardo Ricciardi)

Babcock, B. A. (ed.) (1978) *The reversible world: symbolic inversion in art and society* (Ithaca, NY, Cornell University Press)

Barański, Z. and Vinall, S. W. (eds.) (1991) *Women and Italy: essays on gender, culture and history* (London, Macmillan)

Barbini, A. (ed.) (1970) *Teatro verista siciliano* (Bologna, Cappelli)

Beare, W. (1968) *The Roman stage* (London, Methuen)

Beecher, D. A. (1984) 'Machiavelli's *Mandragola* and the emerging *animateur*', *Quaderni d'italianistica*, 5, 2, 171–89

Beecher, D. A., and Ciavolella, M. (1986) *Comparative critical approaches to Renaissance comedy* (Ottawa, Dovehouse Editions)

Belsey, C. (1985) 'Constructing the subject: deconstructing the text', in Newton Rosenfelt 1985, pp. 45–64

Benjamin, J. (1993) *The bonds of love: psychoanalysis, feminism, and the problem of domination* (London, Virago)

Bentley, E. (1947) *The cult of the superman* (London, Robert Hale)

Bjurström, P. (1964) 'Espace scénique et durée de l'action dans le théatre italien du xviie siècle et de la première moitié du xviie siècle', in Jacquot, J. 1964, pp. 73–84

Blackburn, R. (ed.) (1979) *Ideology in social science: readings in critical social theory* (London, Fontana/Collins)

Bleier, R. (1984) *Science and gender: a critique of biology and its theories on women* (Oxford, Pergamon)

Bloomsbury (1992) *Bloomsbury guide to women's literature* (London, Bloomsbury)

Bonino, D. G. (1977) *Il teatro italiano: la commedia del cinquecento* (Torino, Einaudi, vol. 1)

Borsellino, N. (ed.) (1962–7) *Commedie del cinquecento* (Milano, Feltrinelli, 2 vols.)

Bossy, J. (ed.) (1983) *Disputes and settlements* (Cambridge University Press)

Bottomore, T. (1985) *A dictionary of Marxist thought* (Oxford, Blackwell)

Boucher, F. (1967) *A history of costume in the West* (London, Thames & Hudson)

Bristol, M. (1985) *Carnival and theatre* (London, Routledge)

Brown, J. C. (1986) 'A woman's place was in the home: women's work in Renaissance Italy', in Ferguson *et al.* 1986, pp. 206–26

   (1989) 'Lesbian sexuality in medieval and early modern Europe', in Duberman *et al.* 1989, pp. 67–75

Brucker, G. (1986) *Giovanni and Lusanna: love and marriage in Renaissance Florence* (London, Weidenfeld & Nicolson)

Bruno, G. and Nadotti, M. (eds.) (1988) *Off screen: women and film in Italy* (London, Routledge)

Burke, P. (1978) *Popular culture in early modern Europe* (Aldershot, Wildwood House)

Burns, E. (1972) *Theatricality. A study of convention in the theatre and in social life* (London, Longman)

Butler, J. (1990) *Gender trouble: feminism and the subversion of identity* (London, Routledge)

Carter, A. (1979) *The Sadeian woman* (London, Virago)

Carver, V. and Liddiard, P. (1978) *The ageing population* (Bungay, Chaucer Press)

Case, S. E. (1988) *Feminism and theatre* (London, Macmillan)

Castiglione (1978) *Opere di B. Castiglione*, ed. G. Prezzolini (Milano, Rizzoli)

Cervato, E. (1993) *Goldoni and Venice* (publ. by University of Hull)

Chamberlin, E. R. (1982) *The world of the Italian Renaissance* (London, Allen and Unwin)

Clark, M. (1984) *Modern Italy 1871–1982* (London, Longman)

Clubb, L. G. (1986) 'Theatregrams', in Beecher 1984, pp. 15–33

Cohan, S. and Hark, I. R. (1993) *Screening the male: exploring masculinities in Hollywood cinema* (London, Routledge)

Coyle, M. (ed.) (1995) *Machiavelli's The Prince: texts in culture* (Manchester University Press)

Creed, B. (1993) *The monstrous-feminine: film, feminism, psychoanalysis* (London, Routledge)

Curtius, E. R. (1973) *European literature and the Latin middle ages* (1948) (Princeton University Press)

D'Ancona, A. (1966) *Origini del teatro italiano* (1891) (Roma, Bardi, 2 vols.)

D'Annunzio, G. (1964) *Tragedie, sogni e misteri* (Milano, Mondadori, 2 vols.)

Day, W. P. (1985) *In the circles of fear and desire: a study of Gothic fantasy* (University of Chicago Press)

Dekker, R. M. and Van De Pol, L. C. (1989) *The tradition of female transvestism in early modern Europe* (London, Macmillan)

Delaney, C. (1986) 'The meaning of paternity and the virgin birth debate', *Man*, new series, 21, 494–513

Dietrich, M. and Kindermann, H. (1977) *Das Theater und sein Publikum* (Wien, Verlag der Österreichischen Akademie der Wissenschaften)

Doane, M. A. (1991) *Femmes fatales: feminism, film theory, psychoanalysis* (London, Routledge)

Duberman, M. B., Vicinus, M. and Chauncey, Jr. G. (eds.) (1989) *Hidden from history: reclaiming the gay and lesbian past* (New York, Penguin)

Duchartre, P. L. (1966) *The Italian comedy* (New York, Dover)

Duckworth, G. E. (1971) *The nature of Roman comedy* (Princeton University Press)

Elam, K. (1980) *The semiotics of theatre and drama* (London, Methuen)

Elshtain, J. B. (1985) 'Reflections on war and political discourse: realism, just war, and feminism in a nuclear age', *Political theory* 13, 1, 39–57

Fanning, U. (1996) 'Adultery: the paternal potential', *The yearbook of the society for Pirandello studies* 15/16, 7–18

Ferguson, M. W., Quilligan, M. and Vickers, N. J. (eds.) (1986) *Rewriting the Renaissance: the discourses of sexual difference in Early Modern Europe* (University of Chicago Press)

Ferris, L. (1990) *Acting women: images of women in theatre* (London, Macmillan)
  (ed.) (1993) *Crossing the stage: controversies on cross-dressing* (London, Routledge)

Firth, F. (1978) 'Comedy in Italy', in Howarth 1978, pp. 63–80
  (1994) 'Fixed for death: Pirandello on birth, babies and children in the *Novelle per un anno*', *The yearbook of the society for Pirandello studies* 14, 54–60

Fo, D. (1989) *Venticinque monologhi per una donna di Dario Fo e Franca Rame* (Torino, Einaudi)

Fo, D., and Rame, F. (1991) *Coppia aperta, quasi spalancata, e altre quattordici commedie* (Torino, Einaudi)

Foucault, M. (1985) *The use of pleasure* (New York, Random House)
  (1985a) *The care of the self* (New York, Random House)
  (1987) 'On the genealogy of ethics: an overview of work in progress', in Rabinow 1987

Fratri, L. (ed.) (1928) *La vita in Bologna dal secolo* XIII *al* XVII (Bologna)

Freud, S. (1962) 'The uncanny' (1919), *Standard edition of the complete psychological works*, 17, 217
  (1984) *On sexuality: three essays on the theory of sexuality and other works* (London, Penguin)
  (1984a) 'Fetishism' (1927), in Freud 1984, pp. 345–57
  (1984b) 'The sexual aberrations' (1905), in Freud 1984, pp. 45–87

Frye, N. (1973) *Anatomy of criticism* (Princeton University Press)

Gamman, L. and Makinen, M. (1994) *Female fetishism: a new look* (London, Lawrence and Wishart)

Garber, M. (1992) *Vested interests: cross-dressing and cultural anxiety* (London, Routledge)

Geras, N. (1979) 'Marx and the critique of political economy', in Blackburn 1979, pp. 284–305

Gilbert, F. (1973) 'Venice in the crisis of the League of Cambrai', in Hale 1973, pp. 274–92

Gilbert, S. M. and Gubar, S. (1984) 'The queen's looking glass: female creativity, male images of women, and the metaphor of literary paternity', chapter one of *The madwoman in the attic: the woman writer and the nineteenth-century literary imagination* (New Haven, CT, Yale University Press)

Gilder, R. (1960) *Enter the actress: the first women in the theater* (1931) (New York, Theatre Arts Books)

Giudice, G. (1963) *Pirandello* (Torino, UTET)

Goldoni (1891) *Opere* (Padova, Bettoni, 12 vols.)

    (1972) *Carlo Goldoni: commedie*, ed. K. Ringger (Torino, Einaudi, 4 vols.)

    (1978) *I capolavori di Carlo Goldoni*, ed. G. Ortolani (Milano, Mondadori)

Grosz, E. (1991) 'Lesbian fetishism?', *differences* 3/2, 39–54

Günsberg, M. (1991) 'Donna liberata? The portrayal of women in the Italian Renaissance epic', in Barański and Vinall 1991, pp. 173–208

    (1992) 'Hysteria as theatre: Pirandello's hysterical women', *The yearbook of the society for Pirandello studies* 12, 32–54

    (1993) 'The importance of being absent: narrativity and desire in Sibilla Aleramo's *Amo dunque sono*', *the italianist* 13, 139–59

    (1994) *Patriarchal representations: gender and discourse in Pirandello's theatre* (Oxford, Berg)

    (1995) 'The end justifies the means: end-orientation and the discourses of power', in Coyle 1995, pp. 115–50

Hale, J. R. (ed.) (1973) *Renaissance Venice* (London, Faber and Faber)

Hall, J. (1974) *Dictionary of subjects and symbols in art* (London, John Murray)

Hartsock, N. (1983) *Money, sex and power: toward a feminist historical materialism* (New York, Longman)

Harvey, E. D. (1992) *Ventriloquized voices: feminist theory and English Renaissance texts* (London, Routledge)

Harwood, R. (1984) *All the world's a stage* (London, Methuen)

Hastrup, K. (1978) 'The semantics of biology: virginity', in Ardener 1978, pp. 49–65

Hekman, S. J. (1990) *Gender and knowledge* (Cambridge, Polity)

Herlihy, D. (1978) *The social history of Italy and western Europe 700–1500* (London, Variorum Reprints)

Hermsen, J. J. and Van Lenning, A. (eds.) (1991) *Sharing the difference: feminist debates in Holland* (London, Routledge)

Herrick, M. (1950) *Comic theory in the sixteenth century* (Urbana, University of Illinois Press)

    (1960) *Italian comedy in the Renaissance* (Urbana, University of Illinois Press)

Hewitt, B. (ed.) (1958) *The Renaissance stage: documents of Serlio, Sabbattini and Furttenbach* (University of Miami Press)

Hirst, D. (1989) *Dario Fo and Franca Rame* (London, Macmillan)

Hockey, J. and James, A. (1993) *Growing up and growing old: ageing and dependency in the life course* (London, Sage)

Hood, S. (1994) Introduction, in *Dario Fo. Plays: two* (London, Methuen)

Howard, J. E. (1993) 'Cross-dressing, the theater, and gender struggle in early modern England', in Ferris 1993, pp. 20–46

Howarth, W. D. (ed.) (1978) *Comic drama: the European heritage* (London, Methuen)

Howe, E. (1992) *The first English actresses: women and drama, 1660–1700* (Cambridge University Press)

Hughes, D. Owen (1983) 'Sumptuary law and social relations in Renaissance Italy', in Bossy 1983, pp. 69–100

Hunter, R. L (1985) *The new comedy of Greece and Rome* (Cambridge University Press)

Irigaray, L. (1977) *Ce Sexe qui n'en est pas un* (Paris, Minuit)

Jacquot, J. (ed.) (1964) *Le Lieu théâtral à la Renaissance* (Paris, Editions du Centre National de la Recherche Scientifique)

   (1964a) 'Les Types du lieu théâtral et leurs transformations de la fin du moyen âge au milieu du xviie siècle', in Jacquot 1964, pp. 473–509

Jardine, L. (1992) 'Twins and travesties: gender, dependency, and sexual availability in *Twelfth Night*', in Zimmerman 1992, pp. 27–38

Jay, N. (1981) 'Gender and dichotomy', *Feminist studies* 7, 1 (Spring), 38–56

Kemp, S. and Bono, P. (eds.) (1993) *In a lonely mirror: Italian perspectives on feminist theory* (London, Routledge)

Kennard, J. S. (1967) *Goldoni and the Venice of his time* (New York, Benjamin Blom)

Klapisch-Zuber, C. (1985) *Women, family and ritual in Renaissance Italy* (University of Chicago Press)

Koenigsberger, H. G. and Mosse, G. L. (1968) *Europe in the sixteenth century* (London, Longman)

Kuhn, A. (1982) *Women's pictures: feminism and cinema* (London, Routledge and Kegan Paul)

Larivaille, P. (1983) *La vita quotidiana delle cortigiane nell'Italia del rinascimento* (Milano, Rizzoli)

Laver, J. (1964) *Costume in theatre* (London, Harrap)

Lévi-Strauss, C. (1969) *The elementary structures of kinship* (Boston, Beacon Press)

Machiavelli (1964) *Opere letterarie*, ed. L. Blasucci (Milano, Adelphi)

Mack, M. (1979) 'Rescuing Shakespeare', *International Shakespeare Association* Occasional Paper 1 (Oxford)

Maclean, I. (1985) *The Renaissance notion of woman: a study of the fortunes of scholasticism and medical science in European intellectual life* (Cambridge University Press)

Mangini, N. (1974) *I teatri di Venezia* (Milano, Mursia)

Marker, L. L. and F. J. (1977) 'Sources in audience research: their nature and selection', in Dietrich and Kindermann 1977, pp. 18–31

McLuskie, K. (1989) *Renaissance dramatists* (London, Harvester Wheatsheaf)

Mead, M. (1978) *Culture and commitment: the new relationships between the generations in the 1970s* (New York, Columbia University Press)

Metz, C. (1977) *Le Signifiant imaginaire psychanalyse et cinéma* (Paris, Union Générale d'Editions)

Mills, S. (ed.) (1994) *Gendering the reader* (London, Harvester Wheatsheaf)

Mitchell, T. (1989) *File on Dario Fo* (London, Methuen)

Molinari, C. (1964) 'Les Rapports entre la scène et les spectateurs dans le théâtre italien du xvie siècle', in Jacquot 1964, pp. 61–71

Mulvey, L. (1989) *Visual and other pleasures* (London, Macmillan)

Mutterle, A. M. (1980) *Gabriele D'Annunzio: introduzione e guida allo studio dell'opera dannunziana* (Firenze, Le Monnier)

Newton, J. and Rosenfelt, D. (eds.) (1985) *Feminist criticism and social change* (London, Methuen)

Newton, S. M. (1975) *Renaissance theatre costume and the sense of the historic past* (London, Rapp and Whiting)

Nicholson, L. J. (ed.) (1990) *Feminism/postmodernism* (London, Routledge)

Nicoll, A. (1938) *The Stuart masques and the Renaissance stage* (London, Harrap)

Orbach, S. (1988) *Fat is a feminist issue* (London, Arrow)

Penley, C. (ed.) (1988) *Feminism and film theory* (London, Routledge)

Pfister, M. (1991) *The theory and analysis of drama* (Cambridge University Press)

Pietropaolo, D. (1986) 'The stage in the text: a theatrical stratification of Italian Renaissance comedy', in Beecher and Ciavolella 1986, pp. 35–51

Pilcher, J. (1995) *Age and generation in modern Britain* (Oxford University Press)

Pirandello, L. (1965) *Saggi, poesie e scritti varii*, ed. M. Lo Vecchio-Musti (Milano, Mondadori)

(1965a) 'L'umorismo' (1908), in Pirandello 1965, pp. 17–160

(1965b) 'Feminismo' (1909), in Pirandello 1965, pp. 1068–72

Press, A. L. (1991) *Women watching television: gender, class, and generation in the American television experience* (Philadelphia, University of Pennsylvania Press)

Pribram, E. D. (ed.) (1992) *Female spectators: looking at film and television* (London, Verso)

Rabinow, P. (ed.) (1987) *The Foucault reader* (Harmondsworth, Penguin)

Radcliff-Umstead, D. (1969) *The birth of modern comedy in Renaissance Italy* (University of Chicago Press)

Rame, F. (1992) *Parliamo di donne* (Milano, Kaos)

Robbins, H. W. (1993) 'More human than I am alone', in Cohan and Hark 1993, pp. 134–47

Rose, M. B. (ed.) (1986) *Women in the Middle Ages and the Renaissance: literary and historical perspectives* (Syracuse University Press)

Saslow, J. M. (1989) 'Homosexuality in the Renaissance: behaviour, identity, and artistic expression', in Duberman *et al.* 1989, pp. 90–105

Schor, N. (1992) 'Fetishism', in Wright 1992, pp. 113–17

Sciascia, L. (1987) *The day of the owl*, transl. by A. Colquhoun of *Il giorno della civetta*, first published in 1960 (London, Paladin)

Scrivano, R. (1986) 'Towards a "Philosophy" of Renaissance theatre', in Beecher and Ciavolella 1986, pp. 1–13

Sedgwick, E. K. (1985) *Between men: English literature and male homosocial desire* (New York, Columbia University Press)

Showalter, E. (1987) *The female malady: women, madness and English culture, 1830–1980* (London, Virago)

Silverman, K. (1983) *The subject of semiotics* (Oxford University Press)

Sombart, W. (1967) *The quintessence of capitalism: a study of the history and psychology of the modern business man* (1915) (New York, Howard Fertig)

Sontag, S. (1978) 'The double standard of ageing', in Carver and Liddiard 1978, pp. 72–80

Stacey, J. (1994) *Stargazing: Hollywood and female spectatorship in the 1940s* (London, Routledge)

Stallybrass, P. (1991) 'The world turned upside down: inversion, gender and the state', in Wayne 1991, pp. 201–20

    (1992) 'Transvestism and the "body beneath": speculating on the boy actor', in Zimmerman 1992, pp. 64–83

Steele, E. (1981) *Carlo Goldoni: life, work, and times* (Ravenna, Longo)

Tandello, E. (1992) 'Review of *The rules of the game*', *The yearbook of the society for Pirandello studies* 12, p. 85

Taylor, G. R. (1953) *Sex in history* (London, Thames and Hudson)

Theweleit, K. (1990) *Male fantasies* (Cambridge, Polity)

Vintges, K. (1991) 'The vanished woman and styles of feminine subjectivity: feminism in deconstruction and construction', in Hermsen and Van Lenning 1991, pp. 228–40

Wayne, V. (ed.) (1991) *The matter of difference: materialist feminist criticism of Shakespeare* (London, Harvester)

Weaver, E. (1986) 'Spiritual fun: a study of sixteenth-century Tuscan convent theater', in Rose 1986, pp. 173–206

Woloch, I. (1982) *Eighteenth-century Europe: tradition and progress 1715–1798* (London, Norton)

Wright, E. (ed.) (1992) *Feminism and psychoanalysis: a critical dictionary* (Oxford, Blackwell)

Wright, K. 'A multiple identity politics', paper presented at the graduate conference 'Representation, Identity and Agency', University of Manchester, 13–14 December 1993

Zimmerman, S. (ed.) (1992) *Erotic politics: desire on the Renaissance stage* (London, Routledge)

Subject index

abortion 217, 226

acting 4, 58–61, 206: and prostitution 57, 91; companies 6, 60

actor 5, 10, 21, 42, 43, 49, 51, 57, 60–1, 63, 65, 67–71, 72, 73, 75, 77, 78, 80, 87, 111, 180, 207, 214: boy 56, 57, 61, 70, 211, 240; character as 112; professional 58, 60–1

actress 4, 5, 58, 60, 88, 91, 111, 144, 156, 206–7, 211, 214, 224, 234, 242, 251n.4: as woman 60, 91, 156, 202; *commedia dell'arte* 59, 88; English 58; fictional 112; professional 58–61

address: audience 41–8; direct 42–4, 232, 241–2; *see also* speech, direct

adultery 15, 16, 29, 34, 84, 85, 172, 223: *see also* affair; infidelity

adulthood 77, 173–6, 178, 179, 180, 184, 189–92, 228: and femininity 191–3

adulteress 9

affair 15, 34, 47, 79, 177–8, 182, 188, 197: *see also* adultery; infidelity

affidamento 217: *see also* friendship, female

age 8, 43, 45, 50, 54, 60, 67, 162–202, 205, 222, 241, 253n. 2: and class 166; and ethnicity 166; and gender 1, 63, 162–202; and women 189–202; hierarchy 3, 10, 28, 41, 169, 175

ageing 146, 149–50, 151, 156, 171, 182, 189, 193–7, 200–2, 223, 227, 228, 230

ageism 150, 156, 162, 186, 193, 195, 199, 200, 202

agency 210–13, 215, 221

angel in the house 94–110, 251n.6

angel versus monster 146, 150, 251n.6

anorexia 228, 236: *see also* bulimia; eating disorders

asexuality 132–3, 151, 158, 197

aside 41, 46, 100, 113, 205

audibility 45–6, 207

audience 5, 10, 12, 22, 44, 50, 57–69, 207–8, 224, 241, 246n.27: address 41–8; as fourth wall 43, 155, 232, 241; attention 8, 19, 42–3,

45, 48, 73, 111, 156, 203, 234, 242, 249n.25; composition 50, 61; omniscience 22, 43; onstage 154; positions 10, 41, 43, 57, 66; voyeurism 236, 239–41

auditorium 5, 13, 42, 61, 63, 68, 69, 74, 112, 154, 241, 244n.9, 247n.38

aunt 185–6

authorial impersonality 121

autocoscienza 205, 210, 212, 216–23, 227, 232, 234, 237, 241

autonomy 95, 97, 105, 111, 118, 119, 120, 157, 189–92, 217

bachelor 101

bedsharing 82

bestiality 54

betrothal 31, 85, 115

binary opposition 2, 16, 19, 54, 74, 93, 126, 133, 139, 140, 193, 245n.15

biological versus social 49, 54, 74, 95, 98, 165, 171, 177, 179, 181, 183, 194, 202

bisexuality 54

body 17, 53, 60, 65, 72, 74, 94, 102, 131, 133, 144, 156, 186, 193, 230: commodification of the female 28–9, 31, 39–40, 56, 69, 100–1, 105, 125, 157, 158–9, 245n. 22; female 16, 19, 23, 29, 36, 40, 56, 57, 58, 61, 63, 85, 100, 114, 149, 154–9, 162, 170, 174, 189, 193–7, 200–1, 222–3, 227–30, 233, 236–40, 252n.7; femininity as 141, 145, 193, 202; /home/ house 16–17, 19–20; male 75, 186, 193, 200; size 228–30; surface of the 214; writing the 220; versus mind 16

bonding, male 75–7, 253n.3

bourgeois 93, 112–13, 127, 174: Enlightenment 93, 127; mercantilism 30; morality 113

bride 17, 38, 40, 48, 78, 86, 100, 116

bridegroom 40, 101, 152

brother 32–3, 38, 83–4, 147, 149, 152, 153, 173, 174, 224: -in-law 96, 99, 216, 219, 236; twin 19, 28, 32

263

Name and text index